ISBN 978-1-330-39906-4
PIBN 10051871

1 MONTH OF FREE READING

at

www.ForgottenBooks.com

By purchasing this book you are eligible for one month membership to ForgottenBooks.com, giving you unlimited access to our entire collection of over 1,000,000 titles via our web site and mobile apps.

To claim your free month visit:

www.forgottenbooks.com/free51871

EXPLORATIO PHILOSOPHICA:

ROUGH NOTES

ON

MODERN INTELLECTUAL SCIENCE.

PART I.

By JOHN GROTE, B.D.

FELLOW OF TRINITY COLLEGE, AND PROFESSOR OF MORAL PHILOSOPHY
IN THE UNIVERSITY OF CAMBRIDGE.

CAMBRIDGE:
DEIGHTON, BELL, AND CO.
LONDON: BELL AND DALDY.
1865.

CONTENTS.

INTRODUCTION.

I WILL first give an account of the circumstances of the publication of these 'rough notes', and then of the system of philosophy, if so it is to be called, contained in them.

They represent a continued general thinking on the subjects to which they relate, though they are rather hastily put together as regards their particular form. But there is nothing hasty or extemporaneous in such thought as they may contain.

A not inconsiderable portion of them was written two years since, on the following occasion.

After the publication of Mr Mill's small book on Utilitarianism, I had the intention of writing something in answer to him on that subject, and had actually begun the printing of the result of this intention. I was led, in connexion with this, to put together the intellectual views on which the moral view rested, or which had something of the character of 'prolegomena' to it, and had meant if they should come within reasonable limits, to publish them in an Appendix.

Being of a nature hesitating and irresolute, I altered my mind as to this: and though at first stimulated to controversy, which of itself I do not think I should have shrunk from, I thought that what, in regard of the subject, was likely to be most useful was another course, and accordingly determined rather to put together, in an uncontroversial form, what seemed to me the truth, in opposition to what I thought error.

This, if it please God, is in the way of being accomplished, subject to all the delays which interest in other employments, uncertain health, and some not, I think, uncalled for scrupulousness and anxiety as to what one writes on a subject so important, may throw in the way of it. But in the meantime, I have thought it might be as well to return upon the intellectual views with which the moral view connects itself, and to re-examine them and test them.

The result is the publication of these pages: to which, for reasons which will appear, I have not attempted to give any very regular form or artistic completeness. This explanation is almost necessary for the understanding of the beginning of them, which is abrupt, and refers, it will be seen, to something as going before, and which I thought it was as well to leave so referring. But I have carefully avoided in the following pages all reference to Morals or Ethics, and (except *most* incidentally) all approbation or disapprobation of anything in a moral view or as to moral tendency. I have endeavoured to bring together, for comparison, views, the respective holders of which would probably thank me very little for my trouble : but philosophical controversy is a worse confusion than a battle without generals or discipline, and as we come more to morals and ethics the dust and smoke become tenfold worse. I have wished therefore to examine some things in the earlier and clearer atmosphere. I have nothing to do here with any results to which opinions may lead, or with any supposed opinions held by any one beyond what the books which I notice contain.

I have now to give a short account of the nature of the philosophy which these 'rough notes'
exhibit or involve.

It perhaps may be said, that there are three main
heads or kinds of philosophy in England at present,
each of which it seems to me has appendant error: and
it is against these errors that a great deal of what I say
is directed.

Of these three kinds of philosophy, as I call them,
the first which I will mention is 'the Philosophy of
the Human Mind' or Psychology, and there appears to
me to attach itself to a great deal of *that* a very mistaken view, which I have called generally the wrong
psychology or mis-psychology.

For the particular nature of this error I must refer
to what follows, and will only briefly now say about it,
that it consists, substantially, in the attempt to analyze
our consciousness while nevertheless we suppose ourselves, who have the consciousness, to be particular
local beings in the midst of an universe of things or
objects similar to what we ourselves are. My feeling
about the whole 'Philosophy of the Human Mind'
is this: that at present it is attacked, and with reason,
from two opposite sides; that its philosophy will not
satisfy philosophers, nor its physiology physiologists;
and that it will have to divide itself, for utility and
productiveness, into two lines of thought, very different,
rarely likely to be pursued by the same people, each
very likely to be despised by those who sympathize
with the other, but quite consistent the one with the
other, and *really* of such a nature, that the more purely
and independently each takes its own way, the better is
it likely to be not only for itself, but also for the other.

I am myself very much of opinion that the old

vein of the Philosophy of the Human Mind, or noö-psychology, is worked out, and that whatever there was to be got from it (not much, I think, ever) is got already.

But it seems to me that the way is singularly open and inviting now for a good physio-psychology, as I should call it, by which however I mean something possibly very different from what several who have already treated that subject would mean.

Such a study is a mental and moral human anatomy, and a mental and moral comparative anatomy: but I do not believe that these, or either of them, can ever be pursued with good result unless the pursuers of them dismiss from their minds what I should call philosophy—either looking upon it as a different line of thought, or else ignoring it—in any case not thinking that it is *their* science which will answer the higher questions of the human mind, or tell us what we ought to do.

I have always had a very strong opinion that the later psychology, or Philosophy of the Human Mind, has neglected a large province of consideration which really belonged to it, in its failing to take notice of, and to try to bring into relation with human intelligence, the various intelligence of our humbler fellow-creatures in the universe, the lower animals: mind belongs to them as well as to us. Mental *human* anatomy, which is of two kinds, the anatomy of the body pursued as far as it can be in the direction of the mind, *and* the observation of the results of the action of mind in connexion with this—such psychology always has considered in its province, though lately it has been pursued with special fruit: we want now more of mental *comparative* anatomy, or the study of the varieties of *animal* intelligence, above alluded to.

But for all this we must disengage psychology from the philosophy which it has mingled with itself, and which in all probability it will try still to mingle with itself. Hitherto the result of its doing so has been in the main that confusion of thought on which I have dwelt at length in the following pages. *Now* probably its effort will be to furnish a philosophy (less confused indeed) from *itself* better understood than before, and it will tell us that we must be satisfied with *that* philosophy. In my view, this course will effectually ruin *itself*.

Philosophy, by which I mean the study of thought and feeling not as we see them variously associated with corporeal organization, and producing various results in the universe, but as we understand, think, feel them of ourselves and from within, is something to me of an entirely different nature, and leads to entirely different fields of speculation from the physio-psychology which I have been speaking of. I think that those who have the truest view of the one will also have the truest of the other. It does not seem to me that anything, for instance, as to our moral action waits for a better physio-psychology, except in that subordinate degree in which such action is likely to be altered and benefited by any increase of our knowledge of any kind. In my view, the question of the relation of our mind to our corporeal organization, and the question of the distribution of mind more or less like ours through various organizations, are the two questions of physics far the most interesting: but they are physics after all. Whatever may be found out about them seems to me to have quite a subordinate bearing upon the great questions of the nature of knowledge and of moral sentiments and obligations. These

belong to what I have called philosophy, which rises
high above the other, or if we prefer the language,
underlies it as its foundation: how, I shall discuss in
the following pages.

I think then that the 'Philosophy of the Human
Mind' is now in the way to divide itself into different
branches, all, it seems to me, hopeful and promising
result: the manner in which its method has hitherto
been faulty is one of the matters of my discussion.

The second kind of philosophy which we have among
us is the true and real philosophy, this which I have
described as one line of those into which the Philosophy
of the Human Mind is likely to divide itself: but it
seems to have an appendant error of great importance, which I have described in the ensuing pages
as 'notionalism' and 'relativism', terms in a great
measure, though perhaps not quite, equivalent.

I will only briefly describe this here as the realizing
(and any realizing must be mis-realizing, wrongly
realizing) our logical terms. We get from this what
we may call a philosophy of 'notions', and knowledge,
instead of bringing us into real contact with the thing
we know, appears as something between us and it,
either altering its *real* reality to accommodate it to us,
or forming some screen or barrier between us and it,
or some way disguising it—but on this I shall have
to speak in abundance.

I shall have to consider, against a good deal of the
third kind of philosophy which I have yet to speak
of, that the mind is really active, and that its proper
creations, so to call them, are realities; but, also, against
such views as I have just mentioned, that its *logical*
creations are for a temporary purpose only, and that
the greatest care must be taken *not* to realize them:

that a merely logical philosophy is worse than none, and much worse than that which I am now going to mention.

The third kind of philosophy, though it is not properly philosophy, and is only good in its own place when it does not claim to be so, is that manner of looking at the universe to which belongs the physio-psychology of which I lately spoke: and what I said about that applies to the many other sciences into which this study of the universe divides itself. The error belonging to it consists in its claiming to be philosophy, or claiming to be all that need be considered. This error I have called ultra-phenomenalism or mis-phenomenalism, and I have given the reasons for my language: it is the same manner of thought as is very frequently called 'positivism'.

A real philosophy without notionalism, and a real, honest, thorough, study of nature without the feeling that we are to find our philosophy and morality, more than very subordinately, *there*—these are the two things which I should like to see co-existing, and which I should think not only *might* co-exist, but would each be the better for the existence of the other: and for both alike is needed a good *logic*, in which we are neither on the one side afraid of logical suppositions and abstractions, nor on the other hand disposed to *rest* in them as if the right dealing with them was the knowledge, and they all the furniture our mind needed: and with all these a good *history* of advance of human thought and feeling, upon which depends what I have in these pages called 'Real' Logic: all these things seem to me to *belong* the one to the other: the warfare constantly carried on between the partizans of one and another seems quite uncalled for, and unreasonable. Of them all, the 'philosophy' which I have named the first is in my view the most important, as that on which all the rest depend, and in which they all find their application. It is what all *begins* with for us, for all that we call existence is for us *a thought* of ours, which it belongs to that philosophy to discuss the nature, meaning, validity of. It is what on the other side, is concerned with that which we must know and have settled for ourselves before we can, with reason, apply our knowledge of experience to action: namely, what we want: what we mean to do with ourselves, what ends we wish to gain, what it is well we should do, what we are called upon to do: this is the region of ideals, of freedom, and of choice, where no positive knowledge or knowledge of experience can help us except in those subordinate manners to which I have alluded, as to judge what is attainable, or by what means we may best gain our end.

The purpose then of what I have here written is to clear the ground, or to do what I could to help clear thought, both in respect of philosophy and of physical view of nature : the one is quite as interesting to me as the other, and they seem to me, rightly pursued, to be mutually helpful, not antagonistic. A great deal of the Philosophy of the Human Mind damages both, especially philosophy proper, by its confusion of view— this I have endeavoured to exhibit : 'notionalism' or 'relativism' damages both, philosophy by cutting off from it all life, and fruit, and prospect, the view of nature by making us think and talk of abstractions where they are out of place, and where we want to be in the fresh and open air of good or rightly applied phenomenalism (as I have called it), looking at things as they are before our eyes without perplexing ourselves by thought as to how we know them or what they may be besides. Mis-phenomenalism or positivism damages the study of nature and of fact in this way, that by the expecting from it, and the trying to effect by it, what does not belong to it, it raises suspicion against it, and what is worse, tends sometimes to make its cultivators pursue it with a sort of misgiving, as if this suspicion really attached to it, and as if fidelity to it really required that at whatever sacrifice, we should abnegate, at its apparent bidding, everything which I should call our higher nature, and all our worthier beliefs and aspirations. What I have called philosophy is of course to such positivism of the nature of a dream, and that a foolish and pernicious one.

The manner in which I have tried to help clear thought I must leave the following pages to show for themselves—I will only mention one thing here.

It is in reference to what I may call the coordinating facts of mind and matter, as what go together to make up the universe. This I have variously commented on. I think the purpose of what I have said may be better understood through a few words here to the following effect.

One of the branches of science in which perhaps at this moment (in company probably with many others) I feel special interest on account of the manner in which it seems to promise fruit, is the study of what we may call 'the facts of mind' as we may see, observe, experiment, upon them in the universe, both in various human individuals with corporeal organizations *individually* different, and in various animals (so far as we can thus study them) with such organizations differing *generically*.

Facts of mind of this character are facts of the universe, and may legitimately be co-ordinated with facts of matter, and knowledge about them must be pursued in the same manner in which the study of the facts of matter is—by observation, experiment, induction.

But there are facts of mind, and what are more properly described as 'facts of mind' than these are, which are not at all of this character, but are of such a nature, that so far from being in any way what can be co-ordinated with facts of matter to make up the universe, the whole universe is itself *one* such fact of mind to us—when we say *it is*, we mean that *we believe in it* —it is the way in which we think, something which our thought sets before us—and there are *other* such facts of mind besides this. The *great* fact of the kind is human freedom, liberty, choice. Mind, as we study it for instance in various animal organizations following various laws, is something different from mind *as we feel it*, or *ourselves*, thinking and choosing what we will do: and the generic mind in such organizations, with its future, so to speak, marked out for it by nature, is something different from our mind as we feel it, which is more even than humanly generic or generically human—for we have a free view around us—we may see what is good to be done, and choose what we will act for, not (in this case) as *men*, but as moral beings, who can see even beyond their manhood or proper kind, and can aspire to raise themselves and that kind—when we have chosen indeed, it is as men that we shall have to *act:* we have but human *powers*, though we have a *choice* going beyond known or proper humanity: and thus, in a subordinate way, the facts of mind which may be *physically* studied are of vast consequence: but the real and great facts of mind are the others. And the treatment of these, in both an intellectual and moral view, is what I have called philosophy: the examination what knowledge is, how we know, and what we mean by certainty and truth: the examination what liberty or choice is, what is the meaning of a purpose or ideal of action, what purposes or ideals present themselves to us, what we are to think about them.

Unless we have philosophy of this kind, whatever we can make of it, as a companion or pendant, it seems to me that we cannot follow *either* of the two lines of thought which at this moment are of special interest, without getting into a hopeless perplexity as to the application of them to our action. By these two lines of thought I mean, the one, the physio-psychology of which I have spoken: the other, the past history of the human race, both intellectual and moral or civil. If we wait to know what we ought to think about ourselves and what we are to do (more than subordinately) upon these studies, not only shall we be in an unnatural suspense, but we can hardly fail to get more and more into a logical perplexity, and we shall injure these studies themselves. Already it is evident that the study of human progress, or human developement, or civilization, is in a confusion most difficult to disentangle, on account of people's having failed to present to themselves as two different notions, the progressive improvement, on the one side, of beings with liberty, enterprize, aspiringness, and desire to do the best and the right and to elevate their nature, and, on the other, such a progressive developement as we may conceive to take place in any kind of beings (or *zoöcosm* as I have later called it, *i.e.* system of kinds) in consequence of any natural tendencies in them or circumstances about them, independent of such free choice and aspiringness. In respect of the great and important science of the philosophy of history, as we call it, it seems to me that the prospect is

b

bad for the very reason which makes some think it good: namely, that we are now looking to it for our morality: we want to find out from it what I am sure we cannot find out from it without perverting it, namely, what we ought to do: we shall lose our power of moral judgment in criticizing what man has done, and after all we shall never be able to say why what man has done (whatever it may be) is, as such, the thing which we ought to do now.

The world is in some respects getting old, and its value for the history of the past, whether the intellectual history of man's successive discovery of things, or the moral history of his advance in civilization, may be taken as one sign of this: at the same time the world is in some respects as young as, or, if one might venture the expression, more young than, ever, and never I suppose were hopefulness and enterprize more abundant. No one can feel more interest in history of all kinds than I do: almost, perhaps too much. But the tendency of questions and subjects of all kinds at this time to *run to history*, if I may so express it, amounts, in many cases, to a blinking the great and real questions, which ought not to be encouraged. This historical tendency is a part of the character of mind which may be called 'positivism', though it spreads widely beyond the circle of those who would accept the name. But roughly, the *principle* of this tendency is the following: To understand things, you must understand their history: or perhaps, we cannot understand things: all that we can understand is their history. For things we might put 'men': the study of the history of man is now put before us as that by means of which we are to understand man himself, and know what we ought to do.

I will not say that the truth lies in the exact opposite of this, but I will say that it lies a good deal nearer
to that extremity than to the other. In speaking, in
what follows, of Mr Mill's Logic, I have commented on
the manner in which he gives attention (as I have
expressed it) to what *goes on* in the universe, which we
come to believe upon evidence as we come to believe
any ordinary fact, rather than to what *is* in the universe, which, in whatever way, we come to know, conceive, perceive. And yet what goes on, as the fact, in
the universe, is that the beings and things in the
universe do this and that, change in this or that
manner : the beings and things are of prior consideration really to the fact: we cannot understand the
fact without understanding *them*. We want, in mathematical metaphor, a sort of integration. But if we
ask Mr Mill what *a thing* is, we shall get, I think, but
an uncertain answer: it is something which is, or has
been, or may be named: it is an unknowable substratum with knowable attributes: it is a co-existence of
attributes, in virtue of what nexus or principle we cannot tell. But it is *this*, what the universe is made up
of, what is in it, what makes things things, which we
really want to know before we can properly appreciate
what the things do, their changes, what is going on :
no doubt the study of this latter helps us towards the
former: it is its main interest: but without the former,
so far as we can attain to that, it is what can be but
imperfectly entered into and what the mind will not .
rest in.

It is the same in regard of man and his history :
we ask what man is and what man should do, and we
are answered with what man has done and does. Here
again, we can make nothing of this latter, we cannot

realize or appreciate it, except in virtue of our knowledge of the former. It is the knowledge which we
have already of the former which gives interest to our
study of the latter. No doubt when we can rightly appreciate and understand what man has done and does, it
will mightily add to and deepen our knowledge of what
he is: still, as the general fact, the basis of history is the
more or less knowledge of the nature of that which it is
history of. But *we*, 'men', *are* by our thought and
feeling in a manner much more intimate and real than
we *are* as members of the human race on earth, in such
a manner that history can take account of us. And
therefore the consideration of what we *are* by our
thought and feeling, which is what I call 'philosophy',
is something which no *history* of any kind can make
up for the want of or supply to us, and something without which that history itself loses very much of its importance and its interest.

But I now proceed to describe the method—so far
as there is any method—upon which the following
pages go.

The first three chapters contain a sketch of my own
view as to the double manner of proceeding necessary
in mental philosophy or the discussion of the nature of
knowledge.

I then proceed to review, if it may be called so,
various books on the subject and on cognate subjects :
more correctly however, to compare my views with the
views of the authors of the books which I speak of.
To some extent I give an account of the purpose and
manner of proceeding of the books, not however to a
very great extent.

I will first mention what books I notice, and then say
why I notice any books, and why these in particular.

The first which I speak of is Professor Ferrier's Institutes of Metaphysic. The second, Sir William Hamilton's Lectures on Metaphysics. The third, Mr Mill's Logic. The fourth, Dr Whewell's series of works, representing his former 'Philosophy of the Inductive Sciences'. The fifth and sixth, which however I fear will not occur to be noticed, or at least but very slightly, in what I publish now—I will give the reasons at the close of this Introduction—are Mr Morell's Elements of Psychology and Mr Herbert Spencer's Principles of Psychology. The last is Professor Bain's book upon the Senses and the Intellect, with possible reference to his later book upon the Emotions and the Will.

First then, why do I notice any books at all?

The disposition to comment is one with which, except in certain particular cases, I do not sympathize at all, and the disposition to criticise is not one with which I sympathize greatly. This latter is a disposition which in an age like ours flourishes much : I am disposed to think that the degree to which it does so is due in some degree rather to readers than to writers : I think that what we may call first-hand thought in philosophy is more ready to spring up and appear than it is valued, at first, when it does appear, and that the manner in which the public ear, at any time, is open only to a few or to something said about them has a tendency to make thought more *parasitic* (so to call it) than of itself it would naturally be. This however is by the way. But I have to explain how it is that, if not fond of the spirit of criticism, I apparently so much criticise.

Philosophy has been from the first διαλεκτική, discussion, argument—even when *delivered* in a gnomic and authoritative, or in a poetical form, it must rest, in the mind of the philosopher, upon this imagined—and

it never can be otherwise. Lord Bacon, by most vigorous controversy and criticism, we may say, on his
own part, endeavoured to call men away from controverting each other to the study of the book of nature
open before them : but in mental or intellectual philosophy, not only must we have the vigorous controversy
at the beginning, but even in the carrying out of the
philosophy we cannot get free from it. The reason is
this : the important thing in intellectual philosophy is
to be sure that we are *saying something*. As soon as a
philosopher has in any way made an impression, he
will very likely have some, it may be many, to admire
and adopt what he says : but these are very imperfect
judges as to its substantialness. The test of what he
says being not only words, but *something*, is first his
own inward sight : but this is something for himself
alone, and even he cannot entirely trust it : we cannot
allow that an idea is, by mere virtue of its clearness,
certain and true. Hence mind must be brought into
contact with mind—no man can know even his own
mind without this. And thus the conversational and
discussional form of much early philosophy is not an
artistic accident of it, but belongs to its being : the
philosopher is the man who can διδόναι and δέχεσθαι λόγον
—who uses effort to think clearly himself and give a
clear account of what he thinks, and who besides thinks
it worth while to be patient in trying to enter into the
views of others. Intelligent philosophic criticism is
really what I may call substantial, though not literary
and artistic, philosophic dialogue : it is the meeting of
mind with mind where truth is supposed to be the
object of both, and where truth is of such a nature that
discussion is likely not to confuse, but to clear it.

It is in this spirit that I have noticed the books

which I have noticed—not with the slightest idea of appraising their literary value, or judging them from a superior point of view. So far from this being so, I might mention among the reasons why I have chosen *these* books out of the books on the subject, this, that these, it so happens, are the books from which I have *learnt*. When I say 'learnt', I mean that they are books with which my thought on these subjects has been a good deal associated, and which has suggested much of it: not at all that they are books which I particularly follow, in which case such heterogeneous teaching must produce rather singular results. But it is my nature at least to learn as much from what I differ with as from what I agree with. The philosophical thought is always best which is generated in the mind, and sometimes the thought which is caused by opposition is likely to be the more native, sometimes that caused by acquiescence; not of course mere acquiescence, but such as is intelligent and suggestive. As to this, the case is different with different individuals.

It will be seen in my notices of the books, that I never criticise any views of the writers without giving in the fullest manner my own, in fact not unfrequently making their views only a suggestive of what I say myself. I mention this, lest it should appear that what I have called criticism was my object, which it is not. I care not the least to dispute what any one says, except with a view of clearing my own thoughts and those of others. I have noticed what seem to me various bad arguments, but I dare say I have used some myself: every philosopher ought to make up his mind, that if he does serve the cause of truth, one way in which he will do so will be by his error being the cause of truth in others. I have seen already so much reason, in anything which I have thought about these subjects, to correct previous thought by later, that though, without a reasonable feeling that what I write now is the truth, so far as I can see it, I should not write at all—yet still, when the process of self-correction and growth of thought ceases, I shall consider the cessation a mental senescence which I shall be sorry, not glad, to feel in myself: and of course, what one would correct for one's self, one must not be indignant at having corrected by others.

But in one respect the notice which I have taken of the books which I mention may be considered criticism—that it is taken with an earnest desire to help the understanding and the study of the books: if I had not thought them eminently worthy to be understood and studied, I should have been as little disposed to give so much time to them myself as to take up the time of readers with thought about them. There is no doubt in England at present a want of philosophy—that this is not a character of our minds as Englishmen, I think the literary history of England at other times proves: but at this time it seems to me that the want is rather of general philosophic interest than, so to call it, of philosophic leading, or of minds disposed to philosophic speculation, or of philosophic writers. So far as my own observation goes, there seems to be commencement of germination of the philosophic seed, and there seem to be good philosophical books, which, from the nature of them, can never in any age be numerous: but for what reason I know not, the seed seems scarcely to go on from germination to fruit, and the philosophical books are more admired than entered into: what I have called want of philosophic interest seems to me deserving possibly of a harder name: but there have been certainly periods, and those possibly periods when men's thoughts were much taken up with civil and political excitements, in which men nevertheless found time to think with interest of philosophic problems to which now they are quite indifferent, and to find pleasure in effort of mind about things worth it, where now it seems to them only waste of force.

What however I have mentioned this for, is, that it does not seem to me that there is want of good books of our day on philosophy, and I have chosen for criticism such books as I have with the notion that the philosophic problems which they treat of are treated of by them with an ability which leaves no reason that we should go for the discussion of them beyond our own time and country. I give this of course as a partial reason only for my having selected such books. I leave the philosophy of other countries and the ancient fountains of all our philosophy to others more competent and more acquainted with them than I: but I do say, and that though I fear that those whom I speak of would each one, were they all alive to do so, only in a very limited degree concur with me—that the books which I speak of—and more might be added to the list, for as I have said and shall say more fully, my selection of these is *in part* accidental—form as good a philosophic literature for one period as we shall find at many periods which we much more distinctly should call philosophical. It is not to fill any void, or make good any deficiency that I write, according to what prefaces usually say: it is to help readers to understand and use what they have got: but then by understanding and using a philosophical book I do not mean simply taking in what it says, and thinking, so far as this is thinking, accordingly: I mean studying it, entering into the view, following the arguments (and *watching* them also) seeing the difficulties and seeing whether they are met—and much besides of this kind. It will be said, There cannot be many readers like this: perhaps not. What is really the truth as to the philosophy of different periods and generations, we really cannot tell: we should perhaps consider Bishop Butler's generation a philosophical one in comparison with ours: but as to the readers, his impatience at their supposed sluggishness of thought is almost amusing: and as to the writers, it does not seem to me that we are at all inferior.

I will now mention why I have selected for notice the particular books which are selected. Some of the reasons have been anticipated, but there are others[1].

The books form, it will be readily observed, a sort of scale, spectrum, or gamut, of which Professor Ferrier represents the extreme philosophical end, and Professor Bain the extreme physiological or physical. Towards the centre of the scale, as is natural, there is not much principle of succession. I have put Mr Mill

---

[1] I take the books as representative—as exhibiting, more or less, particular schools of thought. I am not quite certain of the extent to which they are so, and perhaps, in what I hope may follow these pages at a later time, shall remark upon this. Supposing this however to be so, it is evident that in each school of thought there are books to which I make no reference, in regard of which I have not the least wish to pronounce that those which I notice are superior to them. No one for instance could think that I should undervalue what has been written on these subjects by Professor Mansel—but I have considered that what needed saying on his manner of thought would be said sufficiently for my purpose in speaking of Sir William Hamilton—and the same as to Professor Fraser. It so happens that of those whom I notice some are alive and some are dead—it cannot therefore be said that I care to criticise only those who can feel the criticism, or only those who cannot answer. And Sir William Hamilton still lives— a philosopher's best life—in disciples.

nearer the philosophical end of the scale, and Dr Whewell nearer the other for reasons which further on I
have mentioned, and which refer to the *method* of each:
that of Mr Mill being derived in some degree from
the Formal Logic, and having rather a logical and
scholastic character throughout: that of Dr Whewell
resting very much upon physics and physical history,
with much less use of logical manner and language.
If I had looked at the substance more than at the
method the arrangement might possibly have been
different, Dr Whewell joining with his definite physics
much more of what I call the philosophical view.

Of these books, those at the extremes will be found
probably the most suggestive of any thought which
these pages contain, so far as any of them have suggested it, though those in the middle (I may mention
especially that of Dr Whewell) on account of the wider
range of view, may be those in which I have taken
the more interest, and may perhaps think the more
instructive. But there is much less, in the books at
the extremes, of that confusion of thought, as it seems
to me, which one purpose of the following pages is to
call attention to. And also—what may excite some
surprise, but I think it strongly—I think that the
books at each extreme, so far as they do touch any
matter belonging to the opposite extreme, are likely,
from their less confusion of view, to suggest truer
thoughts about it than perhaps the others would. This
is the same thing as what I have meant when I have
said that though philosophy on the one side, and physiology and physical science on the other, are very
different things and may perhaps require different
minds for the developement of them, yet they are not
hostile to each other, and in reality the better and purer

the one is in its way, the better and purer the other is likely to .be. The mixture of considerations *how we know* with the study of *what we know*, the supposition that we not only perhaps do not, but cannot, know reality, that we do not know existence, but only modes and modifications of it, that our knowledge makes some sort of alteration in the thing that we know — and other similar suppositions, which belong to the sort of philosophy which I have called 'notionalism'— all these sorts of things seem to me not only *to be* bad philosophy, but so far as they are attended to, to *make* bad physics. While on the other hand, in studying how we have learnt, or come to the knowledge of what we know, the refusal to look at human mental activity, at the 'how we know', as well as at the fact that there are things which we know and that we know them, is as destructive of any philosophy or true logic of *advancing* thought as the other is of physics.

But I must not anticipate, or give what will not now be understood: I will merely, in this Introduction, say a word or two on each of the books in succession.

I have never known anything of Mr Ferrier except his book which I notice, but I judge that his premature death has been as great a loss to the philosophy of our country as it could suffer. His book seems to me to be eminently suggestive, perhaps the more so on account of much in it which I shall notice as to me very unsatisfactory: it suggests more strongly than any book which I happen to know that which appears to me the great need of our philosophy at the present time, namely, a reconsideration of our Philosophy of the Human Mind, on which we have so many books of so much value, as to its principle and as to the legitimacy of its method: and it takes a genuinely philosophical point of view from which it seems to me thought has with us got too much turned aside.

In what follows, I have said so much upon Sir William Hamilton's Lectures that I will say little of them here. I have had occasion to criticise Sir William Hamilton rather strongly: but, recurring to what I said a short time since about *all* the books, I think we shall have to go a long way back in English philosophic history (if indeed we are successful then) before we find philosophic power of a certain kind united with learning and philosophic knowledge as they are in him. I say 'of a certain kind' because—non omnia possumus omnes—I have had to criticise his reasoning, and altogether I desiderate something which a philosopher needs as much as learning, though perhaps, if he has Sir William Hamilton's learning, it may be difficult for him to have it—something which may be called flexibility, life, growingness of *thought:* but when we owe much to a great man it is idle to blame him for not being everything which one could have wished, and though I do not think Sir William Hamilton's philosophy promises much for progress in the future, I have but little doubt that his books, for one purpose or another, will long be read and referred to.

To Mr Mill I have already slightly referred. There are several things which he has published, and republished, in regard of which I disagree with him far more strongly and deeply than I do probably with any of the other writers here noticed: but they do not at all come into consideration here, and it is, amongst other things, to avoid anything of the kind doing so, that I put together what there is here upon matters

of intellectual philosophy alone, just indicating, in
speaking of Mr Mill, where we pass on to morals, without at all following that road.

Since the following pages have been in course of
printing, I have become aware of a book which Mr Mill
is publishing, or has published, on the subject of his
philosophical differences with Sir William Hamilton.
I speak in this doubtful manner only because I have
purposely avoided learning further. Perhaps this will
be understood. To have waited, and referred to what
Mr Mill may thus say, would have involved a wider
controversy. If criticism of Mr Mill had been in any
degree my main purpose, I should have been bound
to do this: but, as I have said, I have only used
Mr Mill's published views (and so for the other books
which I have noticed) to compare my own with: I
have said as little as may be of approving and dis-
approving, and spoken only of agreement and disagree-
ment: let us suppose Mr Mill, as he has written
hitherto, to be A, a character in rather a lengthened
philosophical discussion, and if the actual Mr Mill
has changed his views, or, which is exceedingly likely,
I have misunderstood him, then let it not be supposed
that it is Mr Mill that I am discussing with at all. For
myself, I am curious to see, when these pages are
published, what Mr Mill may have said on any subject
of which I may have spoken, and I think that such
involuntary controversy may possibly not be the worst
form of it. And after all, since what I have said about
Mr Mill and Sir William Hamilton in conjunction is
not much, it is possible that what Mr Mill says of the
philosophy of the latter may not refer to it, and may
concern some other subject, as, for instance, the Philosophy of the Unconditioned.

With Dr Whewell, my predecessor in the chair which I occupy, and to whom all those interested in Mental and Moral Philosophy in the University must feel themselves much indebted, I have long had the advantage of friendly intercourse. He has set an example in the University (not followed, I am ashamed to say for myself at least, as diligently as it might have been) of energetic and large-minded cultivation of the subjects to which these pages relate, which I should be sorry not to acknowledge. On his books however I think there is nothing which I need say in this Introduction.

Of the remaining writers whom I have mentioned, Mr Bain is the only one whom I know otherwise than by his books. It had been my wish to make the following pages complete as regards these writers: but circumstances have supervened which have determined me to stop at present, in general, with what I have said about Dr Whewell, in the hope that in a month or two, the rest may follow. I have wished, for various reasons, to bring this book out within the present month: one reason being, that ill health has prevented my doing as much in the way of my Professorship during the past academical year as I could have wished, and I wish to do what I can. The preparing for the press what I here publish (concurring with other employments), has taken longer than I had anticipated: and therefore, though much of what I hope to say a month or two hence wants but little of completion, I have thought it best for the present to stop where I have.

After all I have called the following pages 'rough notes' with a real feeling how much the title expresses the incoherence of them, an incoherence which I partly regret and apologize for, and which I partly think is not altogether a disadvantage.

Reading and speculating, and even to a certain extent writing, on the subjects which the following pages concern is something which is so much a pleasure to me, whereas preparing for the press and publication is so exceedingly otherwise, that the hesitation and irresolution which I have hitherto felt have a strong tendency to continue. But I have arrived at an age at which a man begins to feel, that if he thinks he has anything to say, he must say it, without being too particular how: if it shall please God to give the opportunity, it is possible that some things said here confusedly may hereafter be put in a clearer form, but in the interim, as time is passing, it is possible that some things which I say may suggest thought in others, and what I see but indistinctly may be seen by them more clearly, and put in a better and truer light. For the best thing that I can hope, and the thing which I most wish, for anything which I may say, is that it may be improved upon: the present generation seem to have more than one most bright field of speculation open before them, and what I want more than anything is to prevent their enterprize being damped by their being told, whether on the ground of notionalism or positivism, that to know about God, to form a notion of an ideal of what should be done or what they and the human race should aim at — that this and much like it is visionary and beyond the reach of human faculties: nor do I less wish to prevent the truth of their look at nature, and the sincerity of their investigation of it, being vitiated by the suspicion and fear that they will be brought to conclusions inconsistent with all this, and which will force them to renounce their best birthright.

I am not however altogether of opinion that such incoherence as there is in these pages is a disadvantage. For the reputation of the philosophical writer himself, it is best that what he has to say should appear well and artistically rounded : but I am not sure it is best for his readers, if what they want is to know the truth. A large part of the following pages represent the first jet in which such philosophy as is contained in them has cast itself in my mind, after a doubtfulness and effort in which it seemed doubtful whether it would cast itself in any : I am not sure whether, for the real *appreciation* of that which I say, which is what I want, it is not better it should be left in this state rather than more carefully elaborated. But I know that my view in the course of the writing, while in the main more thoroughly commending itself, has in some particulars changed—I think cleared itself : I am aware therefore of weak and confused places, or what seem to me so : while I am also aware that most probably, many places which do *not* seem to me so are so, just as, possibly, the others are not.

I think I have said nearly all that seemed required to be said in this Introduction : there is one thing which is not required to be said, but which I should like to say.

I mentioned that one reason for which I noticed the particular books which I do notice was that they were books from which I had *learnt:* I do not of course mean the *only* books, because, though on these subjects I have not cared to read more than my mind could test, examine and enter into, yet I have taken pleasure, so far as I could, in gaining my knowledge about them from various sources, and have endeavoured mentally to harmonize the knowledge as I best might.

Whatever in these pages is right, and seems to have
been said by others, I beg may be referred to them, for
whether I am aware of it or not, it may very likely
have come from them, and if I have not taken it from
them, I have missed reading something which I very
likely should be the better for having read. But I speak
here about what I have learnt for the following reason.

I have great interest in philosophy and speculation,
no dislike to argument and discussion, and very much
pleasure in imaginative suppositions, sometimes perhaps
of what may seem a wild kind—holding as I do most
strongly, that there is no fruitful reasoning where there
has not been much activity of imagination preceding.
But everything of this kind seems to me circumstance
or accident about philosophy, in comparison with the
one essential consideration in regard of it, What is the
truth ?   It seems trivial to say this—I shall be answered, Who says otherwise ?   But when one listens, and
reads, one seems to find philosophical questions put
really upon all sorts of other grounds : one finds a carelessness in the examination of argument which seems to
show very little value for what it professes to make out:
one seems to find, that mental and moral questions are
scarcely considered worth patience and thought, while
so much is given to others, interesting indeed, but
surely of less importance—and if so, how can it be said
the *truth* about them is valued ?   One seems to find,
that things are talked and written about with sincerity
no doubt, but with little appearance of what I will call
mental *conscientiousness* on the part of the talkers or
writers, that is, with little care or effort to get, so far as
they can, to the bottom of them, to *see* what they talk
or write about—and if so, can we say that truth is *really*
valued ?

Myself, not owing much I think to any philosophical *teaching*, (a thing which I do not think altogether to have been an advantage), I owe almost all such interest as I take in philosophy to what is next best to teaching, if it is not better, to companionship : the companionship of one who did not leave much behind him himself, except a memory with others I think as well as me not likely soon to be obliterated, the late Robert Leslie Ellis. My companionship with him I think was intellectually the most valuable portion of my life, for one single reason, namely, that I learnt from *it* (I say from *it* rather than from *him*, for I think it was from the concurrence and conflict of our minds, which were very different) a something not easy to describe, but which has been the soul of all my notions about philosophy since : one might call it a belief in thought : a feeling that things were worth thinking about, that thought was worth effort, that half-thought or loose thought was something to be despised, that the getting to the bottom of a thing was what would repay the trouble of it : a sort of shame at not being serious and in earnest about matters worth seriousness : without indeed too great a readiness to *think* things this latter. It is perhaps a part of *my* disposition rather than of his, that, in too great a measure, probably, many of the things which seem to people in general worth trouble and thought do not seem to me so : that this feeling is not still stronger in me I certainly owe in part to my companionship with him. But in a time of civilization like ours, when things are talked about, and written about, and read about, so easily and with so little expenditure of attention, one might be tempted to think that our intelligence was really given us only as a means towards material utility or as a something to amuse our-

selves and others with. Without bringing intellect into
any comparison with moral feeling and duty, my own
feeling seems to me to be ever stronger and stronger,
that as rational beings, at once our great duty and our
highest pleasure is something which people do not
in general seem to trouble themselves much about,
whether in life or for education : the seeing things for
ourselves and having an opinion of our own, with care
and any amount of effort that it should be, to the utmost of our power, the true and the right one : a faith
in our intelligence, or, which seems to me the same
thing, a faith in the entire state of things in which God
has placed us, and in the moral universe of which we
are a part, that our intelligence, rightly used, will not
lead us astray, and that the right use of it is something
which is well worth our while.

Robert Leslie Ellis, it is probable, as is the case
with men of abundance of character and richness of
endowment, seemed different to different people, according to what they most sympathized with, but to
me what was most interesting about him was his intellectual conscientiousness : which was marked by the
distinctness and clearness with which, when he expressed an opinion, it always was expressed, and not
less by the readiness to listen to anything which might
appear to throw difficulty or doubt in the way of anything which he might be disposed to think. It is the
going of these two things together which makes the
philosophic readiness to meet the mind of others fairly
with one's own mind, the mingled candour and desire of
truth which I have spoken of : there are abundance of
people with well rounded and neatly expressed opinions,
but they can bear no disturbance of them : there are
abundance who are ready to admit doubts and difficulties,

so ready that they think it hopeless to form any opinion at all. I understand by intellectual conscientiousness the feeling of restlessness and dissatisfaction at anything being confusedly seen or not worked out, and of dislike at seeing it incorrectly put or fallaciously argued, which arises from the feeling that truth is worth effort and patience : this is likely to be encouraged by a mathematical training, or to exist in concert with a mathematical habit of mind, provided (a most important provision) there exists also what I should call a wideness of view, and a feeling of the importance, the higher importance, of other truth besides mathematical. Otherwise the comparison of the directness of mathematical result with the complication and difficulties of philosophy will only produce despair of the *best* truth. The philosopher, as I understand, is a man who means a great deal by believing—means something very different from the easy process which many call by that name : a man in whom desire to believe and desire to believe nothing that is not the truth are equally balanced. There is no real intellectual faith therefore without much of thought, anxiety, and doubt. The philosopher in his search can hardly, I presume, avoid much repulse and even defeat. The true philosopher, in my view, is the man who under all 'non desperavit de veritate': who believes in truth enough to be willing mentally to labour for it, and to forego any substitutes for it.

To me this character of mind seems the reverse of the sceptical, and to be that which gives the proper foundation for religion : it seems to me to be from minds of this conscientiousness and deepfelt seriousness that we learn (and I am sure it is my own experience) very much of what gives religion its claim to be the one great thing which we ought to think of. It is true that I have views on this subject which are not perhaps those of every one : I look upon philosophy not simply as a branch of literature and science, but in its practical character, as intimately connected with human action and the direction of that, and since religion takes that province also, I do not think. they can act independently, or refuse to notice each other. As a man thinketh in his heart, so is he : and to the 'thought' which thus makes the man, I am disposed to. give a wide application. It is of course sadly familiar to us how many neglect and cast away their *moral* selves, their soul : but I am disposed to think, that as regards their intellectual selves, few people value themselves as they might and should : and that if they cared more what they thought, not in view of shining and appearing, but for its own sake, they would be happier and better. Thought is not a professional matter— not something for so-called philosophers only or professed thinkers. The best philosopher is the man who can think most *simply.* Education and learning are wanted for thought just in the same degree to which, on the other hand, fresh view and hunger after truth are wanted : and if the ignorant envies the learned, the latter has some reason to retort the feeling, and to envy the other the intellectual appetite which he *ought* to have. But, like the countrymen in Virgil, the ignorant are insensible of their advantages. I say this seriously so far, that I think if in those who learn, the interest or value of what they are doing as a process of thought could be to a certain degree in mind, the value of what is done would be many times multiplied : how knowledge increases for us is not a thing of near so much conse-

quence as how thought changes. We want and ought
if possible to use our minds in thought all along : for
each stage in the change of thought has its own special
value : and it is as we think at each time, according to
what I said just now, that we are.

But I must not dwell on this : I would only wish
people to consider that thought—and philosophy is no
more than good and methodical thought—is a matter *intimate* to them, a portion of their real selves : when they
think this, they will be to a certain extent good philosophers already, for they will *value* what they think,
be interested in it, and take pains about it : there are
some perhaps, good but mistaken, intercourse with
whom might lead them to consider that what *they*
(such as *they* are) think *themselves* is of very little
consequence, and that they have nothing to do but
to accept something on authority : and there are others,
as mistaken but very far from so good, intercourse
with whom might lead them to consider in the same
way that what they think themselves is of very little
consequence : because there is nothing worth thinking
about : because neither their thought nor that of others
is what will lead them to any result worth speaking
of : because we think according to our place in the
scale of nature and the history of man, and according
to the history of our father and mother, and whatever
else may have determined our physical organization, and
because elevation of our moral selves and of our race is
a chimera, and man is simply a dreamy and imaginative animal, and a grown man of sense will quit such
imaginations, and if I may so express it, let himself
be—do what he must or will do—consider *thought*
for him as what the animal's instinct is for *it*, his ca-
pital or instrument for material life, and the utmost

thing worth thinking of, if he goes so far, that he may use it for the material benefit of others. Fœnum habet in cornu, longe fuge—ultra Sauromatas, or anywhere further still—let us go anywhere to avoid teaching which like this damps as well mental speculation as moral energy—damps all worthy enterprize and aspiringness: teaching which, now occurring as an apparent result of human progress, would have prevented that progress if in earlier times it had been, not only what it always has more or less been, the habit of mind of the less thinking among the human race, but the creed and belief of the more thinking. Human progress has been what it is, under God's Providence, because there have not been wanting in the human race men who have felt themselves free, and who have believed in their intelligence, and who have felt that their race was capable of elevation, and who have seen or seemed to themselves to see, with effort indeed perhaps and obscurely, something of the way in which it could be done. If complaint is to be made at present of the absence of philosophical spirit in our country, it appears to me—perhaps mistakenly—that many men are in a sort of doubt as to what is before them: that they have a kind of fear that religion and the old ways are dying out, and yet are not satisfied with a prospect only of continual multiplication of fresh inventions and new markets, while they do not know what to look to instead. I have but to say on this, let us believe in ourselves, which in this application is not the revolting against, but the believing in God, whose Providence has made men to advance as he has. If we wish, as men, to be wiser, better, happier, let us believe that to *some* degree at least we *can* make ourselves so, and let us try. The following pages are a very humble attempt, or beginning of an attempt, towards advance in the *intellectual* direction: if they are at all a successful attempt, it will be through others taking up anything which may happen to be right in them, and pursuing it: I hope it may be so.

I mentioned a short time since, that it is in the books of the writers at the two extremities of the scale which I have given, that will be found opinions *most* resembling those given in the following pages: and in fact, the main thread, so to speak, of all that follows, is effort to ascertain the relation which the manner of thought at one of these extremes bears to that at the other. I am not going in what is now published, for reasons which I have given, to speak of the writers towards one of the extremes: but to show the line of thought which I shall try to follow, I will anticipate for a moment, and say a word of the one *at* the extreme, Professor Bain.

Some of the leading notions which I have given will be found given in Mr Bain's book more distinctly than in any other, as for instance in his chapter on the Perception and Belief of the Material World. For example "Belief in external reality is the anticipation "of a given effect to a given antecedent"..." Between "the world and mind there is no comparison, the things "are not homogeneous[1]...."—and so in other cases.

But perhaps I had better quote a passage at length, which expresses more clearly than I could express it, in all the first portion of it, what I think myself, and shows in the second what it is that I want to understand and what I desiderate.

"When we come to communicate with other beings, and "ascertain by the signs of communication that they pass through

---

[1] Page 370.

"the same experience as ourselves, this enhances still more the
"constancy of the association between our sensations and the
"corresponding active energies. We ascertain that at times
"when we ourselves are not affected by a particular sensation,
"as of light, other persons are affected by it. This leads us to
"generalize sensation still more, and to conceive to ourselves an
"abstraction that comprehends all our experience, past and
"present, and all the experience of others, which abstraction is
"the utmost that our minds can attain to respecting an external
"and material world. So often as I open my eyes I have the
"sensation of light (the exceptions are not material to the illus-
"tration). I thereupon associate this sensation with this action,
"and I expect in all future time that the action will lead to
"the sensation. Other persons tell me the same thing. I
"thereupon affirm as a general fact that an optical feeling will
"always follow a certain muscular feeling, to me and to other
"sentient beings; and I can affirm nothing more, nor can I
"have any possible interest or concern with anything more.
"The assertion that light and the sun have a permanent and
"independent existence has, for its basis and for its import, that
"I, and all other beings with whom I have had any communi-
"cation, have had a certain optical feeling in conjunction with
"certain activities of which we have been conscious, and firmly
"anticipate the same coincidence in the future. The external
"existence of a stone wall means the association between certain
"optical impressions and a particular locomotive effort, and a
"further and still more decided association between touch and
"another effort, that, namely, which we call the sense of resist-
"ance. Finding the same sequence to exist with reference to
"beings in general, we generalize the fact to the very farthest
"limits, and affirm that it has always been so in the past, and
"will always be so in the future. Our language is apt to go
"beyond this; out of all the *particular* experiences (which
"alone constitute the real evidence for the proposition) we con-
"struct an experience in the abstract, a most anomalous fiction,
"that goes the length of affirming that the sensation is not only
"sure to occur along with the appropriate actions, but that it
"exists whether these actions take place or not. We seem to
"have no better way of assuring ourselves and all mankind that

"with the conscious movement of opening the eyes there will
"always be a consciousness of light, than by saying that the
"light exists as independent fact, with or without any eyes to
"see it. But if we consider the case fairly, we shall see that
"this assertion errs not simply in being beyond any evidence
"that we can have, but also in being a self-contradiction. We
"are affirming that to have an existence out of our minds
"which we cannot know but as in our minds. In words we
"assert independent existence, while in the very act of doing
"so we contradict ourselves. Even a possible world implies a
"possible mind to perceive it, just as much as an actual world
"implies an actual mind. The mistake of the common modes
"of expression in this matter, is the mistake of supposing the
"abstractions of the mind to have a separate and independent
"existence. This is the doctrine of the Platonic 'ideas', or
"'forms', which are understood to impart all that is common
"to the particular facts or realities, instead of being derived
"from them by an operation of the mind. Thus the actual
"circles of nature derive their mathematical properties from the
"pre-existing 'idea', or circle in the abstract; the actual men
"owe their sameness to the ideal man. So instead of looking
"upon the doctrine of an external and independent world as a
"generalization or abstraction grounded on our particular expe-
"riences, summing up the past, and predicting the future, we
"have got into the way of maintaining the abstraction to be an
"independent reality, the foundation, or cause, or origin of all
"those experiences".

Mr Bain's book is a book founded upon elaborate
anatomical detail, expressing then, or trying to express,
the facts of mind in language most concretely (so to
call it) physiological, and proceeding on very rapidly (I
mean with very little of an intermediation or process)
to the more complicated or as we might say abstract
facts of mind; giving, or attempting to give, an account of them in the same manner. With all this there
is united what I should call a better philosophy, that is
a more true and faithful account of the activity of

the mind, than occurs in many books where the philosophy is pursued as the important object, and in the view of which books, Mr Bain's physiology would be looked upon as materialism. I want to understand, how the philosophy and physiology are related to each other. With Mr Bain, *what* exists? In the middle of a book of physiology, we come upon something, upon *thought*, which, like an enchanter's wand, makes everything vanish—makes all explode without even remaining itself—we come upon a universal solvent—for it is not simply the external world, but *we,* corporeally, that vanish—and yet all this occurs in the middle of a system giving an occount of *our* bodies, *our* organs, *our* senses, &c. I will not dwell upon this: so far from mentioning it as any discredit to Mr Bain I mention it rather as an example of what I have said, that where there is the clearest view of the physiology on the one side there will be the clearest view of the philosophy on the other: only that I am not at all sure that we any of us understand how the philosophy and the physiology go together, or what relation they bear the one to the other.

In the same way I want to understand the value of the language (not at all peculiar to Mr Bain) that " we " have *got into the way* of maintaining the abstraction " (*i.e.* the universe of things about us, the phenomenal universe, as I have called it) " to be an independent reality ". (*Could* we have done otherwise?) And in the same way, that the general experience which we construct from particular experiences is " a most anomalous fiction". This is the language it is to be observed of a physiologist or physical philosopher, who has taken this supposed independent reality and general experience for his basis all along. The question with me

about all this is, What *ought* we to think ? Is the way
of thinking into which we have got as to the reality of
the universe a *bad* way of thinking, or not ? If it is,
how did we fall into it, and how may we get into a
better ? And similarly as to the experience—are we
right in constructing this most anomalous fiction ?

So much as this I just mention in order that the
nature of the points to come under consideration in
what I hope will shortly follow that which is given here
may be a little anticipated.

I send out these pages with much misgiving, not as
to the substance of them—all that I can say about this
is that they represent real thought, and of what value
the thought is can only be seen when it comes to be
compared with the thought of others—but as to the
way in which the manner or method (if it is to be
called method) of them may be taken. They are full
of egotism. I can only say that in reading what others
have written it is a matter continually occurring to me,
how much better it would have been if they had been
more egotistic ; how much better we should understand
what they meant if they had described the manner in
which the thing had come to present itself to their
mind, and let us a little see their thought in the forming : and also how many pages of literary history, ending at last in unsatisfactory result, would have been
also saved if this had been the case. What is to me of
interest before all other things, is *thought :* it is because
God, the Beginner of all reality, thought as he did that
things are what they are, and we at once, in finding
out what things are, or what is reality, are following
and tracing, so far as our faculties go, his thought, and
also, in thinking rightly or working out our own intel-

ligence, which is derived from his, are finding out what
reality is. Everything about our intelligence is in my
view interesting and useful : its results, so far as we
can trust them, which are what we call fact or truth :
its mistakes, which are the road to this : the conflict
of intelligences, or discussion (or this same going on
imaginatively within the mind) which ordinarily forms
the way by which from manifold mistake there is struck
out truth. Humanum est errare : it is a prerogative
of man to mistake : what of nature or of fact *is to* impress itself upon each kind of the lower animals does
so almost infallibly : man may learn anything, but to
balance this, he has got to learn each thing by speculation and trial, at the hazard of much mistake. If the
human race were too afraid of mistake it would learn
nothing.

If from my saying so much about what I think myself or what seems to me, it is concluded that I set too
high a value upon my thinking, and that this also is
the meaning of my saying, that human intellect or intelligence is what we ought to have confidence in, I
would answer as follows : Had I more confidence in my
own thought, much of what here appears would probably have appeared long ago. I think, and am sorry
for it, that I have had my full share of a state of mind
too common, I am able to see now that I look upon
a good many younger than myself, which is made up I
think of diffidence, fastidiousness, and an indisposition to
follow thought *out,* and which there seems something in
our literary atmosphere strangely, in respect of philosophy, to encourage. I say unfeignedly, both that my
most earnest wish as to what I have done myself is that
it may stimulate thought in others, and also that to *lead*
the thought of others is a thing to which I feel very

little disposition—it is a cardinal maxim of mine that every one's thought should be his own—I should wish to think rightly myself, and to help, if I can, others to do so in their own way. I should like to make them value their own thinking, and feel, that if it is genuine and their own, it has *some* value for others, and if they are at all in circumstances to follow it out, may very likely have *much*. And when I speak of belief or confidence in human intellect or intelligence, I use the expression more to make people enlarge and heighten their view of intelligence than for any other purpose. Intellect is not something opposed to imagination, not even something opposed to feeling : intellect is what I am persuaded there are very few who have not much more of than they think they have, or than they ever bring out or make any use of. By the philosophical spirit, which is the same thing as being true to our own intelligence, all I should understand is the getting the notion of using intelligence, not merely for advancement in life, not merely for the learning what others have thought, but for individual just and correct thought, and the application of knowledge to the aid of this. But I have said enough.

I may mention here, about the spelling of two words which occur very frequently, that I write 'phenomenon', 'phenomenal' when I use the words in their present English application or in a sense of my own derived from it, and 'phænomenon', 'phæno-menal' when I use them in an etymological reference, or am commenting on philosophers who spell them in this latter manner.

May, 1865.

CHAPTER I.

PHENOMENALISM.

I AM about to try to explain a manner of thought which, in various applications, or perhaps misapplications, of it, I have been in the habit of mentally characterizing, and perhaps of speaking of, as 'positivism.'

I shall now however not use this term, but the term 'phenomenalism.' I understand the two terms to express in substance the same thing, and what the thing is, will appear in what follows. The reason for the change is, because in the purely intellectual application which I shall now make of the term, 'phenomenalism' may perhaps carry with it less danger of extraneous associations being joined with it, and may express what I mean more generally: for the present purpose, I will remount from M. Comte to the times of Plato. I think that if the course of man's study of nature had been more fortunate, and the great onward movement of it which began four hundred years ago had begun in the century following that of Plato, as in many respects it very well might: if then the great bifurcation in philosophy which showed itself in full conspicuousness in that century had been more widely viewed, and not so preponderatingly in reference to Ethics: if Bacon and Galileo had followed Aristotle in the next generation, instead of at the distance of near two thousand years, and if we were to imagine a Greek M. Comte, some time afterwards, descanting on the manner in which science had advanced so as to be fruitful, and denouncing, as in fact many of the Epicureans did, the hindrances offered to it by superstition and fanciful metaphysics: philosophers of his way of thinking would probably have called themselves and been called 'phænomenics' or by some term of similar import. The notion of unreality

involved etymologically in the term 'phænomenon' would not
probably have hindered its use in this application more than
the idea of 'arbitrariness' involved in that of 'positive' and
'positivist' has hindered the application of this: 'phenomenon'
since the time of its first use has been the term most simply
expressing the (so-called) facts of nature considered in contrast
with any (so-called) metaphysical theories as to the origin of
these facts, their causes, or their purposes.

I shall call then by the name of 'phenomenalism' that notion
of the various objects of knowledge which go to make up the
universe which belongs to the point of view of physical science:
and what I shall endeavour to show is that this phenomenalism,
thoroughly true in its own province, and such, that if alien
elements be mingled with it false science is the result, is yet
not the whole of what the human mind, either intellectually
or morally, calls for and should have: that in the view of philosophy or the examination of the nature of knowledge, phenomenalism is an *abstraction* (so to call it) from something
wider than itself, with the truth, real but partial, which belongs
to the notion of an abstraction: that the progress, an undoubted
historical fact, made by both the individual mind and the mind
of the race in clearness of phenomenal view is not an absolute
correction of what has gone before, not simply a substitution of
something better for this, but a correction of it in one particular direction, leaving what thus purports to be corrected
still important and of force in other directions.

If, beyond and *before* this phenomenalism we at all enter
upon the consideration how we, feeling and thinking beings,
come to the knowledge of the facts that it embodies: or if,
beyond and *after* it, we enter upon the consideration how we
are to *act*, for what purpose we are to employ our phenomenal
knowledge: we come into an entirely different region: the
region, as to the method of our thought, not of physical science
but of philosophy or the higher logic: the region, if we are
to employ a term antithetic to phenomenalism, of what I have
called idealism. But the word idea belongs in rather a different
manner to the consideration of the manner in which we arrive
at our knowledge and the consideration of the purpose for
which we should act.

On this difference I will say just now only so much as this : that we gain our knowledge by a succession of mental efforts which are perpetually self-correcting, the correction however being of that kind which I just described, so that while our actual knowledge turns out something different in nature from what we expected, the expectation and previous view of knowledge still remains with its value in its own place. This, I am afraid, is not as yet intelligible, but I shall try to explain how ideas lead us to phenomenal knowledge : how they lead us, in rather a different application of the term, to action, is matter for another discussion. Phenomenalism may be called, if we like it, a step of thought or knowledge between two regions of idealism. The phenomenal world is the fit and as it were intended filling up of the vast, but yet in many respects definite, particular or qualitied, fixedly shaped, capacity for knowledge, which constitutes our ideal or imaginative nature. In this respect the ideal is the subjective, the phenomenal the objective. But the consideration of the relation of this which thus fills our mind to the mind which it fills carries us, as I hope we shall see, to a higher objectiveness or higher idea of existence. I shall consider a little what meaning there is in the notion of the ideal being the true existence, the phenomenal a subjective, and what is more, illusory one.

But there is much to be done first : and what I wish to say now is, that it is impossible to write satisfactorily on a subject such as this without having clearly before our minds the distinction between what, on the one side, is physical, or (in respect of scientific treatment) phenomenal, and on the other what is philosophical or logical. I think both Dr Whewell and Mr Mill err in this respect, I shall try to show how. I think it most likely I shall err myself, for the matter is abstract and difficult, but I hope that our errors will help forward the truth in others. The best way towards avoidance of error seems to me to be to try to exhibit so far as it is possible, independently of each other, in each case as if, so far as we can admit the supposition, the other did not exist, the physical or phenomenal view of the matter or object of knowledge on the one side, and the philosophical (logical or epistemological) view of the fact or process of knowledge, on the other. When we see the two things, so far as they can be separated, separate, we shall put together such parts of each as have to be put together with less likelihood of error.

The phenomenal verb is 'is' in the sense of 'exist', with immediate application of it to certain objects of our thought: the thought itself, the nature of the existence, the grounds of our supposition of it, not entering into consideration.

The verb of philosophy, or when our point of departure is consciousness or our own personality, is one which has scarcely existence in popular language : we might consider it to be 'feel' used neutrally, or 'feel ourselves' (the Greek ἔχω) with an adverb. In this consciousness, in the philosopher's view, is the root of all certainty or knowledge. The problem of philosophy is the finding the relation between existence and this.

Speaking generally, that is with certain qualifications which I may have to allude to, we must understand which view we are taking, and in the philosophical view must talk with great care of 'is', in the phenomenal must talk with great care of 'I', or 'we', 'perceive,' 'feel', &c. this or that. Consciousness or feeling is only a phenomenal fact in certain particular ways which I shall speak of. The phenomenal assumption is that the world of reality exists quite independently of being known by any knowing beings in it : just the same as it would exist, if there were no knowledge or feeling in any members of it : it is only results of such feeling that it is concerned with. The Berkeleian idealism is little more than the easy demonstration that this view, from a philosophical standing-point, is untenable : that the notion of existence, as distinguished from perceivedness, is, nakedly and rudely stated, as abhorrent to the philosopher as that of perceivingness and will in any part of the matter the laws of which he is seeking is to the phenomenalist.

In spite of this, the language of philosophers constantly betokens the notion, held in a manner which seems to me confused, of a double point of departure or source of reality : of the notion, in face of each other, of an independently existing phenomenal world and a perceiving mind, without any preliminary consideration what each of these notions requires, the language indicating sometimes the one point of departure, sometimes the other. What I mean will, as we go on, appear.

Let us for a moment, taking for granted the existence on the one side of our thinking self, and on the other, of an universe the object of knowledge, examine what we mean by 'sensation'.

What we call sensation is something intervening, on this supposition, between us the subject and the universe the object, of knowledge, and supplying the means by which they are brought together. We perceive things: the first and the last word express the supposedly independent realities: the middle word describes a process of communication between them. The point of meeting is a corporeal or physical communication between the various portions of matter which we know and one particular portion of matter which we call our body, which particular portion is constituted or organized in such a manner that according to the nature of the communication there shall accompany or follow it, in the supposed self, or what we call the mind, this or that feeling of pleasure or pain, or this or that felt exertion of will. The sensation is not the communication, but is this which I have described as accompanying it: is in fact a part, and the foundation, of our consciousness. On the one side of the communication, or within it, we may say, stands this sensation: on the other side, the outside of it, stand the various circumstances of body which make the sensation various, and to be of one kind or of another: which we call for instance, qualities. While still further within and without stands something more again: namely on the one side, within, the concentration of our consciousness which makes us use the terms 'I', 'we'; on the other side, without, the understood reality or substantiality which makes us use the term 'things'; which makes us consider that body or matter is something more than its qualities as we are something more than our sensations: which gives to our pursuit of knowledge something of the character, always, of hunting after something which eludes our grasp, of endeavouring, in a way, to understand the meaning of our own knowledge, and to find out why we think in the manner in which we inevitably do think: and, as we shall see, the character of perpetual self-correction and disappointment as well as attainment.

The communication between subject and object or between

'us' and 'things', which is the proper knowledge and the discussion of which is philosophy, may be said to include in the middle of it, as the means of it, the communication between our organs of sense and the qualities of the world beyond ourselves. But this latter communication again requires further analysis. The central part of *it* is a material or corporeal movement (I use the word movement in a wide and loose sense, to include possible chemical modification or change which perhaps may not be movement proper) of parts of our organs of sensation, as e.g. what we call affections of the brain, optic nerve, &c.; and this is the real phenomenal fact upon which our consciousness and our knowledge of the universe depend. What I have called phenomenalism is such a view of the universe as will embrace as a part of it this movement, simply considered as a material and corporeal movement, harmonize with it, and, if we may use the expression, fit on to it. That, in a sphere of thought in which the term 'movement' is without meaning, this movement is accompanied or followed by what we call consciousness, by feelings of pleasure and pain, exertion of will, &c. is nothing in itself, to phenomenalism, which has no means of dealing with, or language to express, facts, (if we may call them so) such as this. It can so far, and so far only, deal with consciousness as that it may recognize or discover the existence of what it may so term, by phenomenal effects which it produces: but it can do no more. We are conscious of what we feel ourselves, but beyond ourselves we cannot perceive feeling, except so far as we judge from effects which it produces, or conclude, doubtfully, from analogy: feeling is the secret, the incommunicable property, of whatever being possesses it: there might be an endless variety of feeling, for all that we know, in different portions of the universe, and it would be all the same to us.

The word 'sensation', in any proper application of the term, expresses a particular variety of feeling, and as such belongs not to the world of phenomenalism but to that of philosophy or the science of knowledge. It is from want of attention to this, that much philosophical confusion has arisen. Movements or changes take place in the subtle matter of our brain or nerves: these may be closely accompanied by feelings, or states of consciousness, however we may like to call them: it is to these latter

that the term 'sensation' properly belongs: but these, as we
have seen, are of no phenomenal consideration. The phenomenon, or fact describable and demonstrable to the common experience of all, which takes place as to knowledge, is simply this:
as to the eye, e.g.: light strikes it according to its own laws,
changes, mechanical and chemical, take place in the eye, the
optic nerve, and the brain, and a change perhaps takes place in
the movements (such as they were previously) of the whole
body, so that (to put the language shortly) the man who was
walking right up against a tree now walks by the side of it.
Physiology here tries, as it can, to make the chain of consecution, or of cause and effect, continuous.   It can follow the impression, and trace back the volitional action, to a certain degree
inwards, and it is conceivable that it might be able to complete
the chain, or follow the phenomenal process from the affection
of the nerves of sense and motion which leads to an ordinary
perception round to the action or changes in the nerves of
motion which lead to our walking one way rather than another:
but however it may do this, it cannot explain sensation, or take
one step towards it.   The physiologist may tell the man what
takes place in his nerves and brain, but the man, and he only,
knows what his feeling is, and he cannot even communicate it.
The physiologist may deny that there is any meaning in the
term 'feeling' as distinguished from the phenomenal process
which he exhibits: if he does so, he only brings out into
stronger relief the fundamental difference between the phenomenal and philosophical domains of thought, so that on the
principles of the one, the other is in the first instance not even
conceivable, and the simplest facts of the one may be denied
by the other without any appeal which can settle the question.

   The phenomenal fact then or the fundamental fact with
which phenomenalism must harmonize is not sensation, which
is a feeling, but the communication between natural agents or
portions of outward nature and the matter of our organs of
sense, that is, in fact, our body.   For our body is in fact one
single sense to us with various sub-senses or special organizations
for sensation, in the same way as, in the point of view of action,
it is one single machine with various sub-machines to obey our
will.   Phenomenally, our body is ourselves, and instead of

sensation we should, in propriety, speak of what I have called communication, just as in propriety, instead of action, we should speak of motion. Of course we may speak of sensation and action, if we attend to what we mean: if we mean sensation in the same sort of way as we speak of the sensibility of plants, as a something, that is, which we judge of by effects, but the nature of which in itself, as felt independently of effects, (or whether it has such nature), we say nothing of. With the same caution of course we may also speak of action. But the term sensation is very constantly spoken of as a phenomenal fact without this caution being borne in mind.

The word 'impression,' used often in a similar way to 'sensation,' is not in the same manner objectionable, but is so in another, *viz.* that it suggests the notion (in ordinary philosophical language) of sensation or perception being only *passive* on our part, or of the communication being only withinwards from without, and not, in a large portion of it, withoutwards from within. In reality, the sensation or feeling is in part an accompaniment of movements or changes in our nerves which the natural agents produce, and in part an accompaniment of movements or changes in them, which, in ordinary and philosophical language, we ourselves make: and which, in phenomenal language, are mechanical sequels of the other changes, to be accounted for as may be. We say a tree in front of us makes an impression on our eye or sense: but in reality what takes place is that the colour of the tree (so to speak) makes such an impression, but that correspondingly with this there are all sorts of movements of the eye by us, by which we measure its magnitude, and (associating our present sensation with many past ones) its distance and other particulars about it: and all this goes to make up that which is loosely described as 'impression'. I shall therefore, to avoid misunderstanding, use the word 'communication'.

The phenomenal world is then that of which *we*, meaning here by *we* our animated bodies, form a part, or, more properly, since a world, or universe, a whole of things, is something which phenomenalism does not suggest to us, it is an extension, loosely speaking we may say a generalization, of that matter of which our body is to us the type. I must here again repeat, that the 'we', or the 'I' spoken of here, is not the 'we' or 'I' of con-. sciousness. 'I', phenomenally, represents one individual of humanity. To find phenomenal reality, we must find that which can be known, so far as it is known, in common by all. Whereas consciousness, as we have seen, is peculiar to each. So far as phenomenal considerations go, each man, by con-sciousness, may have his own world[1]. At this moment, with the distinctest phenomenal conceptions, no one can tell but that what he sees as green may be seen by another as blue (provided the difference of inward view, so to call it, is con-sistent), and no increase of our physical knowledge about blue and green will help us in the least to know this. But phe-nomenal reality, so far as it exists, is what it is quite inde-pendently of the manner in which any one knows it, and even independently of its being known at all by anybody, or of there being any such thing as consciousness, or as mind, to know it, except so far, as I have said, as this 'mind' may produce phenomenal effects. Since we cannot talk except of something which we think and can know about, our talking about matter implies its knownness to us (so far as it is said to exist), without which we could not talk of its existence; this is what I meant when I said some time since, that the phenomenal view is an abstraction from the more general philosophical one: the full fact is, that matter (or however we describe it) is known to us, and we give our attention to it as *existing*, leaving out of account, for phenomenalism, what is contained in the other part of the fact, *viz.* it being understood, or *felt* as existing, by a conscious being or mind. The thing perhaps may be best understood by some by being put in this way: the phenomenal

---

[1] Hence it is that physical facts are after all phenomena only, for we say they exist because we conceive them or think about them, and how deep in us goes the conceiving and thinking of them by each one of us in the same way, is what we cannot tell. Hence too the effort of philosophy from the first to find fact or reality *not* subject to this difficulty, but in regard of which mind might trust mind to the bottom, and be sure of identity of thought. The escape from the difficulty of phenomena *being* phenomena, is, in the direction of what I have called phenomenalism, by a comparison of experiences, and the putting together what will stand such comparison, as a something supposedly existing, in the manner which I have described, independently of being known. The escape in the di-rection of the higher philosophy, which I do not dwell on now, is, in my view, the communication, by means of phenomena, with *mind* above them.

view of the universe is that view according to which its being known to any body, (or any part of it being known), is an inessential accident of it: existence is the fact, knowledge the possibility which may supervene. When, taking the wider or philosophical view, we begin with consciousness, feeling or knowledge is the first fact, involving existence only as a further one: but of this afterwards.

We have nothing then, phenomenally, to do with the way in which the universe is known to us, but we have of course to do with the way in which the different parts of it communicate, as I have said, with our bodily frame. This is so far the centre or type of the phenomenal universe to us, that nothing phenomenally exists so far as we are concerned, that is, can be in any way described by us, unless it stands in some relation to it.

This possibility of communication with our body is our criterion of phenomenalism. But in reality, it is not the centre, but the starting point, for our description of the phenomenal universe, that our bodily frame furnishes to us. Sensation, as I have said, comes into no phenomenal notice except as a property of the human frame, (in the same way as some sort of sensibility may be of plants) quite independently of the consideration whether any extra-phenomenal and incommunicable accompaniments, which we may call in general *feeling*, may go with it. The standpoint of the phenomenalist is free and the same for any one, and we might call it '*cosmocentric*' except in so far as acquaintance with the phenomenal universe being as we shall see an aggregation, or advance from part to part, does not properly admit the notion of such a centre.

To describe summarily the universe as viewed phenomenally, or on the principles here mentioned: space, to begin with that, is what matter (our body for instance), is contained in and moves in, the *continent*, if we might so use the word, of matter: the moving and changing of matter is the result of something which we describe as *force*, and *time* stands in the same relation to movement and change, or to *force* its cause, as *space* stands in to matter unmoved and unchanging; it is its *continent*: space always suggests to us the possible filling of it with matter, and time the possible filling of it with change:

they are the vanishing points or ghosts of these. Space and time are phenomenal realities in virtue of this their relation to matter and movement, not otherwise. And what space and time are filled with, phenomenally, is not *things*, (an expression which really belongs to popular philosophy in the same way as 'qualities,' 'objects,' &c. belong to philosophy more refined) but all sorts of what I have loosely called 'natural agents,' our notions of which, with the advance of physical science, are continually changing and improving. In phenomenal or physical view, it is possible that a hundred years hence what we call *matter* may be looked on as the result simply of the action of various forces: I want now to enter into no details as to the physical constitution of the universe, which I am incompetent to do, but only to disentangle physical notions from (popular or refined) philosophical ones. By the 'natural agents' in the universe which communicate with the nerves of our body I mean the forces (or whatever they may be) in what we call matter which make it produce or resist pressure, which cause it to have what we call weight, I mean light, air as conveying sound, chemical qualities as producing those movements or changes in the nerves of our palate (*e. g.*) which are attended by the sensation of *taste*, and much besides: but I think I have said enough to suggest the sort of thing that I mean.

The phenomenal universe is a complicated play and mutual action of these various natural agents, one portion of their play and action being that which goes on from without to within, and from within to without, between the bodily frame of each of us and the rest of the universe, whether the physiologist, as I have said, can complete the circle within our bodily frame or not.

Things, phenomenally, are units of phenomenal reality, depending upon measurement according to the kind of measurement which the particular kind of phenomenal reality (or the particular natural agent) is capable of. A stone is a piece of matter of such a weight and magnitude : gravity is a force of such a direction and intensity. Proper unity is not phenomenal : phenomenal unity is always a supposition. Supposing matter to be really composed of atoms, these atoms must have phenomenal magnitude, and a microscope is conceivable which would give them such to our sense: they are therefore units only by supposition and for reckoning, the considering them as units being suggested by our inability mechanically to divide them.

Kinds of things result, phenomenally, from the manner of the arrangement of the elements of matter or from the laws of action of natural agents, the special *kind, i.e.* genus, species, &c. in organized beings, being I suppose more or less a phenomenal puzzle. An organized being is, phenomenally, a sort of focus or centre, where, according to the height (or riches) of the organization, more or less of natural agency converges or diverges. *Life* is the name which we give to this, and it is probable that physiological research will more and more enable us to understand what life, phenomenally, is: while, according to what I have said before, life, *as it is felt,* is something which we know, so far as we know it, each one for himself, and no phenomenal research can give us in the least degree more knowledge as to this. It is a physiological or phenomenal fact that, in the case of life, there is reproduction, and like produces like, and this is the most special and marked fact as to what we call kind. And *life,* as I have said, suggests an idea of unity which, phenomenally, is a puzzle.

But I do not want to go into detail as to the phenomenal world or view, and will leave it, to proceed to a similar sketch of the philosophical world or view: after I have said a word first, on the phenomenal test of truth, and then on the phenomenalist mind or spirit.

I conceive that of truth, phenomenally considered, there are two great tests: the one, its answering to our action, the other, its harmonizing all our sensive powers and all the different experience of different men: or, in other words, that we say, phenomenally, a thing *is,* if we are fully persuaded that, if we act in reference to it, such and such results will follow, and also that we say it *is,* if we are persuaded that, though perhaps we only *see* it, yet if we could get to it, we could handle it, and though perhaps nobody sees it but we, yet if another person were present, *he* would see it as well as we. It is probable that our phenomenal notion of existence rests upon these two persuasions. I call them two: we might, if we pleased, call them one, by speaking of the harmonizing together of our active powers, our sensive powers, and our various individual experience. Or, no doubt, on the other hand, we might further analyze and divide them.

Lord Bacon's view as to the relation of physical knowledge to utility has been variously discussed, and Lord Macaulay has described him as in a great measure valuing physical knowledge on account of its utility. On this Mr Ellis has drawn attention to the high degree in which, on the other hand, what Bacon considered was that applicability to practice and use was a test of the reality of the knowledge, and a security against its being merely verbal and visionary. In that ruling thought of his mind, that knowledge ought not to be sterile, but fruitful, Bacon had, as much that he says and his whole temper show, most deeply at heart the utility of which it might be to man, but also strongly the thought, that unless knowledge was tested by being acted upon we could have but little certainty of its life and reality.

I will not dwell upon these tests: but having said so much of the one, will just say this of the other. By *illusion* as distinguished from reality we mean what, given us as apparent fact by one sensive power, will not stand the test of others. Phenomenal reality is the resultant arising from the comparison together of the information (so to speak) of our various senses, or, (so to speak again), our various means of communication with the external world. What is not true for all of these, so far as they can be brought into comparison, is not phenomenally true at all. So far as what any one sensive power presents to us as true cannot, in any of its circumstances, accompaniments, or effects, be tested by another such power, we cannot be certain that it is not illusion. And we only suppose it, even for the moment, to be reality, on account of our experience that what that sense has presented to us has hitherto been in harmony with the others[1].

---

[1] If anything '*is*' (phenomenally) it belongs somehow to all the body. Want of notice, however, will not make it illusion—there must be contradiction. And so far as there is any communication, there is reality of some sort. But where there is communication only of one kind there cannot be description of, or character in, the reality—there is then no test whether there is illusion or not.

Having spoken of the phenomenal test of truth, I will speak a word on the phenomenalist mind or spirit. I am going, after this, to do the best I can to show the actual way in which we come to know what we do know, and to examine knowledge itself instead of the (supposed) *matter* of knowledge, which is *one* part of the whole abstracted from the rest. By the phenomenalist mind or spirit I mean a manner of knowing or thinking which we never have originally, but which, in the advance of knowledge and growth of our mind, we are very likely to have, sometimes holding it with that due qualification and regard for other possible (extra-phenomenal) knowledge which, in my view, is the right state of our mind, sometimes holding it as what we ought to hold exclusively, and to the destruction of all possibilities of truth beyond it or outside of it (this is what, in the physical application of the term, I should mean by 'positivism'), sometimes feeling ourselves disposed to fall into it without considering, nevertheless, that we *ought* to hold it (at least exclusively), in fact being in difficulty of mind about it.

I think the best way of our conceiving this phenomenalist spirit, carefully avoiding, in our *intellectual* conception of it, any moral approbation or disapprobation, is to conceive what exists existing without being known (I can hardly say *conceived* when we are ourselves supposed conceiving it, so entirely is what we are supposing now what I have called an abstraction) by any one: without any mind, or anything like mind, having originated it or having been concerned with its origination or arrangement, so that when we find in it anything which we should describe as order, or form, or composition, it is not that kind of order, or anything like it, which we mean when we speak of putting together anything ourselves with a meaning and a reason. The phenomenalist maxim must be, to put nothing (mentally) in the universe beyond what we find there; and what we find there, phenomenally, is that, and nothing more, which communicates with the various natural elements, nervous matter, &c. of which our bodies are composed. We really, phenomenally, have no right to speak of order, arrangement, composition, &c. in the universe, all which are ideas belonging to our own consciousness of active and constructive powers. The great rule of phenomenalism is to be sure that we do not do that which, as we shall see, we always naturally *do* do, humanize the universe, recognize intelligence in it, have any preliminary faith, persuasion, suppositions about it, find ourselves, if I may so speak, at all at home in it, think it has any concern with us.

To me there is something in the simply phenomenalist spirit, so far as one has a tendency to sink (as I should say) into it, inexpressibly depressing and desolate. We are supposed to wake, not into a world (for even a world or universe is something for the imagination to lay hold of, a unity, a something added to what we wake into from ourselves) but into circumstances to which we ourselves are accidental, and our knowing which or knowing anything as to which, is quite an accident in regard to them: as if we were thrown on an uninhabited island where everything, in a manner which to our actual human experience is impossible, was strange and out of relation to us. And as we go on in our island, in this view, the state of things does not alter. Without the links to bind them together which our mind must supply, one thing is as strange to another as each thing is to us—though here I am using wrong language, as it is impossible to avoid doing, for unless our mind proceeded otherwise than phenomenally at first there would not be even *things* to us; we should separate and distinguish nothing. The progress of knowledge, so far as we can be true to this manner of thought, is the passing on unmeaningly, we might almost say the falling helplessly, from one view to a fresh one in a course which is not advance towards an end but the getting further and further into a hopeless infinity.

I am aware that it will be said that this is not at all the phenomenalist or even the positivist view, but that what we do is to mount up from particular facts to general laws, and to trace again the working of the general laws in the particular facts, and that in all this there is or may be (as is most true) both intense intellectual pleasure and high moral elevation. But what do we mean by 'laws'? Why do we thus take pleasure, and find our minds exalted, in the seeing in the universe these uniformities, and recurrences, and order? It is because we recognize a likeness to what we should do ourselves, and *do* do, that is, we trace *mind*, and here we are going quite beyond the phenomena. When we view things in *this* way, knowledge is not accidental to the universe, or to fact, but so far as either is to be postponed to the other, the universe is accidental to knowledge, and one out of various possible results or expressions of it. And so far therefore as we come to know fact or the universe, we are brought into relation with the knowledge of which it is a result and an example. This is what I meant by our feeling ourselves, as to knowledge, at home in the universe. And this is something quite beside phenomenalism.

CHAPTER II.

PHILOSOPHY AND CONSCIOUSNESS.

BUT I must not dwell longer on this, and must proceed, as well as I can, to exhibit the philosophical or more general view. In using the term philosophical, I am speaking quite without reference to any comparative superiority: I mean simply the view which belongs, not to physical research but to philosophy or the higher logic, and which in some respects, as we shall see, resembles, in its distinction from phenomenalism, the popular or ordinary view which appears in language.

I am not quite certain whether, when I say 'the philosophical or more general view', the language is correct. If we consider simply the process of knowing, or ask ourselves what knowledge is, without any reference to any thing being known, we have again what, in respect of the whole fact, is an abstraction, in the same way in which, on *its* side, phenomenalism is so. If we consider that we have general faculties of knowing (which are the subject of our investigation), with which, so far as we can tell, we might know any thing, and that what we happen to come to know is the facts of the universe, we have the counterpart abstraction to phenomenalism; in which latter we assume the existence, as matter of fact, of the several parts of the universe, which happen to become the objects of intelligence perceiving and knowing them. To keep this consideration of knowledge *quite* in its character of an abstraction, I think will not lead to useful result. Nor are the two counterpart abstractions altogether similarly circumstanced. After we have learned, to forget all about the manner and meaning of our learning, and lose ourselves in what we have learned, which is in substance phenomenalism, is, whatever may be wrong in it, a

more interesting and promising course than to study exclusively
the nature of our instrument or power without reference to its
application or the results which it has produced. If I mistake
not, the suggesting or ground thought of Kant's Critique of
the Pure Reason is, bearing in mind the analogy with Pure and
Applied Mathematics, to disengage the action of intelligence
from all application and actual use of it, and to see what it is
in itself, previously to its being applied in such a way as to
generate particular knowledge. I rather question myself whether
we *can* abstract to such an extent as to make investigation
of this kind really fruitful, or exhibit the primary and most
important acts of the mind in this way as a kind of calculus,
from the application of which to the unknown, or to the un-
informed, unmeasured, chaotic matter of knowledge, knowledge
will proceed.

In place of any process so abstract as this, I shall simply
start from our consciousness, and endeavour to follow it as we
advance in knowledge : I shall dismiss from my thoughts all
previous supposition of there being anything to be known, or of
there being a phenomenal world to make itself known to us—
that is a thing which, so far as we are concerned with it at the
outset of this investigation, may turn out to be so, or may not :
just as, in what I have said about phenomenalism, the phenomenal world is what it is, whether we or anybody else know it
and perceive it, or whether we do not. In speaking about phenomenalism, I described the extent to which sensation was a
phenomenon, or fact of the phenomenal world, which could be
physically reasoned about, and I described the application of the
term in which it was not so—namely, in so far as it is *feeling;* for
feeling is incommunicable ; it cannot be brought into the common
stock of knowledge and thought, or reasoned about phenomenally
according to any logic which we know of. This feeling or consciousness, excluded from phenomenalism, I now assume as the
one thing which we *do* know or are certain of. It is evident
that this is a higher and a more intimate certainty to us than
any phenomenal certainty. Whether anything beyond ourselves
exists or not, we are at least certain that we feel, *i. e.* that feeling, pleasure and pain, are realities, and individual to what, in
virtue of this feeling or consciousness, we call *ourselves :* and

that so far as consciousness is a proof or a fit suggestive of existence, 'cogito' of 'sum,' *we* ourselves exist.

The 'we' or 'I' of consciousness is something quite different
from the 'we', 'I', 'man' of phenomenalism, which, as I said,
is a portion of matter organised and variously endowed, with
phenomenal sensation (*i. e.* liability to affection of certain portions of it in a particular manner by natural agents, which affection produces various results) for one of its properties.

I described some time since the entire process of sensation
on the hypothesis of the existence of ourselves on the one side,
and on the other objective reality or an objective universe
(phenomenally, an independent external world). If the reader
will turn back to that, he will see that the middle point of the
process is what I called a communication between certain natural agents and certain constituents of our body, and phenomenalism is a recognition and following out of this central portion without attention to the extremes. We have now on the
other hand to dismiss from our thoughts this central portion,
and give our attention to the communication which, by the
means of it, takes place between the extremes. Except that we
do not, as in phenomenalism, start with the meeting of two
things of the same nature. 'We perceive things.' But 'we' and
'things' are something different.

Let us imagine to ourselves the successive changes of our
feeling as our consciousness develops itself.

Still however I will make one preliminary observation. The
reader may have observed that I have generally used the
expression 'sensive powers' where most writers would have
spoken of 'senses'. An instance of what appears to me the confusion between philosophy or logic on the one side, and physiology or phenomenalism on the other, appears in the manner in
which the whole question of sensation has constantly been
treated. 'Sensation', meaning by the term an affection or modification (however we may style it) of our senses (to use that misleading expression), nerves, and brain, is a phenomenon belonging to the domain of physiology. It is what I have above called
'communication'. 'Sensation', meaning by the term a feeling
on our part, or a portion or instance of consciousness, which, in
whatever manner, grows into knowledge, is a fact, so far as we

call it one, belonging to a different order of thought, and it is
philosophy or logic which must deal with it so far as it can be
dealt with.

Our whole body is a sense to, or, if we prefer the expression, the sense of, our intelligent self, which latter is the 'We'
or 'I' of consciousness, and the *subject* of knowledge. Every
communication of our body with the remainder of the phenomenal world, whether it be towards the body inwards or
from the body outwards, *i. e.* whether it be the result of impression from without or of exertion of what we call our will
from within, is, I conclude, as the rule, attended with feeling
on our part, and this feeling is sensation as *feeling*. By 'as
the rule' I mean this: that latency of the feeling in consequence of rapid passage of it and want of attention to it must
of course be allowed to some extent, and may perhaps be so to
a very considerable extent—this is a question which I cannot
discuss now. This sensation or feeling is of course a very main
part of consciousness: some might say it is the whole of it:
and that, as every bodily affection is accompanied with feeling,
so every feeling is accompanied with some bodily or organic
modification corresponding with it. The important thing is
to keep in mind that even if this latter is the case, feeling is
not the less feeling, something essentially unbodily and imma-
terial. The only real immaterialism seems to me to reside in
the view of consciousness as, in the idea of it, necessarily distinct from any bodily or phenomenal modification, and those
who think, with regard of consciousness, that any possible physiological acuteness or discovery can ever bring consciousness
or feeling under what we call now the laws of matter, or even
perhaps any laws at all resembling them, seem to me to be
materialists already, subtle perhaps, but really so.

Keeping on the surface of physics, into which I do not wish
to go deep, we may say that the different affections of our body,
(which are *phenomenal* sensation) are of two kinds, chemical
and mechanical: the question whether the chemical ones are
only mechanical of a more refined kind, I do not discuss. The
chemical constitution of bodies affects, under certain circumstances, *any* part of our body to which they can be applied,
and where there can be communication : but there is more par-

ticular communication between certain portions of that constitution and certain particular parts of our body, as the palate
and nostrils. I suppose too that it is the chemical constitution
of bodies which determines how they shall be affected by light,
so as to have what we call this or that colour, and the light
then transmitted from them affects in a manner which we may
for convenience call chemical, our optic nerve. But besides this,
bodies applied to our body (or to which parts of our body are
applied) affect it *mechanically* or displace portions of it, and
here there comes into play our *active* nature, or will: our body
is 'a sense' to our conscious self in a double manner, first in so
far as it is affected in the manner which I have described, and
next in so far as it is not only a frame, vessel, focus, for *reception*, but also a machine for *action*, its different portions moveable at our will, and this movement of them, as movement *by
us*, being of course accompanied with our being aware of the
movement, and of the amount of it; by our, in feeling, *measuring* it. Hence we move our limbs, aware, as we do so, how
much pressure we exert and how much of force producing
change of position: hence we move the muscles of our eyes
with more or less motion, and measure, as well as chemically
feel, what is (phenomenally) before them.

To the philosopher, then, as I have said, the body is all one
sense; it is the glass through which the intelligence looks out
into the phenomenal world. To the physiologist, it is *sensive*
or possessed of sensation (*his* sensation) altogether, but pos-
sessing withal what he would call various special organs of sensation for particular purposes and adapted to particular natural
agents, of which perhaps the chief is the eye. But the attempt
to particularize and enumerate our *senses*, as things or unities,
when under the term are included notions so incommensurable
as that of the eye and what is commonly called the touch,
seems unprofitable.

As I have alluded here to the eye and the touch, I will
make one more observation preliminary to the philosophical view
of knowledge which I am going to try to give. One most fruitful source of the confusion between philosophy and phenomenalism is the treatment of the eye as the main sense, without
thought of the complicatedness of the information which it gives

to us. In reality, philosophers who have treated about our notion of space seem universally to me to have in their minds *lighted* space, which really, whenever we look towards it without a distinct object terminating it, is something which we imagine we *see* (not see *through*), *i.e.* is *matter* to us. In the reasoning about geometrical figures, it seems to me, and I hope to show it, that this error has largely entered in. And it has worked far more deeply than this. Few philosophers seem to have guarded themselves sufficiently against the danger of error which lies in words involving so much metaphor as 'intuition' and other words suggested by light and sight.

But to return.

Let us examine our consciousness or sensation as *feeling* without any thought, at the present, that it is *other than* feeling. Let us try to follow back as well as we can, the stream of our knowledge. Let us try to examine knowledge as it is in the subject, abstracting and separating this, to a certain extent, as I have said, but only to *a certain* extent, from consideration of the object. This is the companion-process to what we did in regard of phenomenalism, when we endeavoured to attend to the matter or object of knowledge without thought of its being known.

I do not think that it can be doubted that the first and original consciousness (to keep that word still for a moment) is *double:* that is, that we no more, and no sooner, feel ourselves to exist than we feel something to exist besides ourselves. When we virtually say in our minds, 'Cogito, ergo sum', whatever force there may be in the 'ergo'—that is, when we look at consciousness as, what it undoubtedly is, an assertion to ourselves of our own existence, it being really the only assertion we ever do make of that, the only meaning, at bottom, of our belief in it—the one thing which distinguishes the notion (if we may speak of notions in this very seminal and embryotic state of consciousness) 'be' from that of 'feel' is that by 'be' we mean something which something else may share with us, by 'feel' we mean something which something else can have like us, but cannot share with us. In this way the separation of the notion of personality or individuality from that of being is coeval with the first consciousness. The matter may be best understood thus: if we, any of us, were the solitary existence, the simple monad, of the universe, though the notion of feeling or individuality would exist in us, I do not think that of exist- ence would—we *feel* for ourselves, but we *are* not for and by ourselves, we *are something;* that is, in other words, in the notion *be* there is something quasi-generic, and it implies al- ready a state of things, an universe.

I do not however mean to dwell on anything so abstract as this—it is more important to think, whether the words 'consciousness', 'to feel', are rightly applied to this initiatory knowledge of the non ego, or something besides ourselves. (We must keep in mind of course that the object of the verb 'feel' here is to be understood after the analogy of 'I feel pleasure, pain, &c.', not 'I feel this table or this chair', which belongs to another order of ideas.) Is it then correct to say, we are con- scious of, we feel, what is not ourselves? Does it, or does it not, violate the idea of consciousness, which is certainly re- flective, and the idea of feeling, which is certainly indi- vidual?

I shall have to discuss at some length the manner in which philosophers have applied the term 'consciousness' to our notion of something beyond ourselves, and the manner in which some of them, especially Sir William Hamilton, have, in my view, *mis-* applied it in doing so. I shall have to compare it with 'common sense', 'original beliefs', and other expressions which have been used in a similar application. The important fact is that even our rudimentary consciousness, so far as it is intellectual, *i.e.* a seed of intellectual development, is a distinguishing ourselves from something: even this earliest of notions is not single, but has its counter-notion. We are born, intellectually, into a state of things, an universe: and here it is, at the very root, that lies the difference between the philosophical and the simply phe- nomenalist view. It is not really correct to say, as an ultimate fact which cannot and need not be accounted for, that we refer our first feelings of pleasure and pain (or some of them) to a cause independent of us, for the distinction begins earlier than this, and as early as we have the consciousness which answers to the language 'our feelings' we have the idea of an universe, large or small, of which *we* are a part.

All our after knowledge is contained seminally in this first particular of it, and our progress in knowledge consists in the gradual making acquaintance with that which is thus revealed to us.

And not only this, but our after knowledge still preserves in one step after another the same character of distinction: and the great mass of notions are not distinct to us or properly held unless so far as we give attention also to their counter-notion or ground, that from which they are a distinction.

A progress of knowledge of this description has of necessity various other particular characters.

One is, that it is perpetual self-correction : it proceeds as it were by hitches, and every step in it together with truth contains error, which the next or an after step corrects.

Another is, that every step in it suggests to the mind a fresh crop of possibilities, with which the imagination employs itself: its employment in this manner is the means by which the notion involved in the last step is familiarized to the mind : and the next or an after step determines among these possibilities which is the truth.

In various ways like these it is that the dim universe which is the ground or counter-notion of primitive consciousness, the reality or state of things in which, so soon as we understand anything, we understand ourselves as existing, takes form and fulness and particularity : I will trace some of the particulars.

The consciousness or feeling from the first is various in kind. Certain forms of it, not many, have been particularized and named in language. All consciousness however is, loosely speaking, pleasurable or painful : it is feeling of pleasure or feeling of pain. Of its more complicated forms, the principal is *desire :* and this forms the link between our sensive nature and another part of our entire nature closely joined with it, our volitional or active nature. Our feelings of pleasure and pain, and the consequent various exertion of our will, with the accompanying feeling that we *are* so exerting it, run closely together.

There is one element or particular, and one only, *entirely* common to the world of feeling and the world of phenomenal fact, and that is, duration or *time,* with its circumstance, repetition, which it always involves to some extent. Our feelings have nothing else entirely in common with the parts of the phenomenal world, except that they last for a certain length of time. If we like so to express it, the duration of our feelings reveals to us or gives to us time : or what we call *time* is something, otherwise unknown to us, which is testified of to us by the duration of our feelings.

Perhaps it is as well to take the occasion of this first of our notions to explain what seems to me to be the proper relation to each other of the expressions 'sensation' (meaning the *feeling*) and 'idea.'

We feel time, or are conscious of its passage, in the manner which I have just described. That is, we have a sensation of it, in the way in which we are now using that word : and if we did not have such a sensation of it, it would be to us and we should be as though it were not. I said however also, it is otherwise unknown to us : that is, though we really can get no further than the sensation, yet still we do not rest in the sensation : we consider, believe, understand, that there is something more in the case than that we feel : we ask, what is this which belongs to *all* our feelings? and answer, it is *time :* we have made a step in knowledge, such a step as I have above described : we have the *idea* of time : we grasp by sensation the end of something which we then mark by a name and set ourselves to think about, and as our knowledge grows, we find out about it more and more.

It will be best however to speak further of this when we have more sensations and ideas to illustrate it by.

Time, I said, is *entirely* common to the world of feeling and the world of phenomena : *space* is *partially* so, and the reason of this partial community is our possession of a body or bodily organization. That is, not only do *we,* considered philosophically and widely, feel and think, but *we,* considered phenomenally, occupy a portion of space, or, in a certain way, our feeling is diffused over space, is local, having of course then this *being local* in common with phenomenal existences. Only that this localized feeling, or feeling phenomenally viewed, is *not* what we analyse in consciousness.

By saying here 'in a certain way' I mean to express a good deal of possible qualification, because I do not want to enter into the question of the real relation of feeling, as local, to *parts* of our body. It is sufficient that our corporeal organization introduces our feeling into phenomenal space (which I defined as the continent of matter), not indeed thereby making it, as feeling, a phenomenal fact, which it cannot be, but bringing it into a relation with phenomenalism, which, as we go on, we shall do our best (it is questionable whether much can anyhow be done) to make clearer.

Phenomenalism, though feeling is thus introduced to it and brought into relation with it, can never, from the nature of the two things, absorb it : nor can any extension of physiology make feeling a phenomenal fact, so as to give us an account of it in terms of matter, force, and the other elements which make phenomenalism. When we make phenomenalism our basis of reality, feeling, though we may know it to exist, must exist as something alien, unique, and insoluble, so that we are driven then to a dualism, or to the admission of a second basis of a reality of a different kind from the first which we supposed. So far as we make feeling or consciousness our basis of reality, which is what we are doing now, the way in which this fact, which we should phenomenally describe as that our feeling is diffused, through our being corporeal, over a portion of space, presents itself, is the following. We feel as what, so far as we feel it, is entirely individual to us and what nothing else is concerned with, the duration of our feelings, or *time*. We feel also the amount of effort which we make in the exertion of our will: but with regard to a portion of this effort, we feel that though we make it, we are not all that is concerned with it, that there is resistance, that we move *something*, that our effort shows something beyond itself answering and measuring it. What we thus feel we call 'space' and 'matter', 'space', so far as our effort meets with no other resistance than such as is involved in its being effort at all (I mean, than such as I suppose would be mechanically described as the inertia of the parts of our own body), 'matter', so far as it does meet with resistance beyond this : in the former case, the amount of motion measures and *feels to us* or is felt by us as space, in the latter case the amount of resistance measures, feels to us, is felt by us as, the solidity of matter.

I must apologize to those who have clearer mechanical ideas than I have for any mechanical misdescription which there may be in this : here, as in former cases, I want to avoid going into detail to which I am incompetent, and I think that the substantial truth of what I say is independent of any, not unlikely, mistake as to that. The important point is, that we feel space, or have a sensation of space, as much as we can be said to have a sensation of anything : or in other words, that the definition of space, in our present line of consideration, is that which we feel when we move, or are moving portions of our body without meeting any resistance. (I say when we 'are moving' in distinction from when 'we begin to move', in which latter case it may be said that the definition would apply properly to the inertia of our body.) Still without entering into detail, though a portion of what we feel may be said to be the inertia of the parts of our body, or resistance in this view, a portion is the distance moved through, or space.

Time we feel without going beyond our feeling, conscious or necessary selves : space we feel without going beyond our phenomenal or corporeal selves, our bodies. Our feeling of space indeed involves to us matter (which time does not), the matter which makes our bodies. But it does not involve, or suggest to us, any matter beyond our corporeal selves (though the notion of these latter may itself do so).

As of time, so of space, we have a sensation, and form an idea : that is, we do not rest in our sensation, but instantly imagine that what we have thus some slight hold of is a great deal more than what we feel; and what we thus imagine behind the sensation is the supposed thing, the *idea* of the thing. On this I will speak again in a moment. What gives time and space the prerogative over all our other and later sensations and ideas, is that which I mentioned in the last paragraph, the fact that we feel them without going beyond ourselves.

I do not know that it is more than a difference of expression, whether we say that we *feel* (*i. e.* have a sensation of) time and space, or whether we say that it is *in* time that we feel our conscious selves, and *in* space that we feel (so far as we

feel) our corporeal selves. I have used the former way of expression for two reasons: one, because I do not see how the
manner of our sensation of space and time, in so far as it is
sensation in the sense of feeling, differs from the manner of our
sensation of anything else: the other, because there is some
danger of our language misleading us when we speak of '*in*
time', and '*in* space'. When we call time and space conditions
or forms of our sensation (perception, or intelligence), all that
this seems to me to mean is, that the sensations which we have
of them stand, in a logical view, in a relation to the others (as
we usually reckon them) of being primary and fundamental;
they enter into all the others, our sensation, as it goes on, becoming highly complicated. But then these others enter one
into other, and some of them are more fundamental and, we
may say, primary than others: and though the sensations of
space and time have the prerogative, above other sensations,
which I have mentioned, still there is a passage *through* them
to other sensations, and it is graduated—there is a sort of
scale. The sensation of space is *lower*, if we like to call it
so, than that of time, for we go beyond our simply *conscious*
selves: the sensation of hardness or solidity, that is, of matter,
(which we feel by the way of pressure and resistance, and of
which I have already spoken slightly), is lower than that of
space, for here we go, at least it is probable that we go, beyond ourselves altogether: but still it is only, in a manner,
partly beyond ourselves, for we may feel one part of our body
by another: our body is, contemporaneously, external to us,
and yet ourselves. And our sense of solidity or of matter
(meaning of course along the whole scale from the closest consistency to the most extreme tenuity) is *almost* as fundamental
to our sensation as those of time and space themselves.

I have already alluded to the mistakes which, to me, philosophers seem to have made, in speaking constantly of space in
its association with the complicated sense of *sight*. To be *seen
through* is what we may call an *accident* of space, for it is only
in consequence of the existence of the particular material agent,
light, and the corresponding existence in us of the complicated
instrument adapted to it, the eye, that this is possible. But to
be *moved* through is *not* an accident of space; it is what, re-

moved, space would not be space, that is, it is a part of what we call our *idea* of space. Is it not better therefore, for clearness and accuracy, so far as possible, to speak of space as moved through, rather than as seen?

Without entering at all into the discussions as to the nature and real basis of geometrical truth, I would say that we shall better appreciate them, at the bottom, by abstracting our mind as much as possible from the figures which are only intended to help our eye. A geometer's straight line, as I understand it, is an attempt to represent to the eye *distance*, if we understand the line as terminated (according to the Euclidic definition), or *direction*, if we understand it as indefinite. These are the things I presume, which he *means*. And *distance* is, in our most simple and earliest understanding, *space*, as we feel and measure this in moving our hand to an object, or from one object to another: while *direction* is the same so far as we suppose the object aimed at, but not attained. It is very likely that we *do* not move our hand what is afterwards called straight, but what is of consequence is that we mean to do it, wish to do it, think probably we *do* do it: in such a way as this it is that comes in the idea as distinct from the sensation: we may be said already to know what 'straight' means, since we are aiming at moving our hand straight, *i. e.* the shortest way to the thing we want, or across the intervening distance. I have described the way in which we have the sensation of space, and have said that, concurrently with this sensation, we form an *idea* of space: in other words, we know already about space much more than is involved in our sensation: we know that there is a spatial way or distance to the thing we want along which we shall get at it with least effort, we know, that is, already in an action what straightness is, or have an idea of straightness as a part of the idea of space.

We should not take the trouble, in our after science, to define (geometrically) what we in the definition call a straight line unless the definition were fruitful in consequences applicable to reality, and this it would not be unless it either represented a truth of reality itself, or were very closely connected with one. There is therefore no meaning in speaking of a science of importance as merely based on definitions. Supposing the definition of a straight line to represent a reality, is the fact, that two such lines cannot inclose a space, that is, that between us and something, or between two things, the distance or spatial interval is one, a thing understood by us ás a necessary truth, or a thing found out by us in the course of experience?

I put this question here without any particular intention of trying to answer it, but only on account of the distinction, real or supposed, between necessary truth and truth of experience which it illustrates, and which distinction, in what I am writing, will recur to us under various aspects.

Whether we begin with knowing nothing, or begin with knowing, confusedly and implicitly, everything, is in my view a question much more of description and of the notions which we start with about knowledge, than of fact which can be made out by observation or argument. We may describe knowledge with equal propriety as the writing characters on the ἐκμαγεῖον (tabula rasa), or as a sort of chemical process like fermentation, crystallization, or any in fact in which something previously confused takes new form and arrangement so that there is produced from it what is clear and definite. ⎽ The description of knowledge as a course of experience and the description of it as a course of analytic and self-correcting judgments—as what many would call sensation, or as reflection in this view of reflection—are both what I call *abstractions:* that is, the historical advance of knowledge is the continued exercise of the mind in judgment in conjunction with the continued communication, by the senses, with phenomenal fact; this latter being the continued consciousness of what we call such communication, or judgment that there is such : knowledge does not advance, as a fact, simply by the succession of our experiences : in regard of these we are passive; it advances by the continual exercise of our will and judgment, not loosely and vaguely, but in conjunction with the consciousnesses which we describe as such experiences. Not that the judgment and the experience can be separated, except, as I have described, by abstraction: they are not two parts of knowledge, but two incomplete views: in judgment, for *it* to be knowledge, there must be something to judge or be judged; in experience, for *it* to be knowledge, there must be *notice* or exercise of will.   I hold therefore that there is no real difference between truth as necessarily known and truth as known by experience: all truth is found out : the question is, what is it that is found out, and what the manner of the finding?

We go on continually finding out, we may say, two things, though really they are but one, namely the bearing of the knowledge which we have already, *and* the circumstances of our environment, or what we consider such: and constantly, as a matter of fact, one thing may come to our knowledge either way, or both, one confirming the other, so far as either is the better for confirmation. The thinker, evolving all knowledge from his consciousness, is the exact pendant, on the one side of our knowledge, to the inattentive wanderer on the other, brought into contact with, and to *such* experience of, innumerable phenomena, and noticing nothing. Consciousness, abstracted from attention to the *occasions* of our sensation, is sterile on the one side, as unnoticed communication is sterile on the other: *neither* is knowledge. But each interpretation of an occasion of sensation is full of *bearing* in all possible directions, if we prefer rather to follow out these bearings than to proceed to interpret a *new* occasion of sensation. The difference between necessary and experimental truth is a difference, and very likely an accidental difference, in our manner of arriving at truth, and not a difference in truth itself. And the urging it on either side as if anything of importance depended on it seems to me to arise from a misapprehension. The experiential is not really, or in itself, fragmentary and desultory, though the effort to make its bounds appear as wide as possible seems generally accompanied with a perverse pleasure in the considering it such, and though the same notion of it is entertained on the other side with opposite feelings. Its appearing so is an accident, not of anything that can be properly called our intelligence or our faculties of knowledge, but of certain circumstances of these, namely our sensive powers and our corporeal frame. Our *reason* is reason of all intelligence, but our sensive communication with the universe is that of the animal man, or rather we might say more generally, of typical terrestrial animalhood, for eyes, for instance, or communication with distant bodies by means of light, belong to all animals, whereas there is in none a special sensive instrument to communicate with bodies by means of magnetism, or various other agencies as real as light. Our knowledge therefore gained by experience or sense is, *as such*, incoherent, not on account of anything in the nature of the things known, but because our powers of sensive communication do not constitute a consistent and universal *physiometer*, so to call it: they put us into communication with *some* things, leaving what we understand to be gaps and can partially, but partially only, fill up, with the important provision however that we have from the first an intelligence or reason which presents to us the universe as a whole, a frame to be filled up, so that we never rest satisfied with the incoherence.

Our sensive power for space is all the variety of our motor nerves, or in fact we may say our whole body, and consequently our sensation of it is full and intimate to a degree to which some of our sensive powers offer no sort of parallel. And in proportion to this fullness and intimateness is the less doubt about its particular informations, and the less need of repeated experience for the testing of them. I find it hard to understand the controversy, whether a geometrical axiom (as that two straight lines cannot enclose a space) is a truth necessary or experiential, in this way: those who hold the latter I suppose do not mean that it is an *accident* of space: those who hold the former do not I suppose mean that we could have known it without ever having moved our body, or had space suggested to us: the questions on the point are really two: is space itself suggested to us by experience? and can space be suggested to us without *distance* and the *singleness* of distance, being so? I think the latter must be answered in the negative: the question then is as to the general nature of space. The answer which I give, a little anticipating what is to follow, is this: that meaning or purpose in a thing (which is really mind or intelligence invested or deposited in phenomena) time, space, force, light, oxygen, are all equally real with the different meanings which *reality* must take in application to them, all equally matters of experience because they are what we successively find out, but all parts of *one* universe of which if we have got hold of any portion we have got *some* hold (little or much) upon the *whole*, a piece of pregnant and developable knowledge already, from which will come truth (such as it may be) without *fresh* experience. *One* sensation of space, so full and intimate, is almost indefinitely developable—one sensation of light, communicating only with the optic nerve and retina, may carry us but a very little way along the road of knowledge there.

But enough of this : I proceed in the next chapter, in continuing the subject of sensation, to the sensation of power.

CHAPTER III.

SENSATION, INTELLIGENCE, AND WILL.

As I have begun to speak of *resistance* it is fit that I should notice the corresponding and companion feeling to the sensation of it, which feeling may be called the sensation of power.

It is not altogether correct to say, that, in its nature, desire, at least so far as we conceive desire to be the result of experienced pleasure or pain, is the necessary foundation, parent, antecedent of volition, and in this way to subordinate our active nature to our susceptible. Impulse to action or rudimentary irritability is, I should think we may consider, something as original to us as susceptibility to pleasure and pain, and the disposition to exert will exists not as a principle, so to speak, intimate and necessary to us in the second degree only—that is, as a remedy owing to our being subject to pain, and an aid owing to our being capable of pleasure—but as something as intimate and necessary to us as our susceptibility or proper sensibility. I do not know but that we can conceive as easily individualities which in the first instance can *act* only, and *feel* nothing but such pleasure as is taken in the action, as individualities which can feel only, without ability to act. With us, the two things from the first go together.

This seems to me an important thing to bear in mind. Of its application to Ethics this is not the place to speak. But it is of importance also in regard of the distinction which I am at present endeavouring to elucidate, between the phenomenalist view and the philosophical, whether this latter be regarded as a wider view or as a companion abstraction. The phenomenalist view considers us as beings (or rather as *something*) susceptible of knowledge, considers knowledge as coming to us (which gives the point to the term 'sensation' as used by Locke and afterwards by most philosophers in the last century), considers such activity as there is, or the spring of movement, to reside in the supposed object of knowledge, so that, before we can form ideas (supposing us to do so) we must have received impressions, we must have *been* somehow affected : there must therefore be supposed in the object of knowledge, in matter (for instance) some power, or activity in this way to impress and affect us, and it is on *that* side that the process begins. Hence while the whole run of language, evincing the human natural understanding, is *we* see, *we* hear, *we* perceive, *we* think, the language of the portion of philosophy which I am now speaking of is, that *objects* begin and impress themselves upon our sense, and that their impressions, transformed or modified in whatever way, constitute knowledge : in ruder or rougher philosophy of the same kind they have been supposed to send forth actual emanations or physical images which did this : this was because a thing could not *act* where it was not, and it was supposed that it was matter, not we, that *acted* in perception.

The phenomenalist view rests on a supposition, one way of putting which is that we are thus *passive* in knowledge (though of course we must be careful about the language). As good an idea perhaps as can be gained of the phenomenalist scheme of knowledge may be gained in this way : the one physical fact which we know to take place in knowledge is that there is, as I have said, communication between particular natural agents and particular parts of our body, *i. e.* that there is, in such a place and body, sensation, so far as physics can conceive sensation. At this communication we are present, as it were, or in the French use, 'assist': the communication between the matter on the one side and the matter on the other is accompanied by a feeling on our part, and that is knowledge. Further, in this way, than there is communication, there is no knowledge. The knowledge and the communication are coextensive. The communication, which in respect of the particular portions of it is called 'sensation', is often in respect of the whole of it called 'experience'. The extension of knowledge, in this view, is the extension of this communication. There are all kinds of abbreviations and summarizations by the help of language, through the means of which we may multiply our communication in a manner otherwise quite impossible ; and there is a world, so to call it, of conditional communication, which is what we express, in this view, by what we call laws of nature: the facts or particulars of the communication have their regular concomitances and sequences, and much perhaps besides: and we as it were stand by (in virtue of the accompanying feeling) and see all this. There is a process going on which we call 'nature', and there is a wonderful, extra-phenomenal power of contemplating this process: the whole is knowledge.

In reality, as I have said, what we do is not to assist passively at a process independent of our real selves, but to look through it at something beyond: and it is upon the amount, and the right application of this *activity* that depend the amount and value of our knowledge.

The roots however of the phenomenalist (that is, the wrongly phenomenalist) view lie deep, going even to the original supposition, that it is feeling (or susceptibility) that makes our being, and not feeling and acting (or willing) as well, or if we like it, something deeper still, of which feeling and willing both, and perhaps other things besides, are equally early attributes. We are sometimes inadvertently led to this view by our language, when we say that it is *consciousness* which shows to us our personality: by this we *should* mean not only consciousness as pleasurable or painful feeling, but consciousness of willing or acting.

Our consciousness of willing or acting is undoubtedly more difficult to be conceived by us than the other. On account of the very intimateness of it to our being, we may say that we only know that we do will and do so far as we measure our action by feeling the amount of it, *i.e.* the amount of effect produced by it, and this is going beyond ourselves, and more thoroughly suggesting, or even making us feel, something beyond ourselves than any merely passive feeling can suggest this. This is true: and though, as I have said, we wake, even so far as feeling is concerned, not to ourselves alone, but into a world of things or an universe, it is our commencements of willing or of action which first begin to distinctify this universe to us, and make us understand it *in particular*. We feel *time* without (necessarily) feeling our activity if we were beings without will, and with only sentience or susceptibility of pleasure and pain, we might feel and measure the comparative duration of our feelings: but with the feeling of *space* awakes to distinctness the feeling of *ourselves* as *active* and as *doing* something.

I have said here 'awakes to distinctness': and I am desirous that what I have said in the former part of the paragraph should be carefully attended to. That we do not *need* space for our activity, becomes abundantly evident in the advance of our consciousness, for effort may be, and is, expended on feeling alone, with no other circumstance therefore but *time* belonging to it. But space, which makes us feel not only that there is something besides ourselves, but that it is something which we can and do act upon, is what at once first brings us into communication with this 'besides', and reveals to us *distinctly* our own active nature.

In saying however that it is *space*, or the feeling of space, which does this, I am probably not speaking correctly, though, as I said a short time since, I must refer to those with clearer mechanical ideas for strict expression on this subject.

Force and matter, I suppose, go together: and so soon as we feel that we exercise not only will, but force, we feel also that what, as thus felt, we afterwards call *matter* resists our force. So far as this is so, the sensation of matter is as early and as intimate to us as that of space. I have said that we feel space without going beyond ourselves: that is, our material selves: to the extent to which we feel ourselves as occupying space, we feel ourselves (to describe a simple thing in necessarily periphrastic language) resisting, more or less, the occupation of it by anything else. I will not attempt to follow out here the relations of space and matter. I have said that while allowing to the idea of space, with that of time, a certain prerogative, I do not look upon it to be fitly described as, in contradistinction to other ideas, a condition of our perceptions.

But our sensation of our activity and of the resistance of matter to it is a step which lands us upon quite a new field of knowledge.

The sketch which I am now giving of the course of knowledge does not aim at being really chronological. We do not have sensations at all in the simple, separate, and marked

manner, which what I have said, were it intended to be historical, would imply. We are always, as the rule, feeling something, and feelings rapidly succeed one another, and become
entangled and compounded together. And thus, though I have
hitherto been speaking of one sort of sensations only that we
have, there is another sort (I call them *different sorts* rather
loosely, for it is not of consequence) which we have quite as
early, perhaps earlier, and which must now be spoken of.

Sensation proper, as a feeling, (I mean by *proper* to distinguish it from the sensation of our activity) is all, in a manner,
as I have said, pleasurable or painful. In a manner: for the
sensation of time is rather as *containing* our feeling of pleasure
and pain, and so far as we have a sensation of time, we must
perhaps rather call it neutral. Our sensation of space is as of
the continent of our motion, of matter as of the absorbent, or
counter-agent of our force: how far these sensations are to be
considered neutral, *i.e.* not of pleasure and pain, seems hard
to determine, and not *now* important. Those who think, in
the manner which I have mentioned, that we are in the first
instance only *susceptible* beings, and not active till our activity
is called forth by something which we want and desire, may be
supposed really to consider that action in itself is a necessary
evil, and that we should be happier and more perfect beings
without it: so far as this is so, the sensations of space and
matter, as arising from our action, must be considered painful.
On the other hand, so far as we look upon action in the manner
in which I have done, as what our nature calls us to for itself
as well as for the gaining of a result, they would be to be
considered in themselves pleasurable. Of course however *pain*
is always a possible and likely accident of them, as in case of
the exertion or pressure being great. Be this as it may, whatever of pleasure or pain these sensations may have in them is
quite inconsiderable in comparison with that which belongs to
other sensations, which may be said to be *of* pleasure and pain,
leaving very little of attention to anything beyond the sensation; that is (in the language which I have used) to the forma-
tion of any idea of the supposed object of them. The cardinal
sensation of this kind is that which we call *taste*. We have
sensations of pain and pleasure variously localised in our body,

but which suggest to us no idea beyond the sensation: but when, in the course of the various parts of our body coming in contact by pressure with matter independent of it, certain substances come in contact with our palate, we have sensation of special pleasure or pain, and this sensation we call taste. Taste may be considered the typical form of the sensation which accompanies the phenomenal fact of the communication between the chemical properties of matter and certain parts of our organization; in other words, the *phenomenal* character of a sort of sensation of which *taste* may be taken as the type is that the chemical properties of matter (I have made such qualifications as are to be made in speaking of this before) communicate with our organism, while the *subjective* or feeling character of the sensation is that it is not of activity, but of pleasure or pain, and that perhaps very strongly.

Our sensation of matter by pressure and our sensation of it by taste constantly go together, as, more or less, in the case of taste proper to which I have alluded: so far as we feel upon the palate the degree of hardness, and the shape (to which we shall come more fully presently), of the thing tasted, the knowledge which we thus gain is not properly by taste, but by the previous sort of sensation.

As we may loosely call our *chemical* sensation of matter (so to speak), which is the etymological *sensus*, 'taste', so we may call our mechanical sensation of it which I have before described, (the etymological *feeling*), the '*handling*' of it (palpatio, $\psi\eta\lambda\acute{a}\phi\eta\sigma\iota\varsigma$), the hand being the portion of our body most naturally moved in this way.

The handling of whatever we come in contact with speedily gives to us the sensation, and suggests to us the idea, of what we call its *shape*. Our sensation of this is simply the feeling of the amount and direction of movement which the hand has to make in tracing its boundaries.

We may now (but we had no business to do so till now) speak of that which, in the advance of knowledge, is of all the most important organ of sensation, the eye: which is in fact a machine for both handling or touching, and also tasting, that is, appreciating certain chemical qualities of matter removed from us, perhaps widely, in space. The instrument of this communication is the particular physical substance or agent, (whatever may be its constitution), *light*.

I am not going to enter into any detail about this complicated sense. Suffice it to say, (describing first the nature of the phenomenal communication) that there are in the atmosphere (or in space) variously coloured rays of light moving in various directions, and on the other hand in our eye various lenses in front of a nervous surface, the whole variously moveable by muscles: after and by means of an action in which movement of the rays from without and the meeting them by volitional (though it may be too subtle to be traced) adjustment of the lenses &c. from within concur, the rays arrive at the nervous surface in a particular manner which, for our present purpose, we need not further investigate. The phenomenal communication being this, the corresponding subjective feeling is, that we, in the language which I have used before, as it were *taste* the colour by means of the nervous surface, in a way in some measure analogous to that in which we taste the taste of anything by the palate: and that, contemporaneously with this (though in a manner the commencement of the other process must be regarded as the stimulant) the movements of the various parts of the eye (really volitional, though so infinitely rapid, and therefore supplying us with sensation of the *former* kind) measure to us space in the same manner in which I have described the movements of the hand or other parts of the body to do so[1]. We generally understand that space in the line in which we are looking (which in most cases is what we call the distance of the object which we are looking at) is not measured to us by the eye, or not a thing which we properly *see*.

---

[1] Imagine the palm of the hand to be sensitive to particles travelling in right lines, whenever these fall upon the parts of it perpendicularly—imagine it to have its present power of turning its face in any direction, and of contracting itself and turning about the portions of its surface—also that it is only the surface, or palm itself, that is sensitive—and we have the same result secured in a different manner as I have described in the eye. The particles must of course give sensations independent of the movements, that is, *taste*, as we may call it. The hand would then be a kind of instrument of distant taste, like our smell, and discriminative in the two ways, chemically and muscularly—intensively and extensively.

On the next sentence, see a note in the Appendix.

But it is very hard to say what we do see, that is, to determine what is the best use of language in reference to the expression 'see', and it is for this reason that I have spoken, in the first instance, rather of other senses than of this. The sensation, *on the whole*, of space is the same, whether the occasion of it is the movement of the muscles of the eye or of those of the hand: and the particular sensations of space are referred one to the other, the later and more remote to the earlier and more intimate. It is possible that we should not understand the *seen* shape of a remote body if we had not actually handled a near one. The eye travels round an object of sight of any magnitude, as the hand travels round a portion of matter near: the result in both cases is our sensation of shape. When I say 'of any magnitude', I mean only to decline any question which may belong to physicists, as to how much may be said to be seen at once, without any movement of the eye. Whether we can or cannot, physically, follow the less and less amount of movement, in the case of the perception of larger and smaller shape, to entire absence of it, I do not know.

Active sensations or sensations of handling, though almost always present to us, are what we may call uniform, being of space and matter alone. Passive sensations or sensations of taste are conceivably infinite in variety, at least as various as the different agents in nature, and conceivably also, in particular cases, such as could be brought into no relation the one to the other. As it is, our powers of nervous or sensitive communication with natural agents are not numerous. Of those which we have, some are in close relation one to another, as taste and smell; some are, I suppose, so far as we can go, out of relation with each other, as taste proper and colour.

I shall now, as the shortest and most natural way of expression, speak of *seeing* objects. I hope that, after what has been said, we may be able to do so without being misled by our language.

But what is the meaning of seeing *objects*?

The sense of sight as it is developed becomes the most important sense, the intellectual sense, or *the* sense in a special manner. The taste-like sensation of colour, always most refined as compared with other taste-like sensations, occupies the atten-

tion rather in its character of a means of discrimination than as
an actual pleasure or pain, except as these latter mingle with
intellectual considerations, and become artistic or æsthetic.
The active sensation, in sight, of space and shape or figure
brings itself into relation with, tests itself by, and grounds itself
upon, the nearer sensations of the same kind which accompany
motions of the whole body or of larger portions of it, and then,
we may say, developes them and multiplies them indefinitely.
The sight of a wide prospect is really a mental travelling over
it.   What we really, in our consciousness, may be said to mean
by saying that we see one conspicuous object, for instance, of
such a magnitude and figure at such a distance off, another
of such another magnitude and figure at such a distance from
that, and these in various relation of magnitude, figure, and
distance, with others, is, that were we among them and in contact severally with each we should have to move the parts of
our body so much and so much in feeling about them, and in
getting from one to the other.   What amounts to movement of
this kind, impossible probably in fact, and if it were not so,
endless probably in duration, sight, through the intervention of
light, effects in a few moments.   Volitional movement of the
muscles of our eye accompanying the arrival of the light at it,
which light arrives in the particular manner in which it does
owing to certain particular circumstances in distant matter, the
effect is the same as if the rays of light were so many sensitive
filaments, so to call them, belonging to ourselves, by which,
across whatever distance, we felt or touched that matter.

The sense of sight being thus, with developement of the
intellect, the most important, takes also a *subjective* importance
of a different kind.   We use it as the typical sense by means
of which we describe, and to which we refer, the operations
of sense in general.   We speak of the feelings which we often
have, closely resembling sensation or feeling, but not accompanied, like it, with communication between our body and the
universe beyond, as *imagination,* by a metaphor derived from
sight.   We speak again of something resembling this last, but
accompanied by a (supposedly well-founded) belief in the importance and groundedness of it, as *intuition* or inward sight.
It is to this use of the sense of sight that are due the terms

'presentation', 'representation', and many similar: for in consequence of the rapidity of the visual movements, we may
have in contact with the sense, or with what is understood as
the internal sense, at what seems the same moment, any
amount of objects.

In the case of persons blind from birth, I presume that this,
the quasi-visual imagination or inward sight, exists to a certain
extent, though there must be an absence of distinction of
colour, and it is hard to understand how space is represented
in the consciousness. Still I conclude that it is more than *dark*
space, or a mere generalization of handling, feeling, groping.
The human organization being *one*, and the eye being a part of
it in such a way that the other parts, if we may use the language, suppose it and take account of it; there being also, we
may suppose, as a part of that internal organization which
every external organization of a being with *will* supposes, an
impulse to the use of the eye, even where that impulse is, from
circumstances, abortive: though the stimulant to any ocular
movement, by the sensation of colour, is wanting, and perhaps
any such actual movement impossible: we may consider it
probable that there is something which supplements the handling and feeling, and enables, in a manner, something like a
prospect to be present to what we call the imagination. It is
a physiological question upon which I do not enter, whether,
when imagination is at work, there is or is not disturbance in
those portions of the body which, if the imagination were sensation, would be correspondently with the sensation, in such
circumstances of disturbance—whether *e. g.* in visual imagination there is motion or affection of parts of the eye, &c., and
so for other senses.

I said a short time since, that it is a difficult thing to say
what we really see, that is, for philosophers, when they are
talking together about seeing, to be sure that they are using
the word in the same application. There is no reason for difficulty of this kind in the case of feeling by touch: we have
indeed in this case much to bear in mind as to the variety of
use of both the words 'feeling' and 'touch', besides the distinction which has constantly to be borne in mind between the
consciousness, whether of effort or not, and the movement or

communication: but with care as to this, the case is simple. Sight, however, is much more complicated.

In reality, Crabbe's lines,

> It is the mind that sees: the outward eyes
> Present the object, but the mind descries:

are happier philosophically than perhaps he meant: so far as we speak, with any reason, of an object of sight, it is the mind that sees the object, and the real sight is *this;* namely, of the (supposedly) independent and more or less distant object, by the mind: the sensive apparatus of vision or the eye with its appendages perform simply the part of presenting or introducing; and it is not any optical phenomenon (image, *e.g.*) which may be ascertained to occur (or be formed) within this apparatus which is what *we see, i.e.* is the object of the sensation as feeling. In the case of sight, the corporeal communication which, taken altogether, is what *presents* the object to the mind, is of a most complicated nature. The light is prepared in a double way for the mysterious point (from the nature of it never to be passed by phenomenal speculation) at which it is converted, so to speak, into sensibility, first by passing through a self-adjusting spy-glass, and then by being converted, so to speak again, into nervous agitation or modification of some kind, which is what our sensation (or feeling) accompanies. It is difficult to follow this process without being in danger of thinking either that the retina sees through the spy-glass, or that *we* see the image on the retina, to do which, I suppose, another spy-glass would be required behind it, like the one before. But in reality, all that can be physiologically or optically made out as to this complicated process is part of the corporeal communication, which our sensation, or feeling, only accompanies. And the sensation which we have is rudimentarily perhaps, simply of a colour, how spatially related to us is hard to trace and perhaps not very much worth tracing. When the sense is at all developed the sensation which we have is that of a coloured *object* having magnitude and figure, and (with still further development), solid shape and definite distance. This is what we call seeing: this is what we see.

But, in this noble sense, the corporeal communication which

is the *means* of it is not more elaborate than the logical result of the sensation, for the growth of knowledge, is important. What do we mean by saying that what we see is an *object*, or thing? Our eye is moveable all sorts of ways, and rays enter it in all sorts of directions, forming all sorts of images: in other words, what we have at any moment before the eyes is a vague confusion of colour, a kaleidoscope only without even apparent order: how is it then that we see *things?* How is it that in this confusion, we individualize, realize, and distinguish any portions from the rest?

In speaking here I must myself, and I hope the reader will, be careful. We never do (saving disturbance by disease) see the confusion I am speaking of, and it may be said that it is not before the eye—but the difficulty which we have here is one which belongs to the consideration of the sense of sight all along. *In fact*, it takes its place with the other senses, and is educated through a use of it conjunct with them, and something more which I am going to mention begins from the first with it, in such a way that by the time that the eye is open to a wide view of colour it has (or rather *we* have) already learnt discrimination of objects in this view. *How* we learn, I shall try to show.

I said some time since, without *then* explaining it, that unity is not phenomenal. I made the statement then in its broad generality, which for my purpose at that time was sufficiently near the truth: more accurately the truth is that unity is phenomenally exceptional, a statement which in its place I will explain. What I mean is, that the communication between natural agents (as I have called them) and certain portions of our organization, which is the physical fact, and upon which the phenomenalist view rests, does not suggest (if we suppose it viewed or understood by a being looking quietly upon it, in the manner I have formerly mentioned, and the result to be knowledge) that *discrimination* of objects from which springs our idea of the universe as composed of *things* or separate unities or individualities. We may hold simply (if indeed we do hold) the phenomenalist view in our developed intelligence, but we never can arrive at it, we never can learn it, except by an unphenomenal process. This amounts to the same as I have formerly said when I called the phenomenalist view an *abstraction*. Unless we to a certain degree shut our eyes, it cannot exist to us without much, we perhaps indeed cannot tell what, existing besides. If I may venture safely to use chemical language, I would say that the phenomenal universe, as conceived by us, is a sort of deposit from our thinking nature, definite, tangible, visible, while our thought besides is fluid and unformed—but still, real as it is, and valuable as it is as against other spheres of thought in some respects, to say that it is all, or that it is the most valuable knowledge absolutely, is not only not true, but is intellectually suicidal. Phenomenalism itself is not true, unless much is true besides it. So far as it may be said without contradiction, if we had been phenomenalists and physiologists from the first we never should have been so at all, for we never should have known anything. If we had understood the mechanism of the eye before we began to see, what we should *really* have rested in would have been the material communication; that through which we should have attempted to arrive at knowledge would have been our own sensations as the physiologist would make them out or judge them likely to be, and we should have *seen* according to these: following these out into matter independent of us, we should have understood, *perhaps*, the laws of light and of other agents which affected us, and should have had, to fill our thoughts, such an universe as this kind of knowledge would produce us: an universe of the *constituents* of things ; a power of following the elements of matter, or such of them as our sensation revealed, wherever they were, with attention chained to *them:* but the universe of *things*, as actual human language or any language we can conceive does or must represent it, would have been entirely alien to us. Our subjective sensation, or sensation as feeling, is not a sensation or knowledge of the phenomenal sensation or material communication, but is a sensation or feeling by means of this of something beyond which is what it is to us on account of the mixture in it of certain elements independent of phenomenalism, and on which the view which we actually have, even of phenomenalism, depends.

The best way of expressing this would probably be to say, that it is not the particular circumstances of the material com-

munication which, more than in a subordinate degree, determine those of the subjective sensation or feeling (the same
thing as by many philosophers is called 'perception') but that
with the nature of this feeling other quite different considerations enter. We understand this most in the case of sight,
because the material communication is longer and more complicated, but it is the same in all sensation. We do not *feel*
all the material communication (as whether the image on the
retina is upwards or downwards), and so far as we know about
it, it is physiological research which tells us.

Perhaps it may help to illustrate what I have here said
about sight if I refer for a moment to what Dr Whewell, following the language of Aristotle, has said, when, in distinguishing
between primary and secondary qualities, he makes it a character of these latter that they are perceived through a medium, as
colour through light. I cannot enter into this language. So far
as it is the subjective sensation or feeling which is spoken of,
that is of an object as seen, of a *thing* as we call it, the sun
for instance, and everything which intervenes between our
conscious self and the thing seen is *medium*, the whole visual
apparatus *together with* light and colour. So far as it is the
material communication which the feeling accompanies, that is
spoken of, *that* is not with the sun, but with *light*, and there
is no medium at all. What Dr Whewell says on the subject
of *outness* is open, I think, to the same sort of criticism. But
to this I may very likely refer again.

I said, in speaking of the awakening of our consciousness,
that the first recognition of our own being is accompanied with
the recognition of something besides it, or of an universe into
which we are born. It is the same as if I had said, that the
first recognition of anything not ourselves, or of the universe,
was accompanied by the recognition of our own being. In
each case the one is the counter-notion of the other: the
notion of the one is formed by distinguishing it from the other.
Whichever is the first distinct and affirmative notion is in a
manner not the first, for the other is the ground and basis
of it. We will suppose however, *ourselves* the first: the universe then (to apply so grand a term), or independent reality
is what we first set *against* ourselves, or set *ourselves* as it

were to measure. The universe has *being* as we have, so far
as we then know being.   There is an original logical genus
with its two species or individualities, subject and object of
knowledge.   At the same time the universe is not only understood as sharing with us in being, but as the ground from
which we stand off: we are in this respect a part of it: and
what is to be contrasted or paralleled with us is not *it*, but
one part of it after another as distinguished from it.

To describe in a sort of exaggerated and magnified, and so
far absurd way, the progress of knowledge, a way however
which may facilitate the conception of it: each successive
reality, as it disengages itself to us from the universe as yet
of confusion, is to us at first a counterpart of ourselves: our
notion of ourselves is what we carry with us, is our primary
idea of being, and what, as one (nervous) sensation after another
stimulates our intelligence, we mingle in our thought with
the sensation: while, as I have said, it is by a continual process of self-correction that we advance in true knowledge.   The
fact is, that every great step in knowledge, besides what it
may have about it of addition to an aggregate, has the double
character as well both of correction of wrong previous view
and of understanding why the wrong previous view was taken,
or in other words, of understanding what there is in it that is
true and right: from the former of these processes, united with
the aggregation of observation, results the phenomenal view:
from the latter result to us, as we shall see, considerations
which suggest to us that the phenomenalist view, though true
in its way, is not all that we have to think of.

To the opening intelligence and awakening will, what meets
and resists our effort appears to live as we do, and is the object
of passion in us as if it were another self; and when this is
corrected, as it soon is, there are left in the ground various
roots or portions of it: one is, that there is something analogous to our will in bodies or matter which nevertheless we do
not conceive to have life, by which they can initiate or make
things begin to be, by which they can be *causes* of things in a
sense distinct from being regular portions of a chain in which
such things occur: another is, that though particulars of the
universe (so as yet to call them) have not *life* they have that

unity, or individuality, or reason why they should be distinguished and separately thought of, which in fact is only suggested to us by our consciousness of our own life and consequent felt self-belonging or independence, and which, like the
idea of cause, is a sort of relic or reminiscence of the life
which the infant intellect supposed in *things*.

It will be seen more fully now why I said that the notion
of unity, or of 'things', is not phenomenal. When we say, we
see a thing or an object, we are using language of the same
kind as when we say, such and such a fact is due to such and
such a cause. Phenomenally, cause means invariable antec-
dent, and thing means portion of matter, or of that which fills
space. But if we had been condemned from the first to think
of 'cause' only as invariable antecedent and of 'thing' as portion of matter, we never should have learnt anything. *Fact* is
continuous, and we should have had nothing to make us dis-
criminate between one portion of it and another, so as to say
that the one went before the other. *Matter* is the interaction
of a variety of what I have called natural agents, elements,
forces, &c., and the phenomenalist, if he *saw* things as he knows
them chemically to be, and really got rid of the kindly delu-
sions (so at present to call them) which are the conditions of
our learning anything (as *e.g.* if he not only knew that, but saw
things as if, the colour of an object was not a part of the
object, but a part of the light which brings it to his eye), I
should think could hardly keep his senses. It would be as if
phenomenal truth required us not only to know that we are,
but actually to feel ourselves, whirling round upon the earth's
surface in space at the rate, whatever it is, at which we actually
are doing so.

When I said that in strictness, unity was phenomenally
exceptional rather than unphenomenal, what I meant was this.
Suppose no reference at all to our own life and individuality,
and suppose, as I have more than once said is the most convenient way of putting the phenomenalist view, that we are in
some way impersonally merely present at and intelligent of the
communication which goes on between portions of our body
and matter besides: *life* is a fact which we should meet with in
nature as so viewed: there would be in it what we should call

living beings. Such beings would separate themselves off, even to our phenomenal view, from the rest of nature as *unities* or individual. I will not follow this out now, for the mixture of various *life* in nature is a thing which I should wish to speak of by itself. I mention it, as a necessary qualification to the statement that unity is unphenomenal. But I do not think any will say that this occasional occurrence in nature of parts of matter of which we may predicate phenomenal unity can account for the fact that our mixed and confused corporeal communication with natural agents takes the form, in the intelligence or to the sensation *as feeling,* of our noticing and distinguishing individual objects or *things.* Nor can the phenomenal fact of spatial arrangements and conditions, as of magnitude, shape, &c. by itself do so. We look upon objects in a different way from that in which we look upon clouds, or masses of cloud. And if it be said that a quantity of other sensations, as of colour, are added to that of spatial arrangement: what is meant by these sensations is nothing more than this same confused communication, with our body, of a variety of natural agents: whence the resulting unity?

There is no doubt that spatial circumscription is one element of it: but it is one element only, and it does not give life to the object *enough.* We notice what we notice and make it *a thing* distinguishing it from what else is within our view, *partly* because, doubtless, it is of such or such a size and shape: but we require more impulse to the notice and distinguishment than *this* furnishes. I think Sir William Hamilton uses the term *interested* in application to our sensations which are pleasurable or painful, to distinguish them from others: in reality all our sensations or perceptions may fitly be called interested: the interest in the case of the intellectual ones being more abstract and remote. For our notice or distinguishment of what then is to us *a thing,* there is required not only size and shape, so far as these are required, but what is in the first instance a comparison of the thing with, or a reference of it to, ourselves. Grammatical gender, as compared with the notion of actual sex and of neutralness or absence of personality, owes its origin, in all probability, to a similar feeling about things as that which I have mentioned, that their reality was a sort of remnant or reminiscence of an actually supposed life, in an infant or mythologic state of the intelligence. And when the members or portions of the universe, the greater portion of them, have ceased to bear to us, as viewed by our intelligence, the sort of fraternal relation which belongs to a similar life, they come, a great many of them, to bear to us another. In the development of our activity, and our imagination, without which our activity would be nothing, we very soon become *constructive*: from using our hands as instruments to *move* matter, we begin to use them as instruments to put it together or to *make*. It is with the first awakening of the constructive impulse that begins what corresponds to the neuter gender, the true notice and distinguishment of *things*. A 'thing' is what we may use or make, or if not we, what others may use or have made. Our notice of things is in this way from the first what I have above called *interested*: what makes them individualities or things to us is originally a supposed relation to ourselves.

It may really be called *a life* which this relation to ourselves, or interest, puts into the universe as we have sensation of it. It is not a life such as our infant intelligence supposes, like our own, but it *is* a life to our intelligence: the idea of the relation to ourselves soon dies away, like that of actual life, but there *is* left what is the soul of thought, namely, the supposition of *meaning* or *reason* of things being what they are. But to this we shall come soon.

The subjective sensation or feeling, though it accompanies the bodily communication, cannot properly be said to correspond to it, for this reason: that while it is highly likely that there are portions of the communication which have no counterpart in the feeling, it is certain that there is much in the feeling which has no counterpart in the communication. It is this latter, when philosophers use such language, which is understood by the *form* of the sensation, or the form superadded upon the sensation, so that sensation as consciousness or knowledge is something different from what it would be, were it simple attention to the communication. The word 'form' is as ambiguous as 'sensation'. We may understand the meaning of it best perhaps in this way: that the relation of *shape* to matter as concretely and rudely understood (stone, clay, &c), is taken as a type, figure, or suggestion of the relation of *something* (the metaphysical form which we want to understand) to incondite or confused *material* (so to call it) of any kind. As the sculptor or modeller gives shape to his clay, so is *something* given to the unmeaning and unsuggestive feeling—which, if we merely felt, as we feel a prick or a pinch, what is going on in our retina and the other sensive portions of our body, would be all that there would be—to make it the meaning and suggestive feeling which the real subjective sensation is. This, which is given, is the *form* of the sensation.

A result of the fact, that our subjective sensation has thus, in comparison with the bodily feeling and any mere feeling of that, a form given to it, is this, that we consider ourselves to be knowing or feeling, not, as in the phenomenal fact, something in ourselves, but something beyond ourselves : and when I said some time back, that at the same time we both have a sensation of a thing, and form an idea of it, I might have expressed the same by saying that the special character of the sensation, as having the form that it has, is that it is something the mind does not rest in. The mind makes *out of it* something which it rests in. The sensation passes away, yielding to the next sensation : but it has done something and it has left something : and this is expressed by saying that we have formed an idea.

Our sensations give form to each other, and the early and great sensation, that which we have of space, goes some way, in the manner which I have mentioned, in giving form to all the sensations which follow it. But it does not do everything.

I hope to make what I have said upon these subjects clearer by comparing it with what has been said by others.

CHAPTER IV.

FERRIER'S INSTITUTES OF METAPHYSIC.

IT is possible that the view which I have endeavoured to exhibit here will be better understood if I make a few remarks on one or two of the most important English works of our time on Psychology and Logic, showing how far they fall in with the distinction which I have endeavoured to draw between the phenomenalist and the philosophical or logical view, and how far they offend against it. I do this with no care for criticizing or controverting the works which I shall name, but simply because I think such a course is the best illustration which I can give of my own view.

The books of which I shall speak have been mentioned in the Introduction, as well as the principle of their selection and arrangement, and the first which comes is Professor Ferrier's Institutes of Metaphysic.

Whatever demerits Professor Ferrier's book may have, it has what I, having given the view which I have given, cannot but regard as a very great merit, namely, that it is free, I should think entirely, from the confusion of thought which much which I have written is directed to prevent. He has invented or adopted the term 'epistemology' for the logical or philosophical exposition which he has given of the nature of knowledge, and has, it seems to me, in a manner of which there are not many examples, kept in mind throughout the assumptions with which he has started, without changing his point of view, or introducing alien and unwarranted considerations. I do not attach much importance to the show of demonstration which his Euclidic method exhibits, for which, I think, the subject is not adapted. In fact, he has omitted from it that most important preliminary, the definitions and axioms, and that this omission *is* important, may appear from the fact that his first proposition, from which all the rest are supposed to follow, and which is treated as almost self-evident, Mr Herbert Spencer, whose book I shall speak of shortly, *totidem verbis* denies[1]. Till axioms then are agreed upon, representing a ground common to various thinkers on the subject, the most perfect consecution in the demonstration is not important. Nor do I agree with Mr Ferrier's notion of the relation of the epistemological view which he gives to the view, in general, which, with great clearness and vigour, he gives as contrasting with it. He describes this latter partly as 'psychology', which with him is a term of great opprobrium, and more generally, as 'ordinary thinking', and something which it is the business of philosophy to correct. This ordinary thinking represents in the main what I have called the phenomenalist view (with a mixture indeed of the 'logical' which I hope at a future time to notice), which, it seems to me, is as valid within its large province as epistemological thinking is in *its* province, the business of the latter being not to correct or simply to oppose the former, but to prevent the misapplication of it. A good deal, no doubt, of 'ordinary thinking' is simply the philosophy of bad philosophers: but the mass of it, as represented by language, is not.

It is not, I think, so much in the direct line of Mr Ferrier's thought as in the incidental remarks, and the *whole* manner of thought which they exhibit, that the value of his book consists. For his direct argument, I can hardly think that his saying, so repeatedly and so barely (this repetition without explanation is due, it is to be observed, to his method of demonstration) that we cannot think or know an object without thinking or knowing the subject (ourselves) or a subject (ourselves as the type) with it, is a sufficient account of what I should call the feeling which we have, that what we know could not have been known by us unless there had been in it something making it possible to be known, or fit to be known, or the possible matter for future knowledge, or however we like to express ourselves. And in the same manner when he tells us that it is not the object of our knowledge, but ourselves as

---

[1] *Psychology*, page 44, et passim.

knowing or apprehending that object, that we know, he seems too much to forget that he has got to give an account of the *second* knowing which he speaks of, or the *apprehending*, which *at least* must be of the object without an apprehended subject going with it.

Whether then Mr Ferrier has thrown any fresh light upon this question by the particular language in which he has chosen to speak about it, I am doubtful; but he seems to me, as I have said, to have the very great merit of seeing the problem clearly.

The examination of the nature of knowledge, when we start from the logical or philosophical point of departure, may very conveniently take the form of an observation or consideration of the difference between what on the one side is known, and what on the other side is unknown—not merely as a matter of fact, because we do not happen to know it—but unknown on account of something in its own nature, or unknowable. For the observation of the difference, we may *suppose* this latter, and we may then *add* to it in thought what suggests itself to us as necessary in order to convert that which cannot be the matter (or in this sense 'subject') of knowledge into that which can. The simplest expression of this is to say, that for anything, whatsoever it is, to be possibly the subject (in this sense) of knowledge, it must have definite qualities or properties, and definite relations to other things, and must be such that one and another thing may be said or predicated intelligibly about it. What is then *not* possibly the subject of knowledge in this sense is what does *not* possess the above character. And the tracing the difference between this and that which on the other hand *is* subject (in this sense) of knowledge, is the transforming, in thought and by successive steps, a something supposed of the latter kind into the universe or system of things as we know it.

Mr Ferrier has in very clear and vigorous language distinguished between this with its analogous processes and the misapprehensions of them which are very probable, and are chiefly of two kinds: the one that this process of logic or thought is an actual, historical (imagined) production on our part of things from nothing, a creation: the other that in such processes, alongside of our thought, we are to suppose things already existing as we know them. Both these misapprehensions are in reality confusions between what I have called the philosophical and the phenomenalist point of view, of the kind which I have endeavoured to prevent. Against the first of these Mr Ferrier has well shown how the distinction, in the above-named processes, is not between existence and non-existence, between something and nothing, but between known-ness, knowableness, knowable existence and what he (in his language) calls 'nonsense' or 'the contradictory'. Against the latter he has shown that the double point of view merely results from confusion of thought.

Mr Ferrier claims for himself much merit for his 'agnoi-ology', or theory of ignorance, of that kind which Sir William Hamilton is very fond of claiming, namely, that he is here original, and the first to break new ground. This merit does not seem to me so great in philosophy as in some other branches of thought or literature, for the reason that the pro-blems of philosophy are all so intertwined together, that from the first, in the touching of any of them, they have all been more or less touched, and to distinguish between what is really new, and what is only the same thing in other words, is diffi-cult. But the calling attention to the difference between igno-rance (so to call it) of the knowable and that mere nescience (so to call it) which must be the state of mind in regard of that which is not matter of knowledge, is an observation of much importance. If borne in mind, it would prevent much foolish talk in depreciation of human intelligence.

I will repeat summarily the view which I have given above myself, and I think Mr Ferrier, with a manner of expression of his own, and a more ambitious, perhaps a better, method, does not in its great features differ from it.

The course of objective knowledge is the growth of the non-ego, which from the first, in conjunction with the ego, we are conscious of, into distinctness. The spring or start in this course is given by (what I suppose we must consider a pri-mary fact of all intelligence) the attribution, in the first instance, to each one of these members of the form of thought under which we view the other: *i. e.* the attribution of objective knowableness to our felt self, and the attribution of subjective knowingness or mind to the non-ego. The latter of these two facts is the spring of objective knowledge. Sensation simply and of itself, considered in its relation to knowledge or the later and grown intellectual sensation, might be regarded (Mr Ferrier has spoken well about this) as the subjective state answering to which, as object or quasi-object, stands what I have generally called confusion or a non-ego of confusion, what Mr Ferrier calls nonsense or the contradictory. It is the projection of *ourself* into this confusion which begins to generate order in it. It is the supposition of an unity in one and another phase of the non-ego, as we are conscious of them, which unity is really a projection or extension of our subjective selves, or taking ourselves, the *first* and most immediate thing we are conscious of, as the type of existence, which makes us (in psychological language) co-ordinate our sensations into masses which suggest to us *things;* which gives law to the disorderly mass, and really (in Dr Whewell's language) informs (gives form to) or *forms* the sensation. The continual correction of this by successive experiences divides our knowledge into two lines, or generates on the one side what I have called the phenomenalist view, on the other that of the higher philosophy. For a *complete* view of things, we in our most developed and instructed thought suppose as much *mind* in the objective universe as we did in our first and most uninstructed thought. The difference is, that we *now* suppose an embodiment of the thought or mind which stands between it and *our* thought or mind: the phenomenal view is the resting, more or less, in this embodiment, without the thought of its suggesting anything beyond: the supposing it a quasi-absolute, an ultimate fact so far as we are concerned, either for some purposes or entirely and for all. If the former, there is simply that view which is true so far as it goes, and is the basis of all physical science: if the latter, there is what I have called positivism or mis-phenomenalism: a simple negation of everything beyond phenomenalism.

Knowledge from the philosophical point of view is a communication of mind with mind through an embodiment or result of the one, analyzed or traced back out of embodiment or result into thought again, by the other. The process or manner of this analysis may be variously described: it is the mistaken, but continuously corrected, attribution to what we are conscious of as different from ourselves, of the mind which is *in* ourselves : one thing after another detaches itself from this supposition, and is considered to exist what we call merely phenomenally, and by the continuance of this process the mind which we contemplate is set further and further off from us: but the *entire* view, if we think rightly, never alters or should alter. The process of knowledge again, logically viewed, is a continued (logical) creation of an orderly universe out of what, but for knowledge, has no properties and cannot have anything thought or said about it: but this creation is always felt or understood by us not as a creation, but as a recognition: while we are really throwing our own mind into the inform (unformed) matter of sensation, what we think is, that we are meeting another mind. The great problem of the higher philosophy, as distinguished from simple epistemology or philosophy of knowledge, is to examine the validity of this feeling, understanding, thought, that we do not, in knowing or perceiving, *make* things, but *find* them. There is a phenomenal outward universe, communicating with our brain and nerves, an *environment* corresponding to our organized or corporeal life: but when we say, the one thing which we are certain of is our consciousness, in the first instance, only, and the development of that; does the manner of this development suggest any antithesis, anything correspondent to, or we may say, communicating with, *that*, through and beyond phenomenalism ? and does it suggest such *reasonably ?*

We are really conscious of a non-ego as of an ego, we are not therefore the only existence, and from this it seems to me to follow, that we have reason in considering that in evolving (by thought), order and character, or *somethingness* out of mere disorder—objects out of præ-objectal possibility—we are not the only mind at work: as much as we feel ourselves mind, we feel ourselves *one* mind, and that there may be others. We know things therefore not only because *we* are, but because there are things which can be known: because there are things which have in them the quality or character of knowableness, *i.e.* a counterpart or adaptedness to reason : which is, however we like to describe it, the same as a mind or reason so far insubstantiated or embodied. I do not wish to follow this out into any conclusions of Natural Theology: only to indicate, that with respect to this, is the *real* difference of view in all philosophy.

The difference as to philosophical view which is a real and fundamental one, whereas almost all differences which cannot be resolved into this have in them more or less of vagueness and mutual misunderstanding, is that between what I have called 'positivism' on the one side, and on the other a view contrasted with this, which has no single name, though in application to ethics I should call it 'idealism'. The point of the difference is that in the former we look upon what we can find out by physical research as ultimate fact, so far as we are concerned, and upon conformity with it as the test of truth: so that nothing is admitted as true except so far as it follows by some process of inference from this. In opposition to this, the contrasted view is to the effect, that for philosophy, for our *entire* judgment about things, we must go beyond this, or rather go further back than it, the ultimate fact *really* (however for the purposes of physical science we may assume the former) for us—the basis upon which all rests—being not that things exist, but that we know them, *i.e.* think of them as existing: the order of things in this view is not, existence first, and then knowledge with regard to this or to parts of it arising in whatever manner; but knowledge first, involving or implying the existence of what is known, but logically at least, prior to it, and conceivably more extensive than it, and not all meeting with application. In the former view, knowledge about things is looked upon as a possibly supervening accident to them or of them: in the latter view, their knowableness is a part, and the most important part, of their reality or essential being. In the former view mind is supposed to follow, desultorily and accidentally, after matter of fact: in the latter view mind or consciousness begins with recognizing itself as a part of an entire supposed matter of fact or universe, and next as correspondent, in its subjective character, to the whole of this besides as object, while the understanding of this latter as *known*, germinates into the notion of the recognition of other mind or reason in it.

The various distinctions, as between 'sensualism' and 'idealism'—between 'inductive' and 'intuitive', 'a posteriori' and 'a priori', philosophy—and others, represent so far a real and neces-

sary conflict of thought as they embody, each of them, more or
less of the above distinction or contrast; and not more.

This may be a convenient place for a word or two upon a
point, in the treating of which I shall refer not only to
Mr Ferrier, but by anticipation to one or two books hereafter to
be noticed, as those of Sir William Hamilton and Mr Mill.
This is the point of the *relativeness* of knowledge, and the
question of ' things in themselves'.

There seems a good deal of misapprehension and confusion
in people's minds about this. To speak first about ' things in
themselves'.

Our knowledge may be contemplated in either of two ways,
or, to use other words, we may speak in a double manner of the
' object' of knowledge. That is, we may either use language
thus, we *know* a thing, a man, &c.: or we may use it thus: we
know such and such things *about* the thing, the man, &c.
Language in general, following its true logical instinct, distinguishes between these two applications of the notion of
knowledge, the one being γνῶναι, noscere, kennen, connaître, the
other being εἰδέναι, scire, wissen, savoir. In the origin, the former may be considered more what I have called phenomenal—
it is the notion of knowledge as acquaintance or familiarity with
what is known: which notion is perhaps more akin to the phenomenal bodily communication, and is less purely intellectual
than the other : it is the kind of knowledge which we have of a
thing by the presentation of it to the senses or the representation of it in a picture or type, a ' vorstellung'. The other, which
is what we express in judgments or propositions, what is embodied in ' begriffe' or concepts without any necessary imaginative representation, is in its origin the more *intellectual* notion
of knowledge.

There is no reason however why we should not express
our knowledge, whatever its kind, in either manner, provided
only we do not confusedly express it, in the same proposition
or piece of reasoning, in both. I am not sure whether Mr
Ferrier, in general so clear, is not in this particular otherwise,
when he speaks of our knowledge as the knowing ourselves as
knowing or apprehending, or the knowing that we know and
apprehend, the object of our knowledge. I have said that he

seems to lose sight of the necessity of giving an account of the last-mentioned knowledge, or apprehension. Is the word 'know' in the two parts of the sentence used in the same or in different meanings?

It appears to me that the notion of a difference between things in themselves and things as we know them arises in the main from the confusion together of these two views of knowledge. If by knowledge we mean acquaintance or familiarity, kenntniss, then we know the thing in itself, partially indeed and indistinctly, but still in the same manner in which we or any intelligence must always go on knowing it till the knowing is exhausted and the kernel (or rather central point) reached. If we begin, as to the thing, with *this* notion of knowing, we must keep this notion to the last. We must not suppose that however we may go on making acquaintance with the thing till we know it in *this* way thoroughly, there is still something to be known *about it* which is the real and important knowledge, and which cannot be attained to. What is defective here is not our knowledge, but our logic.

Perhaps the mistake, as I think it, most frequently presents itself when there is taken, in the beginning, the *other* view of knowledge. Here I must make a preliminary remark on the use of the terms 'subject' and 'object'.

If we wish to try the clearness of a philosopher's thought, it seems to me that the crucial test is his use of the term 'object' in application to knowledge.

'Subject' and 'object', in their common application to knowledge, though they form an antithesis in use, do not form one in proper signification. Or, in other words, they are not proper correlatives. The object is not the object of the subject, or vice versâ. I, the knower or intelligence, am the *subject* of the knowledge, because the knowledge, *here*, is considered a *quality* or property attaching to me or which I possess. What I know is the *object* of the knowledge because the knowing, *here*, is considered an *action* on my part, not a quality. The two terms are therefore, in different views, relatives to the knowledge, and not properly correlatives of each other. They are only antithetic in use.

The appropriation of the term 'subject of knowledge' to the

knowing intelligence has, it so happens, damaged philosophical thought in *this* manner, that it has interfered with the application of it in various other ways in which it was needed. When we speak of knowledge in that which I gave as the second view of it, as the knowing this and that *about* a thing, we want the term 'subject' (as it *is* used in logic) to express the thing *about which* what is known (the proper 'object' of the knowledge) is known. Using it *now* in this sense (I have, where necessary, done so before) I think that the confusion which I have above alluded to as to 'things in themselves' arises from this, that after, with the meaning of knowledge which I am *now* supposing, we have known (if it is so) *about* the thing all that there is to be known, we still, mistakenly, think there is something wanting unless we know, with the first sort of knowledge or that of acquaintance, the thing which all the other knowledge was about. But *that* thing, supposing we use such language about it, was itself no *object* of knowledge, and never entered in thought as such, or even possibly such. The *thing* in *this* view of knowledge, 'is all that can be known about it', and when we have come to this, we have come to the end, not only of our knowledge, but of all possible knowledge, in this direction.

The notion of the relativeness of knowledge is to be considered much in the same manner. There is little significance in saying that knowledge is 'relative'. It is itself a relation; between the knowing mind and the object known: and this relation arguing a prior one between the mind as capable of knowledge on the one side and the matter of knowledge as, whether actually known or not, knowable, on the other: it shows, that is, an existing constitution or state of things to which the knowing mind and the matter of knowledge both belong. And more than this, knowledge not only is a relation, but it is *of* relations or related things: that, of which or about which the knowledge is, must be constituted somehow, must have particularity and character involving relations to other things, or qualities having relations to each other, in order for knowledge to be possible of or about it. The unconditioned, unparticular, unqualitied, unpropertied, cannot be known, there being no means of distinguishing it, and nothing to be known about it.

So far then as we talk of knowledge *in general,* or from the logical point of view, as being relative, what is really meant is that it is itself a relation, and is knowledge of the relative as variously related.

So far as we speak of *our own* knowledge, or the knowledge of any minds of supposed particular constitution, being relative, the notion is different, and what is meant *then* is, 'relative to that constitution'. And here it is important to observe *what,* in or about the knowledge, is relative in this manner. The meaning of 'relative' here is 'different' (more or less) 'according as the intelligent constitution is different'—varying with *that.* But in this case, it is not the knowledge proper which differs, but what we might rather call the means of it; or, if we prefer the language, it is not the important and higher part of the knowledge, but the lower and subsidiary.

Sir William Hamilton's language is, that all that can be possibly known is not existence, but *modes* of existence—and only *some* of these modes, according to the particular constitution of the knowing mind—and then not the modes themselves but only *modifications* of them, determined by the faculties making up that constitution. We do not know existence, or the things themselves, but only modifications of some, out of many possible, modifications of them[1].

This seems to me to be a very vain multiplication of logical barriers between our intelligence and the thing which we suppose ourselves to know. What is added by the particularity of *our* intelligence to the general fact of knowledge is, undoubtedly, that we know *through sense* (under Sir William Hamilton's *modifications,* see the quotation) and that we know, we may say for convenience, through *some* senses, it being possible for us to conceive a larger number (we know *some* therefore only, in Sir William Hamilton's language, of the modes of existence). This is what I have in other places expressed by saying, that we are, whatever

---

[1] *Lectures on Metaphysics,* p. 148, ed. 2. 'All our knowledge is only relative. It is relative, 1°, because existence is not cognisable absolutely and in itself, but only in special modes: 2°, because these modes can be known only if they stand in a certain relation to our faculties: and 3°, because the modes, thus relative to our faculties, are presented to, and known by, the mind only under modifications determined by these faculties themselves'.

we may be besides, phenomenal or corporeal beings, communicating, as such, with a phenomenal or physical universe, and communicating with it in certain definite ways, which ways we might *conceive* multiplied.   It appears to me that Sir William Hamilton's description of all this as 'our knowledge being relative' is language likely to puzzle and confuse both physics and logic.   It seems to imply that if we had more senses (a special organ, *e. g.* for the perception of magnetism, as the eye for that of light) our present physical knowledge would cease to be real, its reality depending upon our having the particular senses, and no others, which we have.   Whereas I conclude that the conception of the physical universe which we form in accordance with our present sensive powers, though it might possibly be absorbed and altered in form by an addition to them, is and must ever remain real and valid so far as it goes. In the same manner this ' relativeness of our knowledge' seems to imply that our knowledge, as through sense, must be considered as what I should call incommensurable, that is, out of relation, non-communicable, with that of any conceivable intelligence which was *not* attained through sense, like ours.   As the other view puzzles physics, this seems to me to puzzle philosophy and logic.   My view is, that though we not only perceive, but even more or less, think, by means of sense, yet that the *results* of our thought, so far as they are to be held as *knowledge* or *true,* must be valid for, and intelligible to, and communicable with, all conceivable intelligence, by whatever means, different from ours, it may have attained to *its* results. *Knowledge* is one and the same.

It seems to me that the proper statement of the fact is, that knowledge, which as I have said is itself a relation and implies for its significance a relation or particularity in *things,* comes into existence in our case owing to what we may call, if we like it, a relation between our intelligent selves and our phenomenal organism, and to a second definite relation between the parts of this organism and the constituents of the material world.   Whether we like or not to use the word 'relation' in this multiplied manner, is a matter of description, carrying no consequences.   We may express, if we like it, by the term 'relative' properly understood, what I have endeavoured to

express by 'phenomenalism.' I have called the phenomenalist
view an *abstraction*, by which I have meant, that though true
in its proper place, it must not be taken to represent the *entire*
of what we ought to think, and becomes erroneous if it *is* so
taken. If the relativeness of our particular knowledge is understood as expressing this, I have nothing to say against it :
nor again if it be taken to mean simply that our generic intelligence, as compared with that of one and another sort of animals, or as compared with that of conceivable incorporeal beings,
is particular, our own, in the means and manner of it. No one
could doubt this.

With regard to the relativeness of knowledge in general,
as Sir William Hamilton has exhibited it in the first of his three
reasons why knowledge is relative, I would refer to what I have
said about 'things in themselves'. The 'thing in itself' if we
use that language, or 'existence' if we use Sir William Hamilton's, may be considered either as a simply *logical* entity, a
manner of expression necessary for us because we wish to consider knowledge as the knowing *about* something, the forming
of judgments, scientia—in which case it is not the *object* of
knowledge at all, but simply the logical subject of the judgments, and the notion of reality attaches not to *it*, but to the
sum of what is and can be known *about* it: or it may be considered as the intended object of the knowledge, what the mind,
acting in the way of intuition, apprehension, kenntniss (not,
i.e. judgment *about*) is always aiming at, to whatever degree it
succeeds. 'Existence,' says Sir William Hamilton, in the passage already cited, 'is not cognisable absolutely and in itself,
but only in special modes.' If cognition is taken in the former
view, then the sum of the modes of the existence is the existence itself, as an object of knowledge, and there is no relativeness, though there may be partialness, some of the modes only
being known, and not others. And this view is what cognition
must be taken in for the word 'absolute' to have its proper
meaning, antithetical to 'relative'. If it is taken in the latter
view, absolute only means 'complete', and cognisable 'completely'
cognisable. The supposition that existence is a reality, and yet
that we can only know it in modes, (*i.e.* the whole supposition
of relativeness of knowledge) seems to me exactly a confusion

of the two views of knowledge (the simultaneous employment
of which is almost a sort of juggling) which I have described.
Supposing us to have exhausted, in knowledge, all the modes of
existence, we are told, you know all *about* it, but you do not
know *it*. In reality acquaintance with, intuition or apprehension or comprehension of, *it*, and judging correctly and exhaustively this, that, and the other thing, about *it*, are two ways of
expressing the same thing, and *either* of them are definitions
of knowledge: the difficulties as to *relativeness* seem to me to
arise simply from a confusion between the two.

It appears to me, accordingly, that the language of almost
all the Kantist-speaking philosophers has been a language of
uncertainty between the saying, It is absurd to talk of knowing things in themselves, or, which is the same thing, of conceiving the unconditioned, and the saying, It is vainly presump-
tuous to think of doing so. The two ways of speaking involve
entirely different views. If the impossibility of conceiving the
unconditioned is logical, because there is nothing to conceive,
(the unconditioned being merely a logical figment, for certain
purposes, of the knowable divested of what makes it knowable) then the refraining from the attempt to conceive it is no
restraint, or subjugation, or submission of the intellect to
limits traced out for it, which it must not transcend: such
attempts then are simply mistakes, and there is no reason why
people should not find out the mistakenness of them (though
of course we may tell them they *will* find it) by making the
attempts, and seeing the absurdity which results. All the
language about submitting or restraining the intellect belongs
to the other view, in which the impossibility of conceiving the
unconditioned is supposed not in this manner logical, but an
accident of our particular intelligence. We are then, supposedly, bound down to certain ways of viewing things which
we see to be *particular* ways, being able, *so far as this*, to
criticize, *i.e.* to rise above, our particular intelligence, while,
at the same time, we are unable to conceive how the things
can be seen in any other way than these particular ones, or
what they, independent of the ways of seeing them, are. This,
of course, puts the intellect in a state of unstable equilibrium,
of a sort of war with itself, of struggle, effort, and difficulty.

All those forms of idealism which represent the present state of things in which we are as '*phœnomenal*', in the original meaning of the term, beyond and through which we may form an imperfect conception of unseen realities, embody more or less *this* view.   And while, as I think, every supposition of religion necessitates this view in a certain measure, there is reason, though the proceeding is not one with which I have myself much sympathy, in the endeavour, for the interest of *definite* religion, to restrain the too great activity of the intellect in these directions, and to enforce upon it moderation and submission.   But what there is *not* reason in is the endeavour to reinforce this restraint by means of a view quite inconsistent with the view upon which the notion of restraint depends, by means, *i.e.* of the view which I have given above, namely, that the attempt to conceive anything beyond the phenomenal world is merely illogical and leads to nonsense.

I have gone into this however rather more at length than I meant *here*.

In taking leave of Mr Ferrier, I would say again, that in giving my own view some time since, and supposing his to be similar, I am not quite certain whether I am justified.   He is, I think, superfluously occupied in making his demonstration inexpugnable, and scarcely, I think, explains sufficiently the exact point of some of his expressions.   Knowledge, in my view, is the mingling our own consciousness with a certain (so to call it) præ-objectal matter of knowledge of which we are so far conscious, as that it is that, by distinction from which we know ourselves: and it is this mingling which generates objects, or converts the supposed occasions of our feelings, a continuous undigested confusion otherwise, into things.   When Mr Ferrier says that we think the subject with the object, I rather question the term 'object' in this application: if, till the subject is added to it, there is no knowledge, it is not as yet, or itself, the *object*.   And Mr Ferrier hardly sufficiently explains whether he means to pass from the notion of ourselves as knowing, or from knowledge being 'knowledge that we know', which of itself, I think, is not very important, to the notion of ourselves, or part of our selves, known in the object, which *is* the important one.   It is *this* which really leads on, in the chain of thought, to

the notion of knowledge being the meeting, through the intervention of phenomenal matter and the conversion of it into intellectual objects, with the thoughts, proceeding in the opposite
direction, of mind or a mind like our own, however wider and
vaster.   This is my version of Mr Ferrier's final propositions.

But I think a great deal of time is wasted in discussing
and rediscussing what one and another philosopher means.   Or,
granting the value of this for the ancient philosophers, of
whom we have very imperfect remains, I think we may very
well do it too much in regard of the modern ones.   Philosophical
language is very uncertain, and it is a good thing, in some points
of view, that it .is so, for this manifold uncertainty is a great
security against mere *unmeaningness* in the language.   No philosopher who reflects on this uncertainty, but must feel the importance of *making effort* to set before both himself and his
readers what he himself means by the terms he uses.   Nor is
any logic or reasoning in a philosophical book of the slightest
value without special care given in this respect.   But beyond
this, a philosopher's view will probably be of most value to us
by our conceiving it in our own way, provided we think about
it *bonâ fide* and without putting force upon it.   In a real
philosopher, the ground of the whole, the fundamental view,
is something very hard, if possible, to put into words and which
he probably labours much in expressing, and perhaps he does
this by using various manners of expression, or perhaps he may
be unwilling to mar such distinctness of expression of it as he
may have attained by illustrations of it which may lead to misapprehension.   In these cases, an infinite literature may be
taken up in discussing and rediscussing what he meant.   The
important thing is how far what he meant or what we may suppose him to have meant is suggestive of what is the truth.

I have said however very little about Mr Ferrier's book
itself.   I will give now a few of his own words, with comments
on them, comparing them with my views.

How my view stands *upon the whole* with his I cannot quite
make out.   His manner of expression is so exceedingly different from mine, some of it being quite unintelligible to me, that
whether what he means is the same on the whole as what I
mean, or something quite different, I cannot tell.   When there-

fore I say that I agree with him, and that what he says seems
to me right, I interpret him in my own way, and if any one
disputes that being his meaning, I have no care to maintain
that it is. What I say *then* is not applicable to him. I have
observed upon the inutility of lengthened controversy as to
whether a philosopher means this or that. Suppose him to
mean either or both or neither, and let us see only how what
it may be thought he means helps the truth, and suggests
thought in us.

Mr Ferrier says[1], " Philosophy is not only a war, but it is a
" war in which none of the combatants understands the grounds
" either of his own opinion or of that of his adversary : or sees
" the roots of the side of the question which he is either attack-
" ing or defending." And again[2], "Now, no" (philosophical) "ques-
" tion comes before the world which does not present many
" disguises, both natural and artificial, worn one above another :
" and these false faces are continually increasing... It may be
" affirmed with certainty that no man, for the last two thousand
" years, has seen the true fiesh-and-blood countenance of a single
" philosophical problem." Mr Ferrier expresses himself strongly,
but otherwise this his starting-point is quite mine. Philosophical controversy is full of confusion, and this is one great
reason of resultlessness of it. But with his remedy I cannot agree :
that is, with the applicability of it. We want, he says, *strictly
reasoned* philosophy : and when we have it, we shall be so certain that we have it, it will be so evidently irrefragable, that
we shall take our ground with the most perfect confidence as
against all possible controversy. His own Institutes, Mr Ferrier considers, furnish such a philosophy, and the language of
confidence with which he speaks about them is extraordinary.

It is extraordinary, because his first proposition, which he
takes as a sort of axiom to build the rest upon, is, as we have
seen, controverted by Mr Herbert Spencer (and in fact by many
more) and is even it would appear, thought to require support
and defence by Mr Ferrier himself.

This proposition is, that the act of knowledge is not knowledge simply of the object of knowledge, but is knowledge of

---

[1] Page 6.   [2] Page 9.

ourselves, the subject, along with the object, and as knowing the object.

I have already hinted a comment or two on this. I agree with Mr Ferrier. Mr Herbert Spencer's view is one which I may possibly touch on further forward: it may be put, as I understand it, thus: the *object* is more important and immediate to knowledge than the subject is: knowledge must have an object, but it may be conceived, *i. e.* at the ultimate point, as without a subject: in knowledge there must be something known, but, conceivably, and for a moment, there may be knowledge without its being anybody's knowledge, without anybody's thinking or feeling it: the basal fact is not 'cogito', not sensation or consciousness, but, as we may say, 'hoc cogitatur', or 'cogitatur de hoc', from which, though still in my view 'ergo sum' may be concluded, it is by a longer process.

I am not going to discuss this point, which is the often discussed one of the nature of personality, and only say, that in point of method I do not see what is gained by Mr Ferrier putting a system of philosophy professedly reasoned in such a manner as to preclude all controversy, upon a point thus controvertible, however, in my view, he may be right upon it.

Interpreting Mr Ferrier, as I have said, in my own way, and translating him into my own language, I might understand, by this master proposition guiding our whole view of knowledge, what I should express as follows: that knowledge is this; thought, justifying itself to us as right thought (belief, if any choose to call it) of ourselves as communicating, acquainted, in contact, with a something not ourselves; but this at the same time requires the accompanying thought (as to which I do not know whether it appears in any form in Mr Ferrier) of ourselves as so to speak *extending* into something not ourselves, or having a being partaking of that which is *not* ourselves besides our simple being in virtue of which we think: this is what I have called our phenomenal or corporeal selves: this second thought being present, it is seen that the communication, the object of the *first* thought, is at various steps: communication of ourselves as thinking with thought, and again of ourselves as phenomenal with physical fact: the communication at the lower stages gives us what I have called 'phenomenalism': this may be treated by itself, as *knowledge* so far as it goes: but it does not represent an *entire* view of knowledge, being all included in the leading *thought* with which we began, and there being knowledge above and beside it.

How far Mr Ferrier's view is really intended to be of the nature of this, which is mine, those who read him and me must judge.

The valuable point in Mr Ferrier, in my view, is, as I have said, his consistency in distinguishing what I have called the philosophical and phenomenalist view. But we must have a transition from one to the other, though we must be careful *what* transition: and in reference to this I will comment on a passage of his[1]. "That which we call 'I' is the object of intel-"lect alone. *We* are never objects of sense to ourselves. A man "can see and touch his body, but he cannot see and touch "himself.......When the cognizance of self is laid down as the "condition of all knowledge, this of course does not mean that "certain objects of sense (external things, to wit) are apprehended "through certain *other* objects of sense (our own bodies, namely), "for such a statement would be altogether futile. It would leave "the question precisely where it found it." This is important and true, true, I think, as against views of Sir William Hamilton and Mr Mansel which I have touched on, but we must take care of overstatement. What is the meaning of 'our own bodies'? Taking 'external things' as our type of 'objects of sense', our own bodies are not, except subsequently and partially, objects of sense to us in *this* way.

I will not dwell upon this, having already spoken a good deal on the subject in another reference. It appears to me that Sir William Hamilton and probably others are obnoxious to what Mr Ferrier says here: but it seems to me that *he* is in error in speaking of our own bodies as if they were merely, in relation to us, external things like the things which surround them. They are a real intermediation between 'us,' (Mr Ferrier's 'I'), and external things: they belong to both worlds in *this* way: not that feeling, or thought is local, for it is not our hand that feels, but 'we'; not, going the other way, that locality is felt with real consciousness, for what we feel with feeling *thus*

---

[1] Page 80.

meant (*i. e.* as consciousness) is the amount of will or force that we exert: but that, in that apprehension of self which Mr Ferrier justly lays down as at the root of knowledge, the self apprehended is not merely the same thing as the self apprehending, in which case the process would be unimportant: the apprehending the apprehended self is the clothing it with various predicates (then, indeed, first understood), among them locality (corporealness or phenomenalness). That is how it is that our bodies are ourselves and not ourselves: we feel by means of them and we do not feel by means of them: it is not they that feel, but we, but we feel that we should not feel without them. However on this I have spoken.

Some of Mr Ferrier's sentences seem better adapted than anything else that I know of to cure in the minds of students the great psychological confusion: such as[1], "The expositors of " Pythagoras's theory of numbers have usually thought" (I do not guarantee the fact) "that things are already numbered by " nature either as one or many, and that all that Pythagoras " taught was that we *re*-number them when they come before " us". And again, "A theory which professes to explain *how* " things became intelligible must surely not suppose that they " are intelligible before they become so". And again[2], "As " if any genuine idealism ever denied the existence of external " things—ever denied that these things were actually and *bonâ* " *fide* external to us. Idealism never denied this: it only asks " what is the meaning of 'external' considered out of all re- " lation to 'internal', and it shows that, out of this relation, the " word 'external' has, and can have, no meaning."

What Mr Ferrier *attacks* he calls *himself*, 'ordinary or natural thinking, confirmed and made worse by psychology'. It seems to me to be *three* things, on the first of which I only partially agree with him, on the other two quite.

On the first point however I am not sure whether his view is single and one. He condemns (philosophically) ordinary or natural thinking, with its 'plausibilities'[3], and considers that philosophy only exists[4] "to correct the inadvertencies of man's "ordinary thinking. She has no other mission to fulfil......no "other business to do". To settle, as a fact, what 'ordinary or

<hr>

[1] Page 89.   [2] Page 105.   [3] Page 25.   [4] Page 29.

natural' thinking is, is difficult enough, as any one will know who has read Bishop Berkeley. And then are 'ordinary' and 'natural' the same? It seems to me that there are two ways of common thinking, which may well be expressed by these several words, and that each, also, is only *partially* wrong.

Suppose we call 'ordinary thinking' that which is represented by common language. This, in the main, I believe in, and think it is right. It represents what may be described as the way we learn, or come to our knowledge: it is only partially what I call 'phenomenalist', containing, besides, a large amount of logical notion, *here* in its place, and most helpful to learning and speculation: the phenomenalism which it *has* represents a sort of normal condition, or mean level, of phenomenalistic thought, at which perhaps the human race will always stand—(I mean we still talk of *the sun rising*, &c.). I am sorry to say, I have always had the feeling, that the language of ordinary intelligent communication among men is better than the language of philosophers. And *the thought* therefore cannot be very bad.

Suppose we call 'natural' thought the thoroughly phenomenalistic view, as I have called it, which is what, with increase of physical knowledge, there is in many ways more and more a tendency to; this, as I have said, is in my view perfectly right in its place and for its own purposes, only not beyond.

With Mr Ferrier's account of what philosophy exists for, just now quoted, I do not agree at all. So far as philosophy does exist for any correction of this kind its use as to 'ordinary' thinking seems to be to prevent any tendency to what I should call 'notionalism', that is, to prevent people's thinking that the 'qualities', 'attributes' &c. which they talk about, and in my view are quite right in talking about, are the *real things* of the universe. Similarly, its use as to 'natural' thinking would be to prevent phenomenalism trespassing, as I should call it, on morals and religion, and becoming positivism.

So much for the first thing which it seems to me Mr Ferrier attacks—the second is 'the philosophy of the human mind', as he with some kind of contempt calls it; psychology, or, as I have called it, noö-psychology (as distinguished from physio-psychology), the Lockian psychology or that of the last century.

I may not despise this, as he seems to do, or think its results, as he does, 'frightful''; but I disagree with it as much
as he.

Under the name of 'psychology' Mr Ferrier includes the
third thing, not quite, it seems to me, the same as the last,
though it is what I equally agree with him in condemning; and
in fact I have, in much that I have written, been attacking it.
It is the doctrine of the 'unknowable substratum', or 'thing in
itself'. I refer to Mr Ferrier at page 128 for an account, too long
to quote, which I go with thoroughly, saving the philosophical
language. The misfortune is, that this philosophical difficulty
is worse than Proteus-like : it is not only infinitely self-transfor-
mative and scarcely any way seizable, but it has the property of
making those who most attempt to grasp it appear to hold
themselves all that is wrong in it, while itself puts on an appearance all innocent and right. People will say that Mr
Ferrier's 'matter per se' is as bad as 'the unknowable substratum'. I believe, myself, that Mr Ferrier is right, and that
there *is* the error which he notices in those whom he criticizes :
but what we want is to be able to do without *talking of* this
horrible chimera which philosopher after philosopher *will talk
about* so much in order to persuade people what, while he does
so, he cannot get them to believe, that neither he nor anybody
can *know* anything about it. Consequently, I do not like the
language of 'matter per se'.

Nor am I certain that I see the bearing, on this question, of
his great law, that we apprehend ourselves in conjunction with
the object. Unfortunately, the method of his philosophy, its
being reasoned, as he calls it, which was to carry irrefragable
conviction and end controversy, is what I can but little enter
into or follow. I can, indeed, translate this 'law' into my own
language, much as I have done: then Mr Ferrier seems to say
much the same as I, or I as he. But if I cannot appreciate
his demonstration, I can the point and clearness of many of
his sentences.

I may say the same, in reference to this subject, of his
Agnoiology or theory of ignorance. His manner of thought
here, as I understand it, is one which might strike many

---

[1] Page 505.

minds forcibly. We do not know this 'thing in itself', to be sure, but then, on the other hand, we are not ignorant of it: our state in regard of it is not that of ignorance, which is what all you who talk about it imply, and even say: it is no more ignorance than it is knowledge: if you can find a *third* alternative, *that* is our state in regard to it: if not, *you* have no more right to say, expressly or impliedly, that we are ignorant of it, than *I* have to say we know it. This, as I understand, is in other language what I meant by saying, that the notion of knowledge is not applicable to it: that there is nothing to know: that talking of knowing it is like talking of eating light, or smelling sound: disparate, incongruous.

I will comment slightly on Mr Ferrier's language as to the necessary and the contingent, that which is, and that which is not, conceivable otherwise: with a view of showing how his language differs from that which I have used.

Nature, he says in one place (if I remember rightly), could have made the sun to turn round the earth, instead of the opposite, but could not have made two straight lines to enclose a space.

Now here I do not go with him, and I allude to what he thinks because it will perhaps illustrate my view, and because my difference with him spreads further.

The difference between the necessary and the contingent (using this latter term of what we know to be fact—to avoid ambiguity, it might be better to call it 'contingential') seems to me only a difference of our manner of arriving at knowledge; that knowledge which we arrive at chiefly by the way of thought and reason has to us more of the character which we call necessity: that which is more of experience, acquaintance, testimony, is contingential: but we cannot draw a line: we cannot say, one portion of knowledge is and must be known to us in the one way, another part in the other: so far as the contingential is true *knowledge*, is *certain*, not approximate only or hypothetical, it might have been arrived at by the road of thought, and then it would have been to be called necessary: and, on the other hand, there is no thought which is not experience: as I have in another place expressed it, we *find out* everything: *after* that which we start with, our own existence.

I think Mr Ferrier's account of what nature could have done in the above case is not correct—it depends on what we mean by the 'sun' and the 'earth'.

If in our notion of 'the sun' and 'the earth' we comprehend only a small number of their actual properties, it is exceedingly easy to suppose the order of things to have been 'the sun round the earth'. Men did long so suppose. The more ignorant we are of their properties, the more easy it is to suppose it. That is, it is the omission of properties from the notion which makes the easiness.

The straight line has got but one property (say), namely, that it is the shortest distance between two points: there is therefore but one thing to omit (to make a parallel case), and the supposition of omission is difficult, because there remains nothing for the notion. But omission thus being scarcely possible, let us suppose, what is very likely, obscure view or inattention: it is then perfectly possible to conceive that two straight lines might inclose a space: and I dare say at this moment many people would so conceive about them.

I am unable therefore to see any difference in nature's power in the two cases: if she had made two straight lines to inclose a space, they would not be what we now understand by straight lines: if she had made the sun to turn round the earth, these would not be what we now understand by the sun and the earth: the solar system would have been different, and very likely we should not be talking of the sun and the earth at all. The difference in the cases is this: common language is constructed on what I have called a sort of normal stage of phenomenalism: hence for things like the sun there is a common, non-scientific, language, but it does not express the full intelligent notion; for geometrical notions there is, I suppose, only the scientific language, expressing the full notion. The sun and the earth which can change their relative circumstances are those of the vulgar, but then what the straight lines of the vulgar may do, or what spaces *they* may inclose, I can hardly tell—we must compare the sun and earth as they are, *i.e.* as we best can know them, with straight lines as *they* are.

The notion of necessity and contingency is important with Mr Ferrier in reference to knowledge altogether. I do not propose to examine what he says, which would take too long, only to say one or two words.

The contingent laws of cognition, he says, are the senses and the circumstances of them: the necessary law of it is the apprehension of *self* in conjunction with the object of knowledge.

So far as I understand this, it seems the same view which I hold if we take care about these notions of 'necessity' and 'contingence', which nevertheless with Mr Ferrier play an important part: there is a fact, a difference to be expressed, but it is not an absolute difference, such as Mr Ferrier probably means to express by these terms.

His fundamental view, that all knowledge is of oneself in conjunction with the object, is, as I understand it, what I should translate in different ways into *my* language: one way would be this. Our second or known self is to our first or thinking self, the great sense or faculty of knowledge, by which the object is known. The notion then of the self (the *known* self) being the necessary, the senses the contingent, accompaniments of knowledge, seems to me to be simply an expression of the subordination of the latter to the former.

All that I say about 'necessary' and 'contingent' here is that they do not express an absolute difference: that they shade off the one into the other; they mean what I have in another place called the comparatively important, and unimportant, parts of knowledge: the important, according to their importance, belonging more universally to all intelligence: the *less* important allowing the conception of a science of comparative epistemology, or of the different knowledge of different beings according to their different cognitive organisations.

One of the boldest efforts of abstract imagination (a sort of thing I like very much) is made by Mr Ferrier in pp. 381, 382, and it seems to me rather to show what *I* am saying. It is too long to quote, and I can hardly otherwise give an idea of it, I will however try.

One and all of our present senses, he says, might be abolished, and provided they were replaced by a set of different senses, a man's knowledge of a tree, for instance, might be as perfect as or more perfect than it now is....But let us suppose the self which a

man, knowing the tree, is cognisant of with the tree, to be ex-
changed for something else, and that some mode of apprehension
different from self-consciousness comes into play—would the
man, in that case, continue to have any cognisance of the tree?
Certainly not. "Withhold any of a man's senses from his cog-
" nisance while he is conversant with external things, and he
" will still be able to apprehend them, provided you give him
" other modes of apprehension." But withhold a man's self
from his cognisance, and he shall not be able to apprehend the
things intelligently—give him what substitute and what endow-
ments you please in place of the self which has been withdrawn
from his cognition.

I have quoted textually the last sentence but one, on
account of an apparent hesitation or ambiguity, which I wish
observed, as to 'any' and 'other'. And I have cited the whole
passage, because the conclusion that *I* draw from it is this: that
'senses' (I do not say *what* senses) or other modes of apprehension (distinct from self-consciousness) are *necessary : any* sense
may be removed, but even then some particular mode of apprehension must be substituted for it: and, on the other side, that
'self-consciousness' is so far *contingent,* that it is possible to
make the supposition of some mode of apprehension being substituted for *that* (as is done in the second sentence—it is one
out of various conceivable modes of apprehension), which indeed
would not give us 'cognisance': but this would go to show that
it is possible to have a wider notion of 'apprehension' of things
than Mr Ferrier's 'cognisance'.

Another way in which I should translate Mr Ferrier's view
into one similar to my own is this: by 'phenomena', using the
word for a moment etymologically, I do not mean appearances
of something necessarily different from the appearances, but
appearances to us, which may be more than appearances, or
may be not—that is of further consideration. I mention in
passing that this hangs on to the view on which natural facts
were first called *phœnomena,* in this way: that they were called
so in distinction from τὰ ὄντα, which latter were variously understood: I recognise such, but understand them to be thought,
which in my view takes the lead of things: by the real being
of things I understand the right conception of them or about

them, by the *phenomenal* being of them (so far as I give *sig-nification* to the term 'phenomenal', besides giving it *applica-tion*, which is my main business with it, to physical fact or the facts of the spatial universe) I mean the conception of them which accompanies our corporeal communication with them: this I look upon as *a* right conception of them, but different from the other as *the* right and complete one.

When Mr Ferrier says then, that what we know is ourselves knowing, one way in which I should translate this is, that the complete or higher knowledge is the observation and criticism of the way in which things appear (are phenomena) to *us: we* are here, as he wishes, in two positions; in the lower, things appear to us; in the higher, we watch the process, and judge from the appearing, so far as we may, what they are.

I think in translating Mr Ferrier thus I am going beyond him : but I think that I am right in doing so.

I will finish with quoting from Mr Ferrier a few words upon the highest matters of philosophy, in which I cordially agree with him, and which are not gratuitous, but are an inti-mate part of his view as I understand it, and certainly of mine (the expression is *his*):

"Neither the existence nor the non-existence of things is "conceivable out of relation to our intelligence, and therefore "the highest and most binding law of all reason is, that under no "circumstances can a supreme mind be conceived as abstracted "from the universe[1]." "To save the universe from presenting a "contradiction to all reason, intelligence must be postulated along "with it[2]." "In the judgment of reason there never can have "been a time when the universe was without God[3]." "Every "mind thinks, and *must* think of God (however little it may be "conscious of the operation which it is performing), whenever it "thinks of anything as lying beyond all human observation, or "as subsisting in the absence or annihilation of all finite intel-"ligences[4]."

We know *more* about God than this, but what we know more about him is what it is to us because we know this *first* about him, and if it is detached from this will cease to fill the mind and stir *the whole* of men's nature as religion has done.

[1] Page 497. [2] Page 510. [3] Page 511. [4] Page 512.

I have spoken about necessity and contingency a little in another place, as well as just now in reference to Mr Ferrier, but I will just put what I have said in still another form, as it is important.

Contingentialness is in substance the notion of a thing existing *as fact*, in other words, of *this* existing, not *that:* necessariness is the notion of a thing existing with reason for its existence. If each notion was carried out to the full, we should mean by the former that *this* is in fact what exists, but that it is quite possible, and for all that we know, equally likely, that *that* might have existed instead (or if we prefer the supposition, *nothing* instead, only that *this* might *not* have existed): we should mean by the latter that *this must* exist, and that we know it must, and that nothing else could have existed instead of it; but that we do not *know* it *does,* and cannot (in effect) imagine *how* it actually does. If we entirely exclude the notion of contingentialness we have no notion of particularity or actuality of existence, if we entirely exclude that of necessariness we have no notion of method or wholeness of existence. And in reality the word 'existence' means *two* things with us, *these* two, and they are quite different. And it means in each case not *one* of the two, but both. If we could absolutely and entirely exclude all possibility of even making the supposition that God did not exist, there would then be no meaning in saying he existed: there would be no ground or counternotion, as I call it, to the notion; it would have no significance. Similarly, if we could be thorough *positivists* (in the proper etymological signification of that word) or, I may say, matter-of-factists, *i.e.* if we could entirely destroy in ourselves all notion of reason for things, and care only for the historical knowledge of *fact* about them—then, if I might so speak, this knowledge would not be knowledge: the mind would be a record of successive experiences, but we should only *really* have had intercourse with fact much as a log of wood tossed about by the sea in various climates would bear traces of them: knowledge is thought, judgment.

The canvass or ground of all our knowledge is the conjunct supposition, 'Everything might have been otherwise than it is, but there is reason why everything is as it is.' The distinct conception of a thing as fact involves *some* degree of imagination that it might have been otherwise: and on the other hand there would be no interest in knowing things as matter of fact at all unless we believed some connexion among the things: a 'necessitudo', a mutual relation.

Of course, beginning from the first infinite possibility, reason of being is in different degrees. Beginning with the existence of God, I think Descartes, and Mr Ferrier in the passages which I have just quoted from him, go too far in this way, that they make the necessity of such a nature as hardly to allow a knowledge of *fact:* consequently to what they describe a great many people would say, we do not call this the knowledge of the existence of God at all: it is not what we mean by it. Therefore when people speak of the knowledge of the existence of God a priori and a posteriori, so far as I understand the distinction, I think it is *both* ways.

Taking then the existence of God as the first necessity, the ultimate point at which nevertheless we cannot *quite* escape contingence, we come afterwards to lower necessities, say mathematical. I see, as I have said, no *principle* in the discussion whether two straight lines not inclosing a space is a truth of necessity or experience, the degree to which it may be called the latter depending in my view simply upon the degree in which people could imagine the contrary. People *might* (there is no saying) try on a piece of paper whether two straight lines could enclose a space, but they would never try on a table whether two inkstands were the same as three.

The various phenomena of the universe have each, and all as connected with each other, their reason, and this makes a necessity, as against what Mr Ferrier says about the sun and the earth, as complete as the necessity which we have just been speaking of. But of all this reason, even the lower and nearer part, the mutual connexion among phenomena, we can know but little of: of the higher and more distant part, or the supposition of purpose for which they may exist, still less. The *means* of our knowledge about them therefore is by the manner of mere experience: contingential: the *more* particular they are, the more contingential. All along we may well suppose gradation of reason or necessity for and in them: some things more important in the universe than others, others less important: some for the sake of others: different ways beforehand of doing the same thing, one chosen: on all this however I could not speak without introducing the notions of will, purpose, ideal, which I do not wish to do here.

CHAPTER V.

SIR WILLIAM HAMILTON'S LECTURES ON METAPHYSICS.

THE next book which I come to is Sir William Hamilton's Lectures on Metaphysics. I wish to test my views by his, and his by mine: or, in other words, to examine how far, in his account of the manner in which we gain our knowledge, he keeps what I have called philosophy and phenomenalism distinct, and whether he falls into the confusion which arises from improperly mixing them.

To recall to the reader for a moment, as cannot be done too often, the difference between them: the point of consequence is, what we start with. The physical philosopher starts, and must start, with the view of things which regulates our material life, according to which *I*, for each one of us, means one of a particular class of organized beings out of an universe of beings contained in space; the whole universe, and this *I*, as a part of it, being composed of various elements and forces variously communicating together. Upon all these we look, as we for *this* view suppose, with a disengaged intelligence, dissecting the *I*, so far as we can, like any other organism, and watching the play of elements and forces between *it* and that which is not it. This view is what I have called an *abstraction;* that is, so far as we look at the *entire* of things it will not stand by itself, for this reason, that we could not have attained to it without certain mental principles being in action which enable us to view things as objects or unities: when however we *have* attained to it, as we all do, we may leave out of account the manner in which we did so, and suppose for the time that the elements, forces, &c., contain somehow in *themselves* the entire reason why they are viewed by us in the manner in which they

6—2

are viewed: such a view, as compared with a supposed view of the *entire* of things, makes what I have called an *abstraction*. This phenomenalist view is what, both in the individual and collective advance of knowledge, we in *one* respect grow more and more to, that it is what experience continually clears and confirms: in another respect, it is simply the view of such intelligence as is possessed by all animals, and we have something about us which protests against its entire engrossment of us.

The original fact to us, the one thing of which we are, before all others, certain, is not the existence of an universe of which we, as organized beings, form a part, but the feeling, thinking, knowing, that this is so, and the knowing that we do know it, or, in other words, that we who know it, are anterior, in our own view of ourselves, to it. If then we begin with *this* supposition, we know nothing about a phenomenal universe, a universe of existing things besides ourselves, except so far as we realize the manner in which one part of it after another becomes known to us or the subject of our thoughts (*object* of our knowledge), and we must not, previously to this realization, suppose them existing. This successive realization is the *logical* genesis or growth of our knowledge. It is not existence of any kind, that in the first instance is supposed to be the object of our knowledge, but what is supposed is feeling, thought, knowledge, and *I* as the subject of them, and only existence in so far as this feeling may, in whatever way, inevitably suggest it. This, evidently, is a *deeper* view than phenomenalism, or, in other words, it mounts to an earlier original fact. But, in the first instance, all that we may consider it concerned about is feelings, thoughts, knowledge, of a supposed *I*. While so restrained, however widely it may trace the manner in which we think and the results at which our thought arrives, it is an abstraction, like phenomenalism, in comparison with what we may imagine an entire view of things. This is what I have called the logical (epistemological) or lower philosophical view.

My notion of the higher philosophy anwers to what might be called, and by many philosophers has been and is called Ontology', or the theory of 'being', as against the theory of knowing, or the phænomenology of knowledge, or various other language: but I do not think the term a good one, for this reason. I do not at all say but that what I have called phenomenalism represents to us, or is to us, a true and real existence. I only say, that we must draw no conclusions from it beyond its sphere, and that if we mount to the primary fact upon which every thing to us, even it, rests, our consciousness, it seems to me that we must consider that the sphere of pheno-. menalism does not represent to us the whole of reasonable thought. Further than this I do not go now.

The purpose with which I am at present examining Sir William Hamilton and other books is to see how far the phenomenalist view and that of the pure philosophy of knowledge are confused: *i.e.* how far there is a vacillation, in the primary assumption, between that of a thinking mind and that of a phenomenal universe.

Sir William Hamilton's Lectures on Metaphysics are I suppose, as to method, a Philosophy of the Human Mind, following more or less the order of considering the subject which was begun long ago, and has been followed, in the main, by the successive Scotch philosophers. He differs from them, or most of them, first, in the greater use of logical conceptions and terms, and next, in what I may call the less prominence, at least, of phenomenalism. I mean that his purpose is described very definitely as being 'the analysis of consciousness'. So far good. 'The phænomena of mind' are however talked of by the side of 'the phænomena of matter'. This is less promising. But effort is then made to get the two into *one* consideration by the establishing that we have a consciousness (I suppose) of matter similar to the consciousness which we have of mind or self. This so far as it is not language only, but represents fact, is what stands in direct opposition to my view, and what, in consequence of this, I shall rather fully examine. But still my view *outflanks* this, so to speak, and the establishment of this is not only impossible, but would not, if successful, serve the purpose needed. Mind is above matter, because even if there could be established a parallel consciousness of phænomena of mind and of those of matter, it is mind which has that consciousness. There would still be a phænomenon of mind at the head of all, namely, this double consciousness itself.

What Sir William Hamilton then has done, is to point out, more distinctly than seems to have been done by others, the doubleness of consciousness, or in other words, he has, it may be, introduced (I am not certain whether that is so) the practice of extending the application of the term 'consciousness' from 'self-consciousness' to (what I may call) the whole amount of knowledge which we have, in the first instance and immediately, in conjunction with this self-consciousness. This is very well: but he seems to me to consider that the amount of this knowledge is greater than it is, and to be confused in his notion of it, and consequently he has applied, as I think, the term consciousness quite beyond the reasonable application of it.

We are aware of the not-self or non-ego quite as immediately and primarily as we are of the self, or ego, the distinction of the one from the other being necessary for the knowledge of either. The term 'consciousness' is therefore very fitly applied, if we like so to apply it, to our knowledge of the non-ego as well as to our knowledge of the ego. But the non-ego as known merely by this consciousness is entirely formless: it is known to us only as the not-self, and in no other character. Difficulty begins to arise when we try to understand how it is that it puts on to us the form of what we call the external world. There requires to be, of course, careful thought here. We are conscious of the non-ego exactly correspondingly to our consciousness of the ego, but no further. We are conscious of ourselves as feeling (say), or thinking, and correspondingly with this we are conscious (if we like so to speak) of something beyond or distinct from ourselves (*ourselves* being determined by feeling or thinking), which, according to the language we use, we describe as being what we feel or think, or what causes us to feel or think, or in various other manners. Over against then, and correspondent to, the feeling of *ourselves* stands a knowledge of something as not-ourselves. But the various qualities or characters of *feeling* are not space, direction, magnitude, solidity, but are pleasure, pain, duration, repetition, &c.: on the other hand, our detailed *knowledge* has for its qualities or characters the *former* sort of things: how is it that the original double consciousness of an ego and non-ego, while, in the line of the ego, it puts on to us those various characters of pleasure, pain, &c., which we can understand as attaching to feeling, changes itself, in the line of the non-ego, into something with which we cannot at all suit the notion of consciousness, the qualities or characters of it (space, magnitude, &c.) being what cannot be characters of feeling?

In reality of course, being an expression of what, in the last resort, is to us feeling, they are in a manner characters of feeling, and we might, in language cumbrous and bizarre, describe our multiplied experience by talking of ourselves as feeling seeingly, feeling hearingly, and by using no other forms of language than verbs and adverbs. What is the reason why we do not do this? In our capacity for pleasure and pain there is the seed of endless variety in our consciousness in the line of the ego: what is the seed of the expansion of our consciousness of the non-ego beyond mere *consciousness*, which is what would be represented by the language which I have given above, into phenomenal knowledge, which is what our actual language represents?

It is strange, but it seems to me as if Sir William Hamilton throughout considered that the saying we were conscious of a non-ego were the same as saying we were conscious of matter[1]. Our body is of course the medium between our in-

---

[1] I have returned to this in another place, and must apologize for much repetition and awkwardness in the treatment of it, only begging that it may be remembered that I never professed to be free from such. What I have here expressed wonder at is I suppose undoubtedly what Sir William Hamilton *did* consider, and his considering it is looked upon by those who sympathize philosophically with him as an important discovery on his part. So far as he did mean this, I have in another place (page 116 &c.) commented on the misapplication of the term 'consciousness'. Independent of the term, all that I can see in Sir William Hamilton's supposed discovery is a fresh form of what seems to me the cardinal error, the putting the phenomena of matter and the phenomena of mind side by side. Sir William Hamilton, starting from consciousness, thinks it a great thing to be able to put the phenomena of matter by the side of the phenomena of mind, which of course are the first thing he supposes: Mr Mill, starting from the supposition of the spatial universe, thinks it a great thing to be able to put the facts of mind by the side of the facts of matter, which of course are the first thing *he* supposes. Sir William Hamilton's supposition of our being conscious of matter seems to me to be wrong in exactly the same manner as Mr Mill's supposition, which I should describe as that we phenomenally know mind—*i. e.* that we may put *its* facts, and that exhaustively, or as our *only* consideration of them, by the side of physical ones. In

telligence and the external world : only that in saying this we must be careful. We may conceive ourselves as we are phenomenally, or in other words, corporeally : we may in this view be said to be conscious of our body : that is, whatever takes place in it (speaking generally) has corresponding to it some kind of alteration of our feeling : our body is in this view a great organ of sense, a vehicle by which we come to feel the existence, as similar to our own phenomenal existence, of a vast external universe in which we fill a place : in this use of the term consciousness, according to what I said just now, that consciousness of the non-ego is corresponding to that of the ego, we are conscious of the external universe in the same way as we are of our bodies, knowing the one by distinction from the other, or (in this case) by the mutual antithetic communication of the two, only the self is what is in the first instance *directly* in thought.

But in all this we are *supposing* ourselves corporeal, corporeal here being a highly complicated notion, which, in its complication, we certainly do not immediately *feel* ourselves, for what we mean by it is that we see and handle ourselves as of such and such a shape and solidity, a tree having such and such another shape, &c. What is the root of this in feeling?

The question whether, as the root of all our after objective knowledge, there can be admitted what we may call a relation of locality of our conscious or feeling self, taking place in consequence of the extension of our body—(we, who feel, are phenomenally *here*—is the feeling *here?* our arm is phenomenally a part of us—is the feeling in *it*, or in *us?*)—is a question which has two sides, a physiological and a logical one. The physiological side, whether, so far as that science goes, we are to be considered as having a locally distributable, or on the other hand concentrated and unitary, feeling self, I do not touch. But the logical side is whether the notion of ascribing locality to *feeling*, the various possible modes of which, I have said, are pleasure, pain, duration, &c. can be even admitted—whether it

respect of Sir William Hamilton—we are conscious of seeing, and just the problem of philosophy is to make out what is our mental relation to the thing we see : what is it but plastering up a crack to say that the word 'consciousness' will cover that also, and that being conscious of seeing is being conscious of the thing we see ?

is not like talking of a yellow sound, a sour colour, or various other incongruities of thought. No doubt locality is abundantly *associated* with feeling, as the language of psychologists runs: but the question is as to the nature of this association, and how we are to conceive it beginning.

Sir William Hamilton's view of our knowledge of an external world seems to be that we feel or are conscious of, locally, the parts of our body and the changes which take place as to them, first, and that then with our body we feel, proceeding onward, outward space and matter.

It seems to me that this is not true physically (or in my language, phenomenally), and that if it were, it would do nothing to explain the logical difficulty.

The logical difficulty is, Why, instead of saying, I feel in such and such a manner, which is all that, with any of us, what we are pleased to call knowledge, when we get to the bottom of it, amounts to, do we use such language as, I see (*e. g.*) this or that thing?

Sir William Hamilton's answer seems to be, There is a part of space (*i.e.* the dimensions of our body) within which if the thing or object be, the knowledge of such things or object and the feeling in such and such a manner, are two identical things, or two ways of expressing the same thing. Our feeling in such and such a way, and our knowing *e.g.* the form of an image on the retina[1] are, we are to suppose, two things which not only are, in whatever way, associated with each other, but which really are the same thing, and the knowledge of the image on the retina leads, in after experience, to the knowledge of an outward object corresponding with it, which is full or developed vision.

Now it seems to me not only that we do not know, except by later science, the form of the image on the retina, nor that, if we did, could our doing so be considered the same thing, the same (not an associated) notion, as our feeling in such and

---

[1] Sir William Hamilton's language is, I believe, and so far as I know, that what we really perceive is the rays of light in contact with the eye. It is Mr Mansel in his Metaphysics who says that what we see is the image on the retina, agreeing in this with many other philosophers (among them I believe Dr Thomas Brown). I suppose the two notions are in substance the same. See forward (p. 145), where passages are quoted.

such a manner. The blank ' in such and such a manner' must be filled up with some possible quality or character of feeling (pleasurably *e.g.*), and this cannot be the same thing as the other.

What takes place is: correspondingly with, in the phenomenal world, certain movements of light, and then of the muscles of our eye, and certain changes, mechanical or chemical, in our optic nerve and brain, there exists in the world of consciousness a feeling on our part, which we call the sight of such and such an object. Of course the feeling is what it is, correspondingly with the changes in our sensive organ being what *they* are: and in this way, if we like to change the word *feeling* from being a neuter verb to being an objective term, we may say we feel those changes, as we say, ' servit servitutem': but we are not conscious of them in the sense of being able to tell, independent of after science, what they are: we only know the variations of them from considering them correspondent to the variations of the feeling.

The fact that our body is the vehicle of our communication (so to speak) with the external world, does not mean that we feel our body and its parts first, and then the external world afterwards. Our body is a part of matter which has these two characters, that disturbances of the parts of it are accompanied with feelings, on our part, of pleasure and pain, and that motion of different parts of it follows at once upon, or accompanies, our will. But whenever it is disturbed, there is a disturbing cause, which we feel, in the sense of being aware of it, contemporaneously with the disturbance, and we cannot move parts of it without moving, or pressing, something beyond it, what we are aware of also in the same manner. Though, therefore, our being aware of *it* is accompanied with pleasure and pain, or with exertion, and in this way it is specially intimate to us, yet we are as much aware of it through the external world as we are aware of the external world through it.

Sir William Hamilton it would seem, considers that he has made a discovery in showing that we are conscious, or immediately aware, of the existence of the external world. It appears to me unphilosophical even to suppose that a discovery can be made of the kind which he thinks he has made.

It cannot possibly be shown, nor would there be any purpose in showing, that we know our own existence (or, more generally, the existence of mind) and the existence of an external world, in the same manner, or with the same kind of knowledge. So far from this, it is evident that we do not. The question is not, as to both one and the other being *certain* to us : we may have no inclination to scepticism either way, but if we try to realize to ourselves the nature of our certainty of the two, we cannot but understand that it is in a different manner that it is realized in the two cases, and that to the extent to which we confine our idea of knowledge to, or let it be absorbed in the one or the other, we have a tendency to lose our certainty as to the other case, or to become, as to that, sceptical. So far as we try to establish the one certainty on the basis of the other, we have the double difficulty, first, that we have no logic applicable to such rudimentary thought, or which can give validity to inference in such very primitive matter : and next, that even so far as we *can* do what we are here wishing to do, the second certainty, whichever of the two we suppose such, would be only derivative and secondary, which does not correspond to the character which *seems* to belong to it. So far as we suppose two independent and original knowledges of different kinds, we must give up the idea of homogeneity of knowledge, and of the necessary commensurability (so to speak), so far as they are known, of the things known in it, *i.e.* of the possibility of their being brought into relation one with the other. If we have one sort of knowledge in which the forms of the knowledge or the qualities of the things known are space, solidity, &c. (whatever language we use) and another kind of knowledge in which such forms or qualities are pleasure, pain, &c.—knowledge then is not a common ground upon which the things which are known can meet—not a way in which they can be brought together : there are two worlds : and though we may *think* of space and solidity, and though we may *see* the space or the solid body in which we understand the pleasure and the pain to be, we cannot bring the characters of the one world into relation with those of the other, or (in different words) establish any relation except a very imperfect one of contemporaneousness, between them.

This being so, we may either, in our thought, start with supposed knowledge of the one kind or the same of the other, and in that case what we have to aim at is (that which it is the object of all these observations to urge) the keeping steady to our first principle or original point of view. The more important and higher point of view is that given by consciousness or thought of our own existence.

But since, in our habitual thought and life, we *both* consider ourselves to exist as thinking beings, and consider the external world to exist also: that is, equally call by the name of existence the being the subject of pleasure, pain, will, &c. and the being the subject of figure, solidity, colour &c.: how are we to deal, or how do human beings deal, with these two kinds of knowledge (so for the present to call them) when they are thus in conjunction?

Practically, where the one has been considered a knowledge, the other has been considered what we may call a *belief*: that is, has been expressed by some term not at all conveying, in the natural sense of it, any less notion of certainty than knowledge conveys, but conveying a notion of the difference of the manner of the certainty.

The most *ordinary* use, in relation to each other, of these two terms 'knowledge' and 'belief' is for 'knowledge' to be applied to right thought in the phenomenalist view or sphere, and for 'belief' to be applied to the feeling (so far as supposed reasonable) which we have of our own unphenomenal or super-phenomenal existence, and to the consequences considered to flow from that—the world or sphere of super-phenomenal relations. A view more or less phenomenalistic is *natural* from the first to our manner of existence here; distinct phenomenalism (as I have already said) is on the one side what experience developes, but it is also on the other a manner of mental action analogous in certain respects to that of the animals, in whom distinct *consciousness* is not begun.

On the other hand, Religion in many forms, the higher philosophy as in Plato, and the lower or logical philosophy (as *e.g.* in Dr Reid), all point out that in reason the name 'knowledge' belongs to the certainty which attaches to consciousness or to the recognition of ourselves as thinking or as mind.

This is what I have at various times expressed by saying that the great original fact to each of us is not the existence of the universe or the external universe, but our feeling ('our' supposing of course the preliminary feeling of *ourselves*) that it exists, whatever may be the value and warrant of that feeling. Knowledge of the external world thus, in the philosophical view, descends a step, and has to be dependent on the consideration what *is* this value and warrant.

Philosophical language therefore has usually been (rather startlingly to the phenomenalist or merely natural habit of thought) that we *believe* in the existence of the external world, on whatever ground. The ground of this belief has been variously assigned as instinct, habit, &c. Dr Reid, whom I particularize here on account of the constant reference to him by Sir William Hamilton, assigns as the ground 'common sense', or the common sense of mankind. The question has been evidently confused. In the first place, it took the form in the last century of a controversy against scepticism, or a defence of certainty altogether, and the possibility of such, against people supposed to deny such possibility. But this is quite an accident of it. The discussion of the nature of our certainty of an external world is of itself a simply philosophical one, and should so be treated.

Again, the question of our knowledge of the external world is the same as that of the knowledge of our corporeal selves. This people are very confused in seeing, nor is it wonderful they should be. For in the reasonings by which the external world, as independent of our mind, was supposed to be annihilated, our corporeal senses, the existence of which was a part of the matter in dispute, had, for the purposes of the proof (and that not a proof by way of reductio ad absurdum) to be supposed existing. Under such circumstances, whatever the value of the conclusion, there was danger as to the validity of the proof.

The point and interest of Berkeley's proceedings seem to have been his putting together two notions which *really* do not belong to the same manner of thought[1], viz. the philosophical

---

[1] Not but that they *might* do so, being both true, and Berkeley on both of them in my view, right. In fact, Berkeley was so thoroughly right (setting aside his affirmative opinions as to the meaning of the spatial universe and the things in it,

notion that the external world cannot be known to exist in the
same manner in which we know *ourselves* to do so, and another
notion, to the effect that by the existence of the external world
is meant the same thing as the actual, phenomenal, existence
of the logical subject of the various qualities, (shape, size,
solidity, colour, &c.) which we speak of matter as having. By
giving his view the one or other of these two forms (that of
the denial of a knowledge of the external world in the same
sense in which we know ourselves, and that of the denial of the
actual existence of the logical subject as above) according, in
general, as he turned it towards the philosophers or towards
the vulgar, Berkeley commanded to a considerable extent,
though always as to a paradox, the assent of both.

Sir William Hamilton seems to consider Dr Reid to have
held confusedly and with mistake the doctrine, in this respect,
which he himself exhibits clearly and right. Really, he may
be said to take Dr Reid's 'common sense', and instead of
describing it as a ground and a legitimate ground of a belief
that the external world exists, to consider it a proof in us of a
consciousness of this external world.

Our being conscious of a thing, and every body that we
know of (apparently therefore in virtue of his human nature)
thinking it, are two very good sources of certainty for us, but
they are different, and the certainty which they produce is
different. If we call the certainty in the former case knowledge, we must call the certainty in the other by some different
name: we will say 'belief'. Sir William Hamilton labours
hard to found our certainty of the existence of the external
world on *consciousness,* or to make it, in his language, the result
of immediate perception. The way to show how far this is so,
is carefully to analyze consciousness: a process at least *very*
difficult. But Sir William Hamilton seems to me in a very
unphilosophical manner to reiterate the fact that the mass of

that what he said would have been quite unremarkable, if it had not been that he
started with the Lockian supposition of ourselves in the middle of a spatial universe, which made the conclusion he came to seem absurd, and invited the unphilosophical refutations of it by kicking things down, or whatever it might be. The
drawing the conclusion invalidated the premises it was drawn from, under which
circumstances the mind gets into the state into which the old sophistical puzzlers
tried to bring it, unless we suppose a reductio ad absurdum.

men *do* think in such and such a manner, as a proof that what
they thus think is a fact of *consciousness.* What they thus
think may have as much certainty as if it were a fact of consciousness—that is not the question: but when what we are
investigating is the nature of the certainty, the fact that any
number of men think so may be a legitimate ground for our
believing in that manner, but can never be a proof of its being
a fact of consciousness.

The analysis of consciousness is so difficult, and when it
goes beyond the simplest observations, so deceitful, that I am
disposed to think (I will not say however altogether) that
nothing should be referred to consciousness in regard to which
even the doubt can arise whether it belongs to consciousness or
not. Pleasure or pain *e.g.* are referred to consciousness or
feeling, for the simple reason that except as matters of consciousness they cannot be conceived as existing at all. But, if
I were called upon to produce a fact of consciousness, I should
be disposed to assign as such the direct *negation* of that which
Sir William Hamilton assigns, and to say that if we are conscious of anything, one thing of which we are so is of our own
existence as feeling, thinking, &c. in a manner not only different from, but out of relation with, that which we, in advancing
experience, understand as the manner of existence of the external world: that consciousness thus, while embracing (if we
like so to speak) a non-ego as distinguished from the ego, distinctly guards itself against, throws off from itself, that non-ego
in the investment which it acquires, in whatever manner, of
phenomenal or sensible existence. It is a fact of consciousness, if any is, that existence as life, thinkingness, feeling-
ness, the exercise of will, is not the same thing with existence
as visibleness, tangibleness, measurableness, audibleness, &c.:
that they are known, so far as they are known, in a different
manner: it is a fact of consciousness again that existence of
the first kind is known to us in ourselves by consciousness: if
any logic is allowed as to these rudiments of thought, we may
surely then say that it is a fact of consciousness, that it is in
some other way than by consciousness that we know, so far as
we know, existence of the latter kind.

I wish most carefully to guard against mere verbal discussions on the .word 'consciousness'. All our knowledge, as knowledge, is consciousness: Sir William Hamilton has·well exhibited the philosophy of knowledge as the analysis of consciousness. But consciousness, thus widely understood, is analysable in two manners: into reflexion or self-consciousness on the one side, and that on the other which is understood to have a bearing, or to relate to something, beyond ourselves: and again into that which is original, and has never had, as to our mind, any other character than that of consciousness, and that of (or *in*) which we have *become* conscious, or which we have come to know, through (or in conjunction with) some sort of suggestion different from the above original consciousness: we know ourselves by self-consciousness or reflexion: we know the existence of a not-self by consciousness, in so far as we do not, and cannot, conceive ourselves as constituting an universe: but we know the form or qualities of this not-self (*i.e.* the sensible world) as something entirely dissimilar to the form and qualities which in ourselves we are conscious of. This ought not indeed (as I have said) to be called *knowledge*, if knowledge is what is built on consciousness: we may call it belief: by which we need mean no more than that, without the slightest doubt as to matter (the form and qualities of the not-self) existing, the certainty which we have of it is not the same (in kind, *i.e.* for in degree, for all that I know, it may be) as the certainty which we have of our *own* existence.

I can see nothing in Sir William Hamilton's doctrine except assertion that it *is* the same, without any attempt at reason for the assertion except what I have already spoken of, the notion (if I may so describe it) of a local coincidence of thinking existence and material existence on the occasion of what we call a sensation in a particular part of the body. We feel that part of our body and what is in contact with it, I understand him to say,—that is, we feel or are conscious of matter—in the same way as we feel or are conscious of mind, our thinking selves. We know thus from the first, in the same way and with a like original knowledge, mind and matter. In different words, we have an immediate knowledge of matter (or the external world), and the establishment of this immediate knowledge Sir William Hamilton looks upon as an important discovery.

All this is exactly that confusion between two lines of thought which it is the purpose of what I am writing to criticize. We feel (say) the prick of a pin, and feel it *locally*, though in the nature of the reference to the locality there is much, I suppose, for physiologists to discuss. But though we may use one word, as *impression*, for the two (so to call it) coincident things, the movement of certain particles of matter (in the pin and in our finger), and our feeling of pain, the two things belong to two different regions of thought, and the only way in which, supposing the two both existent, we can be certain of their being related to each other, is that they are contemporaneous. The supposed locality of the feeling is a complicated fact, and no matter of original certainty. Sir William Hamilton's view is (as I understand it) that the coincidence brings the two kinds of things, our feeling *e. g.* (on the one side, the form of the pin on the other), into the same world of thought, and that we are aware of the form of the pin with the same consciousness, the same immediacy, with which we are aware of the pain which it produces. Surely this is not so. They belong to different kinds of thought, and the knowledge in the two cases is different. If we call knowledge, or if we call immediate knowledge, what we know in the latter case, we may reasonably call the other *belief* or knowledge not immediate. In the one we might, conceivably, be deceived: in the other we could not be.

Sir William Hamilton calls his doctrine of the immediateness of our knowledge of the external world by the name of Natural Realism or Natural Dualism[1]: the mass of philosophers, who have looked upon this knowledge as, in comparison with our knowledge of our own existence, something which required, so to speak, to give an account of itself, a belief, a mediate knowledge (or however they might express it)—being called by him Cosmothetic Idealists or Hypothetic Dualists.

The classification here made of philosophers seems of very little value, making, as it does, no account of the purpose and method of the various philosophies, nor any distinction between what a philosopher assumed at the beginning and the results which he considered himself to arrive at. As to the Hypothetic Dualists, it is to be observed that almost all philosophers have

[1] Lectures, Vol. I. p. 292.

been dualists, (nay, have not all?) in admitting a 'besides-self' as well as a self or mind, Berkeley as much so as Sir William Hamilton: our sensations were not in his view causeless or merely self-modifications, only he did not consider the cause of them to be what we are here calling 'the external world'. The name 'Hypothetic' therefore is little applicable to these philosophers, nor, it seems to me, is that of Natural Dualism to Sir William Hamilton's view, which I should rather describe as a sort of Monism (in language of his own), or an attempt to fuse together, as objects of one kind of knowledge, two kinds of things (if they may be called things) so different as feelings and material qualities[1].

The way in which I should state what seems to me the fact is this: We feel ourselves as mentally living, or know our ex-

---

[1] In speaking of what all or almost all philosophers have thought I speak with unfeigned diffidence, not only because I have a very imperfect knowledge of the history of philosophy compared with Sir William Hamilton's, but because I seem to myself to have a different notion from his of what such a knowledge should consist in. As a branch of study, what I should mean in the first instance by the history of philosophy is a (probably rather loose) general account of the course of philosophical speculation, which is an important branch of literature, and will make a man know, in the general, what philosophy has concerned itself with: but in case any one means to make a more thorough study of it, I think there is another branch of study, so to call it, which he wants first. This is 'interpretation': penetration and conscientiousness in entering into people's thought. And in order to this a man must think much himself. He is a merely superficial (which in this case is *inaccurate*) reporter unless he understands and has felt the philosopher's doubts and difficulties. For thought like this to co-exist with an extensive literary knowledge may be difficult—I will not say—perhaps I may be making the reader think no man can be a historian of philosophy, as Crassus that no man can be an orator, or Imlac that no man can be a poet—but anyhow I hope that I am ennobling his notion of the task.

In the present case the philosophers are bundled up together, and a vast quantity of them represented as allowing nothing but 'modifications of the ego'. But I am very doubtful what this really means. A sentence for instance like the following (Vol. II. p. 29,) quite staggers me. 'Others, again, deny to the mind not only any consciousness of an external non-ego, but of a non-ego at all, and hold that what the mind immediately perceives, and mistakes for an external object, is only the ego itself peculiarly modified.' Whether Sir William Hamilton means here that the philosophers whom he speaks of suppose the notion of external objects, and a wrong assignment to that class of what belongs to another—in which case they would be most thorough Dualists—or whether the mis-psychological iron has entered so deeply into his soul that he can never, in the most abstract regions of thought, get rid of the notion of 'external objects' himself, I cannot tell.

istence as thinking and feeling beings, and with this have what we may call a sub-consciousness of something besides ourselves; or, as I have above expressed it, that we are not everything— not the universe. This is our *most* immediate or absolutely necessary knowledge: without this we should not be *we*, to think and feel. We feel ourselves with less intimacy and less immediateness to be corporeal or (as I have called it) pheno- menal beings, and, what is a part of the same feeling, to be locally portions of a material or phenomenal world. There is no harm in describing this latter feeling as consciousness: in fact it *is* so: only it is a consciousness which *might* be illusion, whereas the former consciousness *cannot:* we feel *as if* we lived in a material universe, and people have been found like Bishop Berkeley to say that though we feel as if we so lived, yet we really do not so live: but there is no meaning in saying we feel as if we felt and thought: here then is real immediate- ness: and no one can say that though we feel as if we felt, yet we really do not feel. Hence the second consciousness, though consciousness if we like to call it so, is still, in com- parison with the other, mediate or belief.

What we are conscious of in this way is not matter, but ourselves as material: and the meaning of this is simply that a certain portion of our feelings, so it is, are suggestive of what, as we feel it, we may call a communication (or in language which has been used by some, ' a conflict') between us and what is not ' we ' going on in a particular manner, (which manner is what is meant by the common confused term, 'sensation'). This com- munication, as our feeling suggests the existence of it, is, as I have described, between us and what is not we. This same communication if phenomenally viewed, or studied as a matter of physiology by what I have called a disengaged intelligence, is only between one portion of matter and another, namely, our bodies and what is around them. That is, the communication, and with it the existence of matter, is only, from the side of feeling, something that feeling, so it is, suggests: and feeling *sugges- tive* (as distinguished from the immediate feeling above) might, conceivably, be all wrong: there might be no external world at all. On the other hand, from the side of phenomenalism, the *communication* is the certain fact, and the fact which can be compared with other phenomenal facts : that along with the communication there go feelings of a sentient being is something which phenomenalism as such, can only take as supposed cause (or causes) of various effects, which *might* be caused otherwise.

The study of this communication, what should have been called *Æsthetics,* is of course most interesting : but the keeping in mind whether our point of view is that of consciousness, or that of physiology, is important for the success of it.

The communication, so far as we are to conceive such, between mind and matter, or (in other words) between feeling and the spatial universe, is a different notion from that of the communication between the matter or nerves of our body and matter extraneous to it, with which latter communication feeling on our part is some way correspondent. Such questions as those of immediateness of knowledge have all really reference to the former communication. In reference to this former communication, we might either consider the notion conceivable and reasonable, but the thing, except by some extraordinary agency (the meaning of this will appear shortly), impossible : or we might consider the notion reasonable and the thing possible ; or we might consider, which is what I am disposed to do, that there is something confused in the notion.

Perhaps it is more correct to describe the first of these views as the considering the notion unreasonable, but still the thing, or something amounting to the thing, by some contrivance (we may almost say) such as a pre-established harmony, or by the continued interposition of divine power, possible. We look now upon theories of this kind as unphilosophical, but the philosophers who made them had the great merit of seeing clearly what *we* do not always see, how feeling and the qualities of matter belong, as I have expressed it, to two different kinds of thought. All that we know, or, it seems to me, can know, as to the relation of the feeling in any case to the contemporaneous nervous or cerebral disturbance, is that they *are* contemporaneous. Theories like that of a pre-established harmony, unreasonable enough it may be, yet exhibiting the two streams running side by side, have the merit of clearly bringing home to us that this relation of contemporaneousness is as far as we can get.

The second view given above, to the effect that the notion of a communication between mind and matter, feeling and space, is reasonable, and the thing possible or the fact, seems to have been held by those philosophers who considered that the primary qualities of matter were like their ideas or mental representations, whereas the secondary were not: this being, as I understand it, equivalent to saying, that in respect of the primary qualities, the mind and matter (or feeling and space) actually met, that there was a communication or something common to both, whereas in respect of the secondary qualities there was only a *correspondence*, or contemporaneousness, between feeling on the one side and the presence of the qualities of matter on the other. This notion as to the primary qualities, which is to the effect, that in the case of knowledge of them, the qualities of matter might be predicable of feeling, for otherwise there could be no resemblance between the idea and the material object, was I suppose suggested by such things as the image on the retina. The image, on the nerves, of a square object, *did* look something like a square idea. The retinal surfaces, at once sensible and capable of square figure, seemed to be a meeting-ground of mind and matter. The thing forgotten was, that what *felt* was not the retina which was thus figured, but *I*, and though, in calling it *sensible*, we imply a particular relation of it to this *I*, the nature of this relation was still the undetermined question.

I can only see, in Sir William Hamilton's doctrine of immediate knowledge, the re-introduction, in different language, of a notion similar to this.

I am aware that, as in a great many philosophical errors, there is a truth involved in this notion of the resemblance of the ideas of primary qualities to their prototypes. The form which this truth bears to me, is this: the matter of our bodies and that of the external world seem to communicate in two different manners, which we may call mechanical and chemical: correspondingly to the first we have feeling of the kind which we call active, *i.e.* we, with more or less of attentiveness, exert our will: correspondingly to the latter we have feeling of the kind we call passive: we feel more or less of simple pleasure and pain. In saying above ' *seem* to communicate in two manners', what I

mean to express is this: it is possible, perhaps, for close physiological observation to make out that the difference in the constitution of one and another of our nerves, which fits them for one
and another purpose, is only at the bottom, mechanical, and that
all that takes place in them is really only motion of homogeneous
elements, and correspondingly with this, it is *conceivably* possible
for us to follow out our consciousness to such minuteness that in
the pleasure and pain (contemporaneous with the movements)
we may discover *really* elements (so to speak) of volitional effort,
attraction and repulsion, acquiescence and shrinking, &c.—
about all this possible *ultimate* analysis I say nothing, only
considering in the meantime the fact to be as I have described.

The fact which the above-named erroneous notion~as to
primary qualities seems to me indistinctly to represent, is this:
that active feeling, exertion of our will, is homogeneous in our
view: pleasure and pain (passive feeling) are both infinitely various, not always even readily distinguishable the one from the
other, neither of them suggesting that kind of attention to them
which could make measurement, and such that the different
kinds of them have scarcely any comparability the one to the
other. And as active feeling is, in its different exertions, homogeneous in ourselves, so it is what we seem to be able reasonably
to assure ourselves is the same in us and in others: with passive
feeling this is in no respect so: as has abundantly been said,
what I see as green another man may see as blue, and the difference be for ever undiscoverable. Hence we feel the *amount* of
exertion of will, and in so feeling we feel ourselves also in
relation with *other* beings which exert will: mechanical sensation is measurement, whereas chemical remains in this particular nearly sterile. The reason why I have mentioned this
here, is, because, in this measurement, we have something like
an actual meeting of mind and matter, of feeling on the one
side, of space and solidity on the other. When therefore philosophers said that the ideas of primary qualities, and not of
secondary, were resemblances of the qualities (the primary
qualities being, speaking generally, those known by mechanical
sensation), they meant, in a not good way, to express what I
will for a moment call an approach to each other of mind and
matter in the way which I have above described.

This approach is in fact by means of the idea of *motion.*
Time or duration belongs to, or is an attribute of, mind or feeling, no one doubts.   Does locality also?   Has feeling 'daseyn'?
The attributing locality to feeling in virtue of *passive* sensation
is as we have seen, very difficult.   When we are investigating
physiologically what we call the *seat* of feeling, what we want
is, to find the portion of the body, with the material modifications of which portion the feeling is *exactly* (*finally* we might say)
contemporaneous.   So far as the feeling or consciousness *itself*
tells us, this part, scientifically found, is rarely or never the seat
of it.   A man's feeling, so far as *itself* bears witness, may be in
his supposed leg, which he has lost long ago.

The attribution of locality to feeling in virtue of *active*
sensation seems to present less difficulty.   A feeling of ours of
this kind, we say, moves or is the means of moving our arm,
and must therefore be locally present or in communication with
the arm to do so.

I am not going to discuss this: only to say thus much.   The
notion implies the unity of the two ideas, force as one of the
ingredients (so to speak) of motion and pressure, and force (or
activity) as the source of change, or that which gives beginning
to what did not exist before.   That our volition is a real cause
of the movement of our own body, or, in other words, that our will
is a reality and our supposed consciousness of it not a delusion,
I hold most thoroughly, and if we like from this to draw the
conclusion that our will, acting locally, must have locality,
valeat quantum. · But I think that the only way in which we
are able to conceive these things, and to investigate them fruitfully, is to keep, even *here*, the two lines of thought which I
have endeavoured to exhibit, separate: to put no stress upon
the phenomenalist to admit what cannot be expressed in qualities of matter, nor on the other hand, to assert against him
that we are conscious of anything which he from his premises and
by reference to those qualities, can disprove: keeping however
in mind that we, in the position of consciousness, are nearer the
source of the stream of knowledge than he, and that he can
have none of it, in the *entire* view of things, except as we allow
it to pass to him.   It may be a question whether we have an
arm at all (for all our *immediate* knowledge is that we feel or

think we have), and if this is denied, the matter, as to certain
knowledge, is settled for him and for us alike.   Only every
reason which goes to justify our belief that we have an arm or
that our arm exists, goes also to justify our belief that we move
it, and that it rests with us, uncertain till we determine it,
whether it is moved or not.   But for the purposes of research,
there are two sets of things or considerations—on the one side
the circumstances which determine our will, on the other the
qualities of our arm as matter—which, like oil and water, will not
mix together.   We create then, or abstract, the phenomenalist
view, from which *origination* is excluded, and in which there are
instead of it only relations of time and perhaps of mechanical
force: and since feeling, whatever it may be susceptible of besides, is susceptible of these relations of time, we let feeling *so
far* into phenomenalism, or in other words, we let the two lines
of thought run together in *this* particular, though further than
this we cannot do so without confusion.

What I have said is not exactly as I meant to say it, but
I think there is conveyed in it what I should have said, namely,
the reason why I think that even the *idea* of a communication
between mind and matter, feeling and space, further than as
a relation of contemporaneousness is such, is not reasonable.

The measurement which I have last spoken of, or in other
words, the mental conversion of so much effort of will into so
much space traversed or so much motion resisted, is a manner
of sensation, and far the most important manner, its importance arising from this, that by means of the relation of amount
or magnitude (measurableness) the qualities of matter and of
mind do seem to, or do in some measure, approach each other.
But they do not meet or mix: amount of will exerted, and
amount of space traversed, though both amounts and so far in
relation, belong to different worlds of thought.

In respect then of that kind of form of objects which is
given by relations of space and solidity, mind and matter
(feeling and space), though they in a manner *approach*, do not
meet or mix.   The kind of form of objects in relation to which
they do meet is the εἶδος, principle, meaning, purpose of them,
that which gives to each its unity.   This kind of form may be
considered at once an attribute of the material object and of

the knowing mind.   The colour of an object is not transplanted
from matter into mind in any degree—colour cannot be at all
a quality of our thought: the length of it only partially—it
is so much distance, and our will may have for an attribute of
it quantity of exertion corresponding to this distance: but the
meaning, reason, purpose, of it, that is, the expression of the relation of the parts of it to each other, which gives it unity,
thinghood, reality, may be transferred to the mind altogether
—it may be with equal propriety described as *a thought* and as
the thing, as something in our mind or something in the object.

I do not think that the metaphor or manner of speaking
conveyed in the word 'transference' and in such expressions as
'in' the mind can really here cause any deception.   Of course
I am not speaking of any movement or any locality, and the
reference to such which the words convey (and it is impossible
to find words un-extravagating in this respect) does not enter
into the thought or argument.

I have not lately been making much reference to Sir William
Hamilton, and will now for a short time leave him entirely, in
order to discuss some points connected with what I will call the
scale of sensation or knowledge.

CHAPTER VI.

THE SCALE OF SENSATION OR KNOWLEDGE.

I DO not know that there is any harm in saying that we have sensations, or the sensation, of time, space, solidity, and even of unity or genericity. After all, *sensation* is the general term to express the consciousness, feeling, thought which we have correspondent with (so far as we assume the existence of the external world, but), more correctly, *supposed* by us correspondent with, the presence of any portion of existence independent of us. We may conveniently imagine two kinds of this sensation, in no degree rigidly separable the one from the other, viz. feeling and thought: *feeling*, that kind of it in which self-consciousness, reflexive attention, pleasure or pain, is strongly present: thought, that in which the attention is directed rather to the non-ego and to the exertion of the will. The former is clearly that in which there is the least approximation to each other, in the qualities of the feeling and those of the matter. To this extent there was reason in the language of many philosophers, that the ideas, as they called them of secondary (chemical) qualities were unlike the qualities. A feeling embodying pleasure or pain must be most thoroughly incommensurable and out of relation with any quality which can be supposed in unliving matter. As at the extremity on the side of feeling the incommensurability is complete, so at the extremity on the side of thought, or the sensation of unity, thinghood (so for the present to call it), the meeting is complete: this we have seen. Half-way along the line stand the relations of space.

At one end then of this line the mind has feelings, the matter qualities, contemporaneous, but not mutually compar-

able: at the other the mind has thoughts, and the matter
something in it which we may call (for the present) thoughts
embodied: near this extremity must be relations of time and
half-way those of space.

At every step of what we call perception, *i.e.* the advance of
our experience or conception of the external world, sensations
of all these kinds are blended together. It is obvious that
sensations belonging to the feeling end would be of themselves,
for intellectual result, mere confusion. What makes this confusion orderly is in a less degree sensation belonging to the
middle of the scale, in which there is measurement; and in a
higher, the highest degree, sensations belonging to the other
end, to which belong special distinction, arrangement, classification.

I carefully guarded the word 'transference' where I used it
before, but I will now resume it with a little less care. We
will speak of mind and matter as if they were things between
which there could take place something like movement.

In what I have called feeling the mind is passive, and since
it is supposed there must be activity somewhere, the *matter* is
considered active, and the mind or subject of the feeling is
spoken of as 'affected' or in some similar way. In reality
there is no importance in this, for in respect of the sensation, there
is no more activity of the matter than of the mind. Under
certain circumstances of the one, there is feeling of the other:
activity must have been required for the putting the former in
these circumstances, and that is all.

The passivity of the mind is tolerably readily comprehen-
sible, but what is the meaning of its *activity?* and as it is all
passive at the *feeling* end of the scale, is it all *active* at the
thought end? And what is it half-way?

There being at this latter end, on the one side, thought in
the mind, on the other, thought embodied in the matter, is the
relation of these two thoughts one of coincidence, or of identity?
In other words, Is the thought which meets us in the matter
thought which we have first put there? Here the mind would
be active.

Again, half-way, the qualities of space and those of the
mind being capable of being brought into some relation, has

this which is common to the two, its source in the mind, or from the other side?   Is the mind here active or not?

The describing *space* as a form of thought, or as a form given by thought to sensation, seems to me a manner of speaking in some respects exactly analogous, from the opposite point of view, to the manner of speaking about primary qualities of Locke and other philosophers, which I before commented on (namely, that the ideas of them were *like* their prototypes); to be in the same manner itself an error, but to be representative of the same truth which *that* represented.

To say 'we think spatially', which is the kind of language we ought to use on the supposition of space being a form of thought, seems to me language in some respects of (exactly) the same kind as the supposition of a square idea.   The way we think spatially, so far as we do so, is to will a certain amount of exertion, which exertion we understand as carrying our hand (say) through a certain amount of what then we call 'space'.

I have before said, that if we liked to use language in that manner, all that we ultimately or immediately are certain of is that we think or feel in such and such a manner.   There is therefore certainly no harm in the description of our having the sensation of space (so I have expressed it) as 'thinking spatially'.   But the point is, Is there *more* reason, in the above case, for using the language 'think spatially' than there is for describing our sensation of a red colour as 'thinking redly'?   In other words, is space *more* a form of thought as distinguished from a quality or relation of body or matter, more *subjective*, as some would describe it, than colour is?

I do not think we can understand the manner in which it is so without here making a most careful distinction.

When I said just above, "may we speak with more reason "of 'thinking spatially' than of 'thinking redly'?" I follow the same line of thought as Berkeley, when he considers, Is there any difference in the manner of our perception of primary and secondary qualities, giving everything of a higher or more important character to the perception of the former?   He decides that there is not.

But the prerogative of the primary qualities above the secondary, against which he argues, *viz.* that the ideas of them are like their prototypes, whereas those of the others are not, is, in one view, exactly the opposite of the prerogative which is claimed for them when space is described as a form of thought, so that we might use the language 'think spatially', whereas we could not say reasonably, 'think redly'. If, in the case of primary qualities, the idea was like the quality, whereas in the other it was only correspondent or contemporaneous, it was clear that the object in the former case came into the mind in a manner which it did not do in the latter, or that the perception in the case of the primary qualities was objective, and that of the others subjective, possibly therefore illusion. And it was on this supposed subjectivity of the perception of secondary qualities, and the disproof of any prerogative of primary perception above them, that Berkeley built what we know as his doctrine.

If we describe space as a form of thought, in contrast with secondary qualities as qualities or relations of matter, we of course do exactly the opposite to this, and make the primary perception the subjective, the other the objective. This is what I referred to in saying, that the Kantian language had an analogy with that of Locke, from an opposite point of view.

Now what we must keep in mind about all this is, that our thought must start from the phenomenalist or the philosophical assumption, and that whereas in the former objectivity is the test of truth, in the latter subjectivity is. On the philosophical or epistemological assumption, knowledge is not the bringing of one thing which is, into the relation which we call knowledge with another thing which is: such a description would be absurd, involving in the description the thing which we are describing (we cannot describe the things without supposing them *known*): knowledge is the view as orderly, formed, having reason and meaning, character and qualities, in it, of that which, but for the knowledge, would have to be viewed (if it could be viewed) as confused, inform, characterless, undistinguished. On the phenomenalist assumption, on the other hand, we begin with supposed existence independent of us, of which we are a part or with which we coexist, and taking for granted what knowledge is (which cannot be investigated on *this* view), we investigate the particular ways in which we come to the knowledge of the par-

ticulars of this existence. On this view what we see first is
things, then we see them of such and such a shape and size, then
of such and such a shape, size, and colour: by which of course I
do not mean that this is the historical order of perception, but
I mean that if we take up a book of this kind, we see first
things talked about as what are supposed (or very often, with
much confusion of thought, *objects*)—these *things* are supposed
from the first to have various powers to do this and that, and
the course of the investigation is to make out how the shape,
size, &c., which is assumed as belonging to them comes to be
known by us, and then how the colour, taste, &c., similarly
assumed, does so: and the old doctrine as to primary and
secondary qualities was to the effect that the shape, size, &c.,
really belong to them, as a part of the thing, but that the
colour, taste, &c., are something, as compared with *those*, superadded, and which the thing might be without—and are more-
over known to us much less perfectly than the others, we only
knowing, as to them, that we have certain feelings to which
there must be something, though we know not what, correspondent.

Now, exactly to the degree to which anything (the reader
will not be deceived by the necessary word 'thing') on this
assumption, is a more necessary quality of external or objective
reality, so on the other or philosophical assumption, is it more
subjective, or in a higher degree a form of thought.

The order of consideration on the philosophical assumption is
exactly the reverse of that on the phenomenalist, which I have
described. On the philosophical assumption the confused mass of
chemical or secondary sensation gives the confused and chaotic
matter of (in *this* sense), or preparation for, what is afterwards
knowledge. To this *time* and *space* (which viewed from *within*, are
in fact a higher degree of self-consciousness and so much volitional
exertion) give form and order of the first or lower description,
in the sense of shape, magnitude, relative position, &c.   Then
finally form of the higher description, εἶδος, quality or *qualitied-
ness*, kind, true reality, is given by a higher self-consciousness,
and there begin to be *things*. The things are specially *things*,
they are noticed and distinguished as *unities* out of the confused
mass of sensation of which they are a part, in virtue of various

suppositions, most thoroughly subjective or matters of thought, about them : that they are like ourselves: that they are a contrast to ourselves: that they are what we can handle or use: that they are like what we can construct: that they are what hurt us: and a variety of other suppositions of like kind. They are made *things* to a *certain degree* by the lower description of form or by relations of space: but it is evident *things* mean to us much more than solid shapes, of one and another colour, &c., and if *this* was all the character which they possessed, we should very slightly notice and distinguish them, even if we did so at all.

Of course this is not meant as a *historical* order of perception, any more than the order which I gave as to phenomenalism.

Of the actual or historical course of such perception, I shall speak in a moment.

It will be seen that the discussion whether space, *e. g.* is a form of thought (*i. e.* a form given by thought to our sensation, experience, or lower intuition) or a relation (circumstance, quality) of matter is one which I do not regard as important, or, more strictly, I think the supposition that it must be one *or* the other unphilosophical. As that discussion is sometimes conducted, people seem to think that the supposition is, that there are things with their secondary qualities on one, the objective side, and we, out of various possible forms which thought might have, have for *our* form of it the supposing these existing in what we then call space. So far as space is a form of thought and not a relation of matter, it is when the subject of our investigation is not what matter is, but how we think about what we call so.

Space is very fitly described as giving *form* to that which is commonly described as sensation, that is, to the confused semi-perception which belongs to what I have called the 'feeling' end of the scale. Any dwelling upon this would come more fitly in speaking of Dr Whewell's books: but I will say now thus much, that so far as relations of space are considered to give form to that sort of sensation, they want higher relations still, those which I have described as of unity or reality, to give what is more properly called 'form' to them. Relations of space, in consequence of their being, as I may say, perceived by measurement, or measured in the perceiving, have a character of exactitude about them which has caused great attention to be given to them as exhibitions of accurate truth, in a way in which nothing else is. All this may be made to mean too much, or may have more philosophical importance given to it than it should have. From the time of Plato downward, more strongly however in followers of his than in himself, this has been so. But mathematics, though giving exact truth, give truth only of a very poor sort: and what is more, they require, even for this, to be *informed* (or to have form given to them) themselves by higher considerations than those of space, time, and number. As I have said, it is not the *shape* (or size, or position) of a thing which to us, except in a very limited degree, constitutes it *a thing*, but it is what Aristotle called the λόγος of it, that in it which Plato conceived to correspond to the idea, that which I have variously called (for indeed one can give it no one name) the meaning, purpose, &c., the reason, in a manner, embodied in it which is a kind of principle or soul to the arrangement of it. This is what, in order to have a fixed point round which growing knowledge may group itself, we *suppose*, and mark by the name, and take for the logical subject of the adjective things or predicates which one after another we go on learning about the substantive thing or originally noticed and distinguished unity. This first *principle of notice* so to call it may be a mere supposition, may turn out to have been a mistake—this is not of consequence to the after knowledge: for every real step of knowledge, as I have before remarked, is as well a correction of error as, if we like so to view it, an addition to an aggregate. The important point is this—that the *thing*, unless it is a mere mathematical representation, is a *thing* or object of our thought in virtue of something (supposedly) in it or about it more important and of a higher reality than its shape or size, which, in comparison with this, are only accessory features.

It is the same in regard of *number*. The great importance of this at all times in philosophy has been assumed (and honour has thence accrued to mathematics) to arise from the exactitude of which the calculations which it deals with are susceptible.

But this is quite a subordinate reason of its importance, the great reason of which is in the conception of a *unit* which such calculations suppose. Such *unit* is really a logical *individual,* a conception most complicated: that is, not merely an object singular (what in common language we loosely style an individual) which is all that relations of space can separate and distinguish for us, but an object of a sort or kind, involving therefore the idea of such sort or kind, or of order and arrangement, that is, invested, embodied, *mind,* in the universe. Number, setting apart the pleasure of calculation, has no importance except as it is number of *things,* the bringing of which together implies, so far, generic identity.

What I have last said explains, sufficiently for the present, the *thought* which I have supposed to stand at the opposite end of the scale from sensation as mere feeling.

Historically, in every act at all important of perception, sensation enters of every kind, all along the scale. It may be said in this respect that all the operations of our mind are homogeneous, or that into all perception, or intelligence, what we commonly describe as the later mental operations really enter. In the same manner also all perception or intelligence is acquired or composed—an aggregate, cemented by past experience.

If we analyze the operations of the mind, or which is the same thing, analyze itself as we know it, assigning to it various faculties, what I have called sensation will probably be divided among several of these. The *thought* at the head of my scale, the measurement at the centre, and the feeling at the bottom, have from very early times been allotted to three separate faculties, called once νοῦς, διάνοια, αἴσθησις, and this sort of triple division, under various names, has been frequently recognized.

The course of the school often called Sensationalist or that of Experience (now perhaps the Inductive School) has generally been to blend together the central and lower part of the scale, as involving no important difference, and to leave out of account, as more or less visionary or fictitious, the upper part (that of *thought*), thus making the whole homogeneous.

The question whether relations of space (*e.g.*) are modes of thought or of objective reality, is as I have said, at least unim-

portant, perhaps wrong in the conception: but it is otherwise
with the question whether they are of the same nature as the
secondary qualities, or those of mere feeling.

Locke as I have said, and I suppose Kant, maintain the
difference from opposite sides, the former (following the old
philosophy) making the primary qualities more objective or
more intimate to matter than the others, and therefore in *his*
view more real, the latter making them more subjective or
more a part of thought than the other, and therefore *more* real
than they, so far as his view is to be considered the philosophical, *less* real so far as it is to be considered the phenomenal.
On this I say nothing. It seems to me that the general effect
of Kantism in England, owing perhaps to a phenomenalist application of it belonging to our habit of mind, has rather been to
puzzle philosophy and to strengthen what seems to me scepticism, and that when applied in the other direction, it has had,
as perhaps with Kant himself, too much of a merely mathematical (or drily logical) character. We in England use the word
subjective often as almost synonymous with visionary: and the
saying that space, upon the reality of which depends whether
or not the external world (or what we think so) is an illusion,
is subjective, would be taken as the saying, with a different philosophical reason, much the same as Berkeley did. And so for
much of Kantism besides.

What I have said hitherto about mind and matter has been
very general—I will now speak of them a little more with
reference to the particular circumstances of *our* perception.

I use the word 'perception' for the gaining of fresh knowledge in what I have previously called the way of acquaintance
with things, kenntniss. 'Sensation' I rarely or never use,
though I use it constantly, without describing what, in the
particular application, I mean by it.

At the lower or feeling end of the scale of sensation which
I gave a short time since the two things which stand opposite to
each other are not properly feeling and matter (sensation and
body), but are sensation or feeling on the one side, and on the
other side a communication between two kinds of matter, that
of our body and that which is external to it. It is *possible*, as I
have said, that *here* there may be a mechanical measurement

and corresponding to it a latent, because infinitesimally minute, consciousness: *e.g.* that the real character of *taste* might be an action and reaction (the force on the one side being our will) between the separate portions of our organ of taste and the particles and minute forces of the thing tasted. But this, though we might possibly follow it out on the side of physiology, we could never possibly follow out on the side of feeling, having no microscope for consciousness. We can only say then, that the communication between the tasted substance and the palate is *accompanied* by what we call a feeling (the sensation of taste) entirely, as feeling, out of relation with the communication. And the contact or contemporaneousness is not between feeling and matter, but between feeling and the mutual communication of two kinds of matter.

At the middle of the scale, to which correspond relations of space, the case is not exactly similar. Here the sensation or feeling (not like the last) does enter in some degree, though not in a great degree, into a relation which we can understand with the supposed matter without. It is still the phenomenal fact, that matter on the one side (in our bodies) communicates with, on the other side, space, or what is traversed, and external matter, or what resists or is resisted: but the feeling on our part which accompanies *this* communication, is one which, starting from the phenomenalist side, we *can* to a certain degree take account and speak of: it is not *entirely* out of relation with the qualities of matter: it is what we understand as not simply accompanying, but more or less giving the reason for, the communication. When we say that it is an effort or force of will that moves the arm, of course we do not mean more than to *a certain degree* to compare what takes place in the world of feeling with the phenomenal forces in the world without: but *to that degree* we *do* mean to compare them: between the one and the other there is some relation which we can understand: they are mutually commensurable or the one is understood as measuring the other: the will-force has in this respect not that entire subjectivity which belongs to feelings of pleasure and pain (which, as I have said, might be entirely different in different people, and the thing, of itself, never come to be known), in so far as, having an imme-

diate measure in the world without, we are able in some degree
from this direction to judge of it. At this part of the scale
then, though *still* feeling and matter belong to two worlds, and
we must say that what is on the one side is feeling, and what
is on the other side is the communication between two sorts of
matter, yet the feeling is associated with *one* of the sorts of
matter in a way which we can more or less understand: it acts
upon it, and that means *something* though it may not mean
much: feeling is here in relation not merely with a relation
between two kinds of matter, but with matter itself.

At the upper end of the scale, that of *thought*, the case is
exactly the opposite of what it was in the lower. As *there* there
was communication between two kinds of matter, and over
against these a corresponding feeling or mode of mind, so *here*
there is communication between two different forms or modes
of mind, and matter, phenomenalism, appears distinct from them,
as simply what has brought about the communication. The
perception, in its completeness, of an existing object of knowledge, is really a sympathy with its constitution, arising from
the fact that we know *ourselves* more or less as constituted
beings, and that we can make or constitute things ourselves for
purposes for which we need them. We recognize therefore in
the objects mind kindred to our own. The feeling and measurement which build up the knowledge thus completed, and
through which this final (far indeed from *final* in point of time,
for it is the spring of the others) perception strikes the life of
unity, are the crude material of the knowledge on our side, just
as the qualities of matter are on the other side the material in
which the mind which we recognize has been invested, embodied, immateriated.

It is in consequence of the complication of all this which I
have endeavoured to exhibit, that the words 'presence', 'presentation', &c., and the words 'inward', 'internal', have rarely
been used in reference to these subjects without confusion.

If we mean by 'presence' a sort of abstract contact, which
phenomenally or concretely, is only contemporaneousness, then
what is 'present' to the feeling (obscure, not *known*) is, at the
lower end of the scale of sensation the communication between
the two sorts of matter: in the middle, either (or *both*) that,

or (and) matter itself: at the upper end the mind embodied in the matter.

If we mean by 'presence' *local* presence, then by 'ourselves' (the one side) we must understand our corporeal selves, *i.e.* the organized matter of our bodies, to which our mental selves, our feeling, is, in whatever way, related.

With the confusion of these two notions, that is, with the failure to keep in mind whether our assumption is the phenomenalist or the logical, and with the taking the sense of sight for the typical sense, there arises an entanglement almost inextricable.

A thing cannot act where it is not. This, as to phenomenalist things and forces (or, if any prefer the expression, when spoken concretely and without metaphor) is true. Hence an object (*e.g.* a tree) affecting the eye, must in some way be present at the eye: and even, affecting the mind, must in some way be present *there* (somewhere, as those who speak thus have usually supposed, within the body) too. All this is only carrying out the language. Hence the endless theories about 'images' of things, and hence too the discussions and rediscussions, whether or not Dr Reid's adversaries meant by 'ideas', images, whether or not he meant that they meant images, whether if he *did* mean that they meant it, he *really* refuted them—and much more. The disentanglement of *this* may be left to those who have Sir William Hamilton's interest in clearing up points like these.

Perhaps the thing will appear most clear if, looking back to the sentence in the last paragraph which refers to an object affecting the eye, I try to point out to the reader which portions belong to the logical, which to the phenomenalist view. '*Object*' (in other words the saying that it is *the tree* that we see, the tree which out of the whole field of view is in relation with us) and then afterwards, 'affecting the mind,' 'being present at the mind,' are logical or philosophical: 'affecting the eye,' 'being present at the eye,' are phenomenalist.

Logically, the object, or the tree as such, may be said to affect the mind and to be present at it, so far as that is a good description of what really takes place, *viz.* that we have a feeling in our mind that there exists in that relation to us which we call sight, one particular object of knowledge out of a spatial universe, which object we call a tree, and understand to be such in virtue of certain qualities, forming together a whole or unity, which we suppose it to possess, vegetable life, greenness, &c. &c.

Phenomenally, what the eye is affected by is light, one circumstance of the light which so affects it being that it is interrupted, or reflected, or modified in whatever way by the portion of matter which, when the perception is completed, we call the tree. The saying then that the tree affects the eye, though there is no harm in it, is insignificant, and carries no conclusion of the kind above. But the speaking of any one thing affecting the eye is dangerous. The whole is a process highly complicated, one part of which is various change (of position &c.) in what we call the eye.

It would take me too long to go further into this confusion, illustrations of which will recur.

It is not so easy to discover how far there is or is not confusion in the use by philosophers of the terms 'presentation' and 'representation', or e.g. 'presentative and representative consciousness'. 'Presentative consciousness' should mean the feeling (which we regularly and naturally have) of our phenomenal existence, and in conjunction with this the feeling also, to which latter it is that the attention is directed, that there exists in actual communication with us through the bodily senses an object, which in this character we fix and name, independent of us. (In this view of presentativeness there is no room for discussion whether the knowledge is or is not *immediate*. The speaking of it as 'immediate' would have no distinctive significance.) In contrast with this stands consciousness *representative:* which is the feeling, first as before of our phenomenal existence, and then (with attention given to it) of there being in our thought something which *might be* in communication with us by the bodily senses, but which, so far as the representation goes, is not. I say, 'so far as the representation goes', because the feelings of presentation and representation may be, without special attention, undistinguishable, or may be concurrent. Philosophers generally have considered that the only way in which we can consider that a thing *might be* in communication with our bodily senses is from the knowledge that every separate portion of it has been.   In this respect representation *must* involve memory, and may involve besides what we may call an *active* power in the mind of recomposing.

How do presentation and representation thus viewed, stand related to the notions of mediacy and immediacy of knowledge? In this way: Representation, in the notion of it, might be described as *bi-objectal* knowledge, that is, knowledge in the case of which we might use the word *object* in either of two senses, *either* to express what is thought, *or* (in common language) what is thought *of:* there is supposed something (for the moment we will say) in the mind, and something also, possibly but not necessarily existent, out of the mind, which that *in* it represents.   We know then the thing out of the mind by virtue of (through the medium of) that *in* it.

It is important to observe that the notion 'mediate' or 'immediate' is really wider than that of 'representative' or 'presentative,' and that they ought not at all to be used as equivalent. Bi-objectalism is only *one* form of mediateness.   What is really meant by knowledge being *immediate*, when we are speaking of the foundations of knowledge, is that from the most intimate of it there is no break, but that it is continuous, in a manner homogeneous.   Thus, if our most intimate knowledge is considered to be of ourselves, we have not an *immediate* knowledge of an external or phenomenal world: there is a break: and so far as the word *knowledge* belongs to the former, some word like 'belief' belongs to the latter.   This is in fact only saying, that we have no means of demonstrating the latter from the former.   But this does not mean, that we know the external or phenomenal world by *representation:* if the reader will look at the description given of representation above, he will see that this cannot be.   The whole notion of *representation* is in fact borrowed from the supposition of an external world, and cannot be applied back to that.   Nay more, it is borrowed, at great danger of confusion, from one particular manner of viewing the external world, or the suggestions of one sense, the eye.

The difficulty of language in these respects may appear from the word 'immediate', as I have above applied it.   Continuousness of knowledge (by which is meant the absence of a break or gap) may be denoted by immediateness or mediateness, really as we choose to apply the word : immediateness may mean no *chasm* between, or no *road* between. I have made it mean the former.

Our knowledge of the external world is not a knowledge gained (in the first instance) or gainable, by demonstration, and in *this* respect, so far as it is a knowledge, it is *immediate :* but at the same time it is a knowledge separated by a step or break, and that a most important one, from our knowledge which *is* immediate, our proper consciousness, and in *this* respect it is *mediate.* The two things, the reader will see, are the same ; there is different use of the same word. It is from the supposition of their being different things that arises what is often called scepticism : such, *e. g.* as that knowledge which is mediate, and yet undemonstrable, must be no knowledge, and that *such* is our knowledge of the external world.

I will just signalize what, in the endlessly confused controversy as to immediate or mediate knowledge, presentative or representative perception, which carries away in its torrent alike clear metaphysical thinkers like Mr Ferrier, masters of philosophical history like Sir William Hamilton, and masters of phenomenalist logic like Mr Mill (as we shall see), seem to me to be the real points of importance.

Our knowledge of the phenomenal world is not, if we take as standard of immediateness our proper consciousness (*i. e.* self-consciousness with a formless non-ego as accompaniment) immediate. The latter has the higher degree of certainty.

We know, but besides this we know that we know. It is not proper to say that this latter statement, as against the former, is the true one : both because in this way, as Aristotle would say, the thing goes on εἰς ἄπειρον, and the same reasons which recommend to us *this* degree of abstractness of consciousness or double use of the word know, would seem also to recommend to us a higher degree of it, and a triple use of the word (we know that we know that we know, &c.) : also because (as I mentioned in speaking of Mr Ferrier) it is very possible that this double use of the word know may be applied by us, or may tempt us, to give the word ' know ', improperly, a double meaning. But though this is so, there is reason in making the latter statement by the side of the other, because, besides knowing the object of knowledge, we do know the fact or phenomenon (the first and greatest of all phenomena) of knowledge, and upon this knowledge, in the higher philosophy, many important conclusions depend.   But this is only saying that the object of knowledge may be, if for a particular purpose we choose to make it so, the fact of knowledge itself.   Sir William Hamilton seems to me to make all knowledge, even as knowledge, mediate.

We know the external world by our feeling ourselves something, which I have called phenomenal beings : the fact being, that we feel, consider, imagine (however we may describe it) ourselves in communication, not merely with a formless non-ego, but with a regular and various universe independent of us, by means of a part of that universe which we call our bodies, with which part also, in various manners, we consider our feeling associated.   Of some portions or characters of this universe (secondary qualities) our feelings are only suggestive : some (primary qualities) they directly measure : some (the composition and order in the universe) they identify themselves with or entirely appropriate.

With what reason we think or feel all this, is the problem of what is commonly called 'Ontology'.   Upon this I will not enter now, nor upon the question, whether there is reason in proposing such a problem.

This being so, calling our knowledge of the particulars of the universe ' perception', are we to consider it immediate or mediate, presentation or representation ?

The answer to this really depends on what we mean by the word 'thing' or on what we consider, in perception, to be the object of knowledge.

I described some time since the two kinds of words by which, in most languages, knowledge has been expressed.   One chief particular of the difference between the two, is our placing ourselves in imagination, when speaking of knowledge, lower or higher upon the scale of sensation.

Knowledge of acquaintance with things is the notion of knowledge which is suggested by the lower portion of the scale of sensation, where are the secondary qualities of matter : (the primary qualities enter both into this and as we shall see into the other kind of knowledge, most specially perhaps and necessarily into this). This is kenntniss, connaissance : the type of it is usually taken to be the sense of sight, which embodies both secondary and primary qualities : hence the philosophical name of it is 'intuition', 'anschauung': and hence the great tendency in the term 'representation', &c., as applied to it, to give the notion of an actual image. It would have saved some confusion of thought, at the expense of some picturesqueness, if instead of words referring to the sense of sight to express notions of this kind, we could have used or coined some referring to the sense of *touch* (in the double character of feeling and handling, nervous and muscular perception), such a word *e. g.* as 'betouchment'; the term 'apprehension' and words of this kind have something of the character which I mean : here, however, there would have been danger of confusion too : for whatever sensive power (even the simplest) we refer the term we use to, the reference to the sensive power will be something of a metaphor, for we *mean* to express something more general, more abstract than the reference to the sensive power would imply, though something which the sensive power suggests to us. Any feeling distinctly attended to is more or less of an intuition, and any recurrence of such feeling, similarly attended to, is more or less of a representation.

If we take knowledge of acquaintance, or by way of intuition in this use of the term, for the type of knowledge, and mean by the word 'thing', as is its real meaning, 'the object of our knowledge', then of course our perception or knowledge of things is immediate : the words intuitive and immediate in this sense will mean the same thing. The 'thing' in this view is what we see, handle, smell, taste. I have expressed the fact *this* way as the way in which it would be expressed, and to shew how many philosophical disputes arise from mere inattention to language. *Is* here expresses a relation of co-extensiveness or identity: it does not mean that what follows it is a predicate or part of the description of that which goes before. The proposition is true converted : what we see, handle, smell, taste, is the thing. Even *so* it is not absolutely safe from misapprehension : and it is this misapprehension which gives rise to.

the notion of something mysterious contained in the word *what*. *What* is it we see, handle, &c. people *will* ask : with some reason we shall see presently, though not with the reason they sometimes think. What is the substratum or substance of which these qualities which we perceive, seeableness or colour, handleableness or shape, taste, smell, &c. are attributes? The answer is, there is, in the sense you mean, none such : the thing itself is really, so far as knowledge is concerned (on *this* view of knowledge as acquaintance), determined by these particulars which you perceive about it, which are really therefore the elements or constituents of it. But because you do not know how many of these constituents there are (and for another reason too, which we shall see) you choose, in thought or language, to suppose the thing itself unknown, and to call all these things qualities or adjuncts of it. In reality, on this view of knowledge, there *is* nothing more *to be* known than the sum of these qualities.

But of these qualities of the supposed thing there is one of transcendant importance, which is its *thinghood* or reality, which is really the same notion as that of the relation of its parts to each other, and of itself to what is about it. In the view of knowledge as acquaintance with things, this is not to be treated as a mysterious substratum of the qualities, but is a quality itself, only the most important, and the particulars of which we are always endeavouring to discover. I have mentioned, that all the discussion about things in themselves seems to me to arise from the treating as two different *portions* of knowledge what are really two different views of the same knowledge. The cardinal quality of a sensible object of knowledge, which is what I have called its 'reality' or 'unity' vanishes out of the field of knowledge of acquaintance with things, for this reason, that it belongs to a higher part of the scale of sensation and thought than that knowledge will really apply to.

It is possible however, that we may take acquaintance with things, instead of being the type of knowledge, to be no knowledge at all, and to resolve all intellect at bottom merely into a sort of habit or familiarity : just as from passing a tree every day we might know, entirely without intellectual exercise, every branch and leaf of it, or might know to little purpose every

line on the face and every button on the coat of a man whom
we meet every day, but to whom we had never spoken. We
may take for type of knowledge the knowledge of facts about
things, judgment.

This is the *logical* notion of knowledge, and it is because it
is so that, in the manner which I have mentioned, knowledge
or acquaintance, in order to enter into thought and language,
is put into this form, and the thing we make acquaintance with
is split into substance and qualities, to which correspond, logically, subject and possible predicates.

Knowledge, when the *former* type is taken of it, is a matter
of communication, the suggestion of which is given by the communication between our body and the external universe: when
this latter type is taken, it is a matter of question and answer,
of dissection and analysis: we stand as it were behind the great
web of reality, of which we do not, so far, see the face; or
rather, seeing the face, we *endeavour* to get behind it.

Of knowledge of this type there are continually varying
actual objects, which are the facts we know about things: these
facts put together make up in this view the *thing*, and we are
said to have a *conception* of the thing, as distinct from an intuition.

Truth, in the intuitive view of knowledge, is simply undis-
turbedness or purity: in the conceptive, it is thinking rightly
or *as we should* about things: the highest notion of truth altogether is perhaps the accordance of the two descriptions of
knowledge, or the agreement of the results of the one with
those of the other.

CHAPTER VII.

SIR WILLIAM HAMILTON—CONSCIOUSNESS OF MATTER.

IN the last Chapter but one I have made some general remarks on Sir William Hamilton's Philosophy, but have as yet made little or no quotation from him.

I shall probably have occasion, in a later Chapter than this[1], to refer to his philosophy again : in the present Chapter I will try to exhibit the part of it with which I am most concerned in his own words as well as the proof which he gives of it.

Upon this part of his philosophy, our (supposed) consciousness of matter, I have myself written, I fear, with some confusion (and I must apologise for it) in this way : I have done my best to enter into Sir William Hamilton's view, by putting it to myself in various ways, and have seemed to myself thus to come to see it more clearly—it is probable that what I have written will bear the traces of this effort. But certainly, the more I seem to myself to understand it, the less do I agree with it.

I should almost be disposed to consider it the master-confusion, the 'temporis partus maximus' of mis-psychology—but we will see.

I have myself not the slightest objection to say that we are conscious of matter, if these are the terms we like to use, in *this* way. Matter is a thing we know, and whatever we know we may be said to be conscious of, if we talk of 'consciousness *of*' things : all our knowledge, even all our thought, is consciousness, as I have said myself as strongly as I can : what we know then, and not only that, but what we imagine, what we conceive, what we remember, we are conscious of : this very simple fact, or rather manner of expression seems to me to be all the substance of many pages of Sir William Hamilton, where he proves that the different faculties, by which, in the language of some philosophers, we are said to do these various

[1] In the next part.

things, are only so many manners of consciousness. Matter, then, is a thing that we are conscious of: this is *my* cardinal doctrine: I put it two ways: it is because matter is *after all*, so far as we can tell, *only* a thing that we are conscious of— a thought of ours supposed warranted, a mental creation properly created, a something the certainty of the existence of which depends for us on the certainty of our own existence, and the trustworthiness of our own feeling—that the study of consciousness is higher than the study of matter (in my language, philosophy than phenomenalism) and that we ourselves, who are conscious, know ourselves, preeminently, with a different knowledge from that with which we know matter, *of* which *we* are conscious, just as we know also our own thoughts and feelings with a consciousness more intimate and immediate than that with which we know matter, since we mean by matter something which we suppose to give occasion to varieties of such feelings: that is one way: again because matter is a thing which we are conscious of, therefore there is a study of it *as* we are conscious of it, which we may pursue without at all troubling ourselves what the *being conscious of it* means, and *this* is what I call 'phenomenalism'.

My hesitation in treating of Sir William Hamilton's view has arisen from an anxious desire not to misinterpret him: but the more I study what he says, the more I think that his view is nothing like such consciousness of matter as this, but something quite different. Whatever we are conscious of must be, so far as we are conscious of it, an object of consciousness, a creation of the mind: I really suppose that what Sir William Hamilton means by saying that the whole body of philosophers only allow us to be conscious of modifications of the ego, is that, in fact, they say this, which I have said above: and that he himself really says against it that we may, making the phenomenalist (which, used in connection with philosophy, is the mis-psychologist) supposition to begin with, that the things, or matter, are actually, spatially, existing before us, describe our relation to such things as the being conscious of them, without altering the meaning of the word 'conscious', but using it still in the same manner, drawing the same conclusions from it, as we do when we use it as to the previously supposed objects of consciousness, mental conceptions, mental states, self. Matter is supposed first as existing, described, defined, quite independent of consciousness: Sir William Hamilton is not finding matter by examining consciousness, but knows it already and lays down what it is. Consciousness then, which is variously synonymized, defined, particularized, as thought, feeling, will, and by other such notions or expressions, all, for that is the condition of them, referrible to a conscious or sentient subject, is examined as to its 'contents', in Sir William Hamilton's expression, which of course must be in some way homogeneous with, or predicable of, *these* things, thought feeling, &c.: and then among the contents of it there comes to be found this matter known otherwise, so entirely heterogeneous, with its constituents of oxygen, light, &c., and its qualities and predicates of shape, colour, taste, sound, &c.: and from its being thus supposedly found the conclusion is drawn that matter with *its* constituents or qualities exists to us in the same manner and with the same reality as the thought, feeling, &c. which are the other contents of consciousness, and this conclusion is supposed to be necessary to obviate scepticism.

Against this incongruity I will endeavour to put what seems to me the truth.

We are conscious of beliefs, thoughts, feelings, occupying our mind with various degrees of conviction or cogency, and next in conviction to the *central* belief that we exist at all, is the belief that we exist with what we call a body, by which we communicate with much which is not only independent of our primal selves, but external to our corporeal selves, and what we thus, speaking from our primal selves, think we communicate with, or, speaking from our corporeal selves, actually do communicate with, we call the universe of matter.

Taking this universe of matter, with our corporeal selves in the middle of it, up *here* and with these considerations about it if we are philosophers, and, if we do not care to philosophize, simply *up* without these considerations at all: and proceeding in the reverse direction to that in which, if we *have* made these considerations, we have *hitherto* proceeded : this universe of matter communicates with our body and all its various sensive organization, and concurrently with this various communication there is various consciousness, with which *this* course is brought to a halt—the other is complete, this is not—for in the consciousness thus come to we say *I, I know*, and other such things of which *this* way of consideration can take no account, and which, belonging really to the other, absorb everything which belongs to *this*, and make *this* appear a something secondary, included, an abstraction.

I hope the reader will give me credit for a wish to make Sir William Hamilton's view intelligible to him, so far as it can be so made—of course he *may* think it would have been better without my aid—and for being thus long, both upon the view itself and the opposite view, with *this* purpose.

But we will now take Sir William Hamilton's own words. I will give first his various enunciations of his view, then his proof of it: and on his proof I will first examine whether it proves what he wishes, and next, if it proves anything, what it proves.

First of all, however, I will make a general remark on his reasoning, and on his frequent quotation.

His reasoning is, it seems to me, sometimes very doubtful: I think I could find more instances like the following.

Philosophers, he says[1], refuse to admit the fact of consciousness, the immediate perception of external things, declare it to be impossible, and give reasons for thinking so: these reasons, he continues ought, if they are good for anything, to establish the absolute necessity for the rejection of this testimony of consciousness : he will endeavour to refute them, 'by showing that they do *not* establish the necessity required'. He finds five such reasons given : the second is, " Mind and matter are sub-"stances of different and even opposite natures : mind cannot "therefore be conscious or immediately cognisant of matter." Sir William Hamilton conceives it is an answer to this to say: "But the very first fact of our experience contradicts the asser-"tion, that mind, as of an opposite nature, can have no imme-"diate cognisance of matter : for the primary datum of con-"sciousness is, that in perception, we have an intuitive knowledge "of the ego and of the non-ego, equally and at once " (knowledge of the non-ego and of matter being not, with Sir William Hamilton, distinguished) [1]. The philosophers reject what Sir William Hamilton considers the testimony of consciousness, because the fact which, it is averred, it bears witness to, they say is impossible. Sir William Hamilton undertakes, against five reasons, to prove the possibility. The above is the way in which he does so against one of them. To prove the possibility, he thinks it enough straightforwardly to re-assert the fact which is in dispute on the ground of its being impossible. The philosophers say, What you assign as a datum of consciousness cannot be admitted as such, because mind can have no immediate cognisance of the non-ego or of matter: he thinks it is an answer to this to say, You are wrong in saying mind cannot have immediate consciousness of matter, because that which I have assigned as a datum of consciousness *is* such a datum, and the primary datum [2].

I notice this, which I hope the reader will examine for himself, not in respect of the consideration, which here is wrong or which is right, but because it shows a notion of argument which, in the case of any with whom, as with Sir William Hamilton, argument is so main a feature, rather affects one's confidence in him. The passage here quoted is not something occurring *obiter*, or an apparent inadvertence, but is introduced as is often Sir William Hamilton's wont, with much parade.

Next, on his quotations.

Sir William Hamilton's Lectures, as published by Professors Mansel and Veitch with full references, form a book the

---

[1] Vol. II. p. 122.

[2] I do not lay so much stress upon another thing which I will just mention here, which is a certain degree of inconsistency of view in what is said in different places, because some uncertainty of view, possibly even involving inconsistency, is by no means a defect in a philosopher in my eyes, if only it seems to arise not from confused thought, but from a continued *nisus* in the conception of truth, a struggle and a feeling after it. But if we compare Sir William Hamilton's language here with the first portion of his proof, which I shall shortly notice, it is certainly remarkable. This supposed fact of mind and matter being opposite, is what he rested upon *there* as a strong argument *for* the knowledge of the two being one knowledge, viz. consciousness: *now*, what *he* had then brought forward as an argument *for* the thing, the philosophers are represented as bringing forward as an argument *against* the possibility of it: and he, as if he had forgotten his own argument, instead of retorting the argument upon them, or doing anything of that kind, answers as we see, by simply re-stating the matter in dispute.

value of which cannot be over-estimated to the student who has opportunity to turn to the references. But I trust that the notion of learning, and of its meaning and value, which made Sir William Hamilton quote so much, is going out of fashion. I am quite ready to consider, that for reporting a philosopher's opinion, no person could have been found better, both in the way of conscientiousness and of penetration, than Sir William Hamilton. But I should have thought that his own endless and complicated discussions as to Reid's misconstruing of those before him, and Brown's misconstruing of Reid, and I know not what more, would have suggested to him of how very little value an off-hand report of a philosopher's opinion on an intricate and disputed matter is; so that his frequent citations of philosophers and quotations of them, in strings and shoals, might as to value have been spared, though I fully acknowledge the interest of them. When we come to Mr Mill, we shall see perhaps the value of one such string.

In my own opinion, but that is my own only, there is something depressing in this weight of learning, in this manner: nothing can come into one's mind, but one is told, Oh, that is the opinion of such and such a person long ago: and naturally therefore on the other hand if anything should come into our mind which we cannot find in any body, the air of a discoverer is put on for very little, and in a manner which seems to me unworthy of those whose business is simply truth. So long as a philosopher's meaning is as discussible in the case of our predecessors, as Sir William Hamilton has in practice shown, I am suspicious both of the professed originalities and of the references of opinion to this or that philosopher. And I can conceive nothing more noxious for students than to get into the habit of saying to themselves about their ordinary philosophical thought, 'Oh, somebody must have thought it all before', and about one or two particularities perhaps, 'Ah, but this is something which I have been the first to say'. The progress of philosophy is a thinking, and a re-thinking, and a re-thinking still more clearly and better, about the same matters of everlasting interest, and the philosophic disposition is to value correct thought about these greater things, rather than small originality, if it be so, in detail.

I will now proceed to give the various manners in which Sir William Hamilton enunciates his doctrine, that we are conscious of matter.

1.   The primary datum of consciousness is described to be: "That we are immediately cognitive of the phænomena of "matter and of the phænomena of mind[1]".

2.   This is called in the passage cited a short time since: "That we have an intuitive knowledge of the ego and of the "non-ego, equally and at once[2]".

3.   Again: "Consciousness declares that we have an imme- "diate knowledge of an ego, and of an external non-ego[3]".

4.   Again: "The fact to which consciousness testifies is— "that the object, of which we are conscious in perception, is the "external reality as existing, and not merely its representation "in the percipient mind[4]".

5.   In the following passage the two portions of this intui- tive knowledge are looked at separately.

"The acquisition of knowledge can only be accomplished "by the immediate presentation of a fresh object to conscious- "ness, in other words, by the reception of a new object within "the sphere of our cognition. We have thus a faculty which "may be called the Acquisitive, or the Presentative, or the Re- "ceptive".

"Now new or adventitious knowledge may be either of things "external, or of things internal, in other words, either of the "phænomena of the non-ego, or of the phænomena of the ego: "and this distinction of object will determine a subdivision of "this, the Acquisitive Faculty. If the object of knowledge be "external, the faculty receptive or presentative of such objects "will be a consciousness of the non-ego. This has obtained the "name of External Perception, or of Perception simply[5]".

6.   Again: "The great fact"—is—"that we are immediately "conscious in perception of an ego, and a non-ego, known to- "gether, and known in contrast to each other. This is the fact "of the Duality of Consciousness[6]".

---

[1] Vol. II. p. 86.   [4] Vol. I. p. 278.

[2] Vol. II. p. 122.   [5] Vol. II. p. 11.

[3] Vol. II. p. 29.   [6] Vol. I. p. 288.

7. But in the same page: "Such is the fact of perception "revealed in consciousness, and as it determines mankind in "general in their almost equal assurance of the reality of an " external world, as of the existence of their own minds. Con- "sciousness declares our knowledge of material qualities to be "intuitive or immediate—not representative or mediate".

I will comment for a moment on each one of these passages.

The first of them (I will not discuss the exact meaning of *immediate*) belongs in substance to that view which made me some time back put together in a note Sir William Hamilton and Mr Mill. The passage may be regarded as a parallel passage from a different point of view to Mr Mill's saying that the universe is made up of mind and its attributes, and body and its attributes. In reality what *we are conscious of* (beginning from this side, *viz.* the side of consciousness) is the phænomena of mind (to use this language), and a large class of these phæno-mena are interpretations of the felt non-ego or supposed occasions of our sensation, which interpretations constitute our *thought* of an external world, while we call this thought 'perception' in virtue of another important phænomenon of mind, *viz.* our belief that there is an objective reality in what it leads us to—I mean by objective reality, a reality as certain to us, though differently known, as our own subjective reality, which is our type of reality. So much for *that* side. From the other side, that of the universe, what *the universe is made up of* is matter variously constituted and put together, more or less filling space, and two phænomena or attributes of this matter (if so we are to call considerations more important than the matter itself) are, one that there is an order, a system or constitution to which belong the laws or principles of the above constitution, the other that certain portions of the matter, our bodies to wit, are so constituted as to communicate in a special manner with (in the language of many philosophers 'to be impressible by') various natural agents &c.—hence there are in the universe the great phænomenon of *order,* or a sort of organization of the whole, and the scarcely less phænomenon of *life,* or the particular organization, with sensation for accompaniment, in parts: but all as to these that is *phœnomenon*, to be connected with what communicates with our bodies, is that there *is* order, and that there *is* sensation. I will not say but that from the side of the universe, physiologists may make something of sensation as a part of *life*, nor have I any wish to prevent them making as much as they can. But beginning thus with reality as indicated to us by our bodies and what communicates with them, what happens in regard of facts of mind is that if we proceed further with them than I have just indicated we find our first supposition or our universe *absorbed* by them, and must go over to the view which I gave before, from consciousness. 'I' is not a phænomenon of the universe, but a something of which, as we then saw, the universe itself is a belief or a thought.

We are conscious then of phænomena of mind : the universe consists of phænomena of matter, thought of by mind, which thinks also of much besides (the language, 'phænomena', 'mind', &c. belongs to others).

I wish I had not been so long on this, but in fact the whole object of my writing these pages is to enforce what I have given just here.

The second and sixth passages in substance I agree with, and anything which I may have to say besides about them will come shortly, when we speak of Sir William Hamilton's proof. It will be observed that the 'Duality of Consciousness' as thus described is independent of any notion of 'externality' or matter : what Sir William Hamilton can mean by refusing the name of 'Dualism' to a large portion of philosophy when *this* is his Duality, is to me inconceivable.

That there should have been some confusion on my part in making out Sir William Hamilton's view may perhaps appear excusable, when we pass from these passages to the third, where we are told that we have an immediate knowledge of a non-ego and of an external non-ego. Here we have a duality given essentially different from, or going beyond, the last. It is this 'external' which is the point. And the fourth passage is to the same effect. So also the seventh, where for 'external' we have '*material* qualities'. To this we shall return.

The fifth passage shows what I call the wrong psychology in its fullest blossom. There is a parallel drawn (continued

in what follows, if the reader will refer) between the presenta-
ation or consciousness of things internal, and of things external.
Now the things *internal* are feelings, thoughts &c., and the
making them present, or their becoming present, to consciousness, is reasonable enough: in Sir William Hamilton's wide
view of consciousness they are in fact always so, they *are* (in
their nature) presentations: but then, next, there is supposed a
material object already existing with its material qualities, and
Sir William Hamilton seems to think that by merely using the
same word he can make it be believed that in respect of (or between) consciousness and something so incongruous with it as this
there takes place a process in some way similar to that which takes
place in respect of (or between) consciousness and the thoughts
or feelings.   What is of consequence, of more consequence than
the criticism of Sir William Hamilton, is that the reader should
see what these errors spring from, or what I have called the bad
psychology—it is the confusing together the difference, on the
one side, between thought and matter, or in other words the mutual independence of them, and, on the other, the externality,
the distance from us, of the object, or the difficulty of its communication with the bodily sense.   Of course, when Sir William
Hamilton begins with supposing the existence already of the
material object, he cannot but have in mind the thought of
this latter communication: and as soon as he thinks he has
solved the difficulty as to *this,* so that object and sense can
come together without anything which he would call *representation,* he thinks he has solved the other difficulty.   But what he
has got to do is to show that there is, or can be, any meaning in form, smell, sound *being present to thought* except that
they *are* thought, thought of, thought to exist and to occasion
sensation in us.

   The last thing which I will notice is the 'almost' in the
last passage, which at first sight one might be disposed to
take for a misprint.   In fact there is a carelessness in the sentence altogether, which would lead one to think that perhaps
further attention would have put it differently.   For what has
philosophy to do with qualifications like this 'almost'?   And
what is Sir William Hamilton's 'consciousness of matter' good
for at all, if it does not furnish an *altogether* equal assurance of

the reality of matter and of that of mind? And what is the meaning of his supporting, as he does, his opinion by the voice of mankind against the voice of philosophers, if all that the voice of mankind goes to is this qualified, partial, assurance? If the expression is genuine, it seems to me to show a sort of unphilosophical misgiving, which really I think *does* belong to all the psychology with its notions of 'common sense' &c. I hold a secondary and mediate (if Sir William Hamilton likes the term) *knowledge* of an external world compared with the knowledge of ourselves, but a perfectly equal assurance of its reality: *i.e.* the assurance is in each case, in its own way, complete: what is the use of establishing a primary or immediate knowledge, to come after all to an *almost* equal assurance?

So much for Sir William Hamilton's statements of his doctrine: now for his manner of establishing it.

Reid, in Sir William Hamilton's view, had in his doctrine of Common Sense taught truly on the subject of our immediate knowledge of an external world, but had been wrong in restricting the meaning of the term 'consciousness' to self-consciousness or reflection, and in saying that the knowledge which we had in the former case was by a faculty, 'perception', different from consciousness. Against this Sir William Hamilton argues that it is wrong so to restrict 'consciousness', and that 'perception' is a 'consciousness'. The discussion has a double character, one character quite indifferent to me, and I should hope to many of my readers. It is a convenient often and useful way of speaking to speak of different faculties of thought or knowledge, but the *realizing* them to such an extent as to make it a matter of importance whether this or that piece of thought belongs to one or another faculty, is a thing I do not care for. But the discussion has another character more important. Sir William Hamilton makes *use* of the description of perception as 'consciousness' to give to the supposed 'immediate knowledge' a meaning (so far as meaning of the kind is possible) very different from what the term 'Common Sense' or any such term would suggest (I beg I may not be understood as giving any opinion as to what Dr Reid meant). This meaning I have endeavoured to describe above.

We are conscious then, says Sir William Hamilton, (1) not

only of ourselves, but of the not-ourselves: (2) not only of perception, but of the object which we perceive.

I will begin with the latter of these, and quote at length the reasoning on it, with a few remarks on it: the reason why I take the other last will be seen[1].

"Reid's assertion, that we are conscious of the act of per-"ception, but not of the object perceived, involves, first of all, "a general absurdity. For it virtually asserts that we can know "what we are not conscious of knowing. An act of perception "is an act of knowledge; what we perceive, that we know. "Now, if in perception there be an external reality known, but "of which external reality we are, on Reid's hypothesis, not con-"scious, then is there an object known, of which we are not con-"scious. But as we know only inasmuch as we know that we "know,—in other words, inasmuch as we are conscious that "we know,—we cannot know an object without being conscious "of that object as known; consequently, we cannot perceive an "object without being conscious of that object as perceived.

"But, again, how is it possible that we can be conscious of "an operation of perception, unless consciousness be coextensive "with that act; and how can it be coextensive with the act, "and not also conversant with its object? An act of knowledge "is only possible in relation to an object,—and it is an act of "one kind or another only by special relation to a particular "object. Thus the object at once determines the existence, and "specifies the character of the existence, of the intellectual "energy. An act of knowledge existing and being what it is "only by relation to its object, it is manifest that the act can "be known only through the object to which it is correlative; "and Reid's supposition that an operation can be known in "consciousness to the exclusion of its object, is impossible. For "example, I see the inkstand. How can I be conscious that my "present modification exists,—that it is a perception, and not "another mental state,—that it is a perception of sight to the "exclusion of every other sense,—and, finally, that it is a per-"ception of the inkstand, and of the inkstand only,—unless my "consciousness comprehend within its sphere the object, which

" at once determines the existence of the act, qualifies its kind,
" and distinguishes its individuality?   Annihilate the ink-
" stand, you annihilate the perception ; annihilate the conscious-
" ness of the object, you annihilate the consciousness of the
" operation."

This proof, so to call it, seems to me to have three members, each, for a different reason, wrong.

In the first paragraph, so far as I can make out, there is a
non-sequitur at the point of the conclusion : 'we know an object
inasmuch as we are conscious that we know an object' (or 'we
cannot know an object without being so conscious') is treated
as if it were the same sentence as, 'we cannot know an object
without being conscious of that object as known'—the whole
question in dispute is the legitimacy of the application of the
term 'consciousness' to the object—Sir William Hamilton
settles the dispute by simply so applying it, which he is at
liberty to do, and then, which he is *not* at liberty to do, concluding that his so applying it is a reason why it *ought* to be
so applied.

The second portion of the argument, occupying the first
half of the second paragraph, is a piece of what I call 'notionalism'.   Knowledge is described as 'an act'; an act must have
an object, and can be known only through the object—whether
there is meaning or not in this, I recognise no cogency in it.
Knowledge might be described in many other ways than as
being an act, and in calling it an act I should in no degree
mean that it was thereby brought under the laws of a sort of
general science of acting or agency, supposing that there was
such.

The third or remaining portion of the argument seems to me
to belong to the wrong psychology.   I do not understand the
phrase, 'unless my consciousness comprehend within its sphere
the object'.   Consciousness doubtless comprehends within its
sphere the object of the consciousness, but what it is that is the
object of the consciousness is just the question in dispute.   Sir
William Hamilton wants to prove that consciousness comprehends within its sphere the inkstand, and seems to think that can
be done by calling the inkstand an object.   The expression 'annihilate the inkstand, you annihilate the perception' shows the

wrong view: *i. e.* the phenomenalist view trying to swell itself out to include consciousness, which makes the bad psychology. I should say: Are we in the spatial world? then I know nothing about consciousness of things—it does not belong here —I know about things, and communication of what we call external things with one important thing which we call our body, and accompaniment of this communication with sensation— which we have to stop with: annihilate the inkstand, there is vacant space, no communication, no accompanying sensation: call the sensation perception, if you like, use the language if you like 'perception of the thing': then with the inkstand, you annihilate the perception of the thing: but all this cannot prove, when we start with phenomena, that consciousness of the thing, or perception of it, represents any *fact*, anything to do or done between the mind and the thing—any relation between them. The thing is what it is—the feeling or con-sciousness is what *it* is—there we have to stop.

If instead of starting with the spatial world and coming in to ourselves, we are awaking without any previous knowledge or remembrance, and *opening,* as a sailor might say, the spatial world point after point, feature after feature, thing after thing, to ourselves—*then* the truth is not perhaps exactly the converse of what Sir William Hamilton says—annihilate the perception and you annihilate the inkstand—but something like it—sup-pose no perception of an inkstand where perception of an ink-stand ought to be, and (barring sensal defect or disease, which is not our present business) there is no inkstand.

So much for the second portion of Sir William Hamilton's proof: the first is of a different nature. Having quoted the other portion at such length, I cannot do the same with this: I trust the reader will refer to the book: but I will endeavour to give as good an account of it as I can.

Dr Reid then 'maintains', says Sir William Hamilton, 'that we are conscious of our perception of a rose, but not of the rose perceived'. 'That we know the ego by one act of knowledge' (viz. consciousness), 'the non-ego by another' (viz. perception). This doctrine he proceeds to refute[1].

I will now quote: "It is not only a logical axiom, but a

[1] Vol. I. p. 225.

"self-evident truth, that the knowledge of opposites is one.
"Thus we cannot know what is tall without knowing what is
"short,—we know what is virtue only as we know what is vice—
"the science of health is but another name for the science of
"disease.   Nor do we know the opposites, the I and Thou, the
"ego and non-ego, the subject and object, mind and matter, by a
"different law.........Unless we are prepared to maintain that
"the faculty cognisant of self and not-self is different from the
"faculty cognisant of not-self and self, we must allow that the
"ego and non-ego are known and discriminated in the same
"indivisible act of knowledge".   And this faculty or act of knowledge he proceeds to describe as 'consciousness'.

This is a line of proof with which, if we examine what
it really proves, I heartily concur.   But what does it really
prove?

Let us look at Sir William Hamilton's catalogue of opposites.   The nature of the antithesis between subject and object
I examined before.   Whether here Sir William Hamilton considers all these as different oppositions, or different views of the
same opposition, I cannot tell.   But what is the nature of the
antithesis between mind and matter?   Mind and matter are
repeatedly called by Sir William Hamilton *opposite*.   I suppose
that what at the top of the same page, he puts into the mouth
of the partisans of Dr Reid, but it would appear, fully admits,
may be taken as an explanation of what he means by this opposition.   "Mind and matter are mutually separated by the whole
"diameter of being.   Mind and matter are, in fact, nothing but
"words to express the series of phænomena known less in them-
"selves, than in contradistinction from each other".   This loose
manner of speaking, 'known less in themselves than ...', which
resembles the 'almost' on which I commented before, and
which is quite inconsistent with the argument, seems to me
to denote a want of confidence in the opinion held, a fear of
going through with it, or it may be a want of full sight and
hold of it.   The first of the two sentences I have just quoted
may be perfectly true, but has nothing to do with the opposition
which we are now concerned with.   An opposition of such
'separation' as that could not make the two things object of
one faculty.   But an opposition of 'contradistinction' such as that

mentioned in the second sentence, (if we omit the qualification which destroys the argument) would. Only the argument bears to me a different aspect from that which it does to Sir William Hamilton, and I should use it to draw from it the conclusion that the two things (or any two things) which, in the manner which he describes, are the objects of one faculty or one act of knowledge, must be opposites of each other, and must be known in mutual contradistinction. This the ego and non-ego are. But what is the case as to mind and matter?

The fact of the contradistinctional opposition of matter to mind is, it appears to me, *my* great fact, not his—it belongs to the *philosophical* view, not to the psychological—and, coupled with the inevitable existence to us of mind, thought, ourselves, it is what makes *my* fundamental view. For I recognise two manners of existence, in mutual opposition or contradistinction, thinkingness and thoughtness, and it is this *latter* which, when we believe the thought correct or justified, we call phenomenal existence or matter. In *this* view I have no objection to speak of our consciousness of matter.

But matter, from Sir William Hamilton's phenomenalist (which here is the wrongly psychological) point of view, is something quite different from this. He supposes the matter existing as we know it: I have myself, at the beginning of all that I am now writing, described how it does thus exist: it is, if we like to call it so, a succession of natural agents acting according to their various laws: it is body or matter, if we like rather to call it *so*, with its various attributes or qualities: mind, on the other side has *its* attributes or qualities: (for this logical language, and it is its great advantage, being kept in mind as referring to *notions* only, may be used without implying, as to the things of which it is used, any commensurability of existence or possible co-consideration). And the thing to be observed is, that the attributes of matter and the attributes of mind as thus understood are not contradistinguished or opposed: they are simply *incongruous* with each other. They belong, in my more ordinary manner of expression, to different worlds. Sir William Hamilton, as in fact every body else, allows and teaches this abundantly when *that* is what is before his consideration—strange that he forgets it here, for, so far as we speak of faculties, this incongruity most thoroughly shows that the two sorts of things must be the object of *different* ones. A moment's consideration will show the reader that there is no meaning in memory being contradistinguished from light, or imagination from weight—the things, as I have said, belong to different worlds.

I reserved the discussion of this first part of Sir William Hamilton's proof till last just to show what the fact is which he misapprehends and misdescribes—to show, as I said in other words, what his argument *does* prove. The knowledge of something besides ourself is, so far as we can judge, a necessary accompaniment of the knowledge of ourself—*here* we may speak of contradistinction and opposition, and may with reason use, if we like it, the word *consciousness* for the double knowledge. But the word *consciousness* thus used, to keep any value or to serve any use, must retain the notion of the contradistinction to self which is the point of it when used of this non-ego, and when we come, by sense, perception, or however we may call it, to develope this non-ego into the phenomenal universe or matter, and come thus to a set of things or qualities entirely incongruous with the facts of mind of which we are conscious—then, if we choose still to apply the word *consciousness* to our knowledge of them, we simply destroy all value in the word, and can conclude nothing from it.

If the reader will turn back to a previous passage[1] of Sir William Hamilton's, where he is showing how consciousness is a discrimination, and examine it, I hope it may help his understanding what I am saying. Sir William Hamilton speaks of *three* discriminations: between self and not self: between one state of mind and another: between one external object and another. In these three ways consciousness discriminates. The distinction therefore between mind and matter is considered, I presume, identical with that between self and not-self. This is in harmony with all that I have been noting in Sir William Hamilton: I call attention to it as just the wrong psychology, or the misapplication of phenomenalism, which I wish to condemn. As I have no objection to our speaking of consciousness of matter, so I have no objection to our speaking of

1 Vol. I. p. 203.

a self distinguished from external or spatial objects: this is what I called our phenomenal or corporeal self: only let us then remember that our starting point is *matter*, and no more expect *phenomenal* knowledge of thoughts and feelings, than in the other case we expected *conscious* knowledge of weight, light, and oxygen.

In commenting, a short time back, on the expression 'almost equal assurance', I alluded to Sir William Hamilton's opinion[1], that on the doctrine which we have been treating of he has with him the universal voice of mankind, and against him the almost universal voice of philosophers. This I think of little consequence either way, on account of the exceeding difficulty, as it seems to me, of ascertaining what, on a point of philosophy of this kind, *is* the common voice either of mankind or of philosophers. I will however notice it now for two reasons: first, because, as I have already slightly noticed, the assertion that the opinion in question *is* thus the common opinion of mankind throws, in my view, a little suspicion upon the assertion that it is a fact of consciousness—suspicion, lest really this latter should mean no more than the former, in which case it is liable of course to the same doubt as the former, in reference to what the opinion of mankind really is. Sir William Hamilton changes Reid's expression 'common sense' into his own 'consciousness': but a passage like the following leads one to doubt whether what he *points to* is after all much more than *popular opinion:* "The fact that consciousness does testify to an immediate "knowledge by mind of an object different from any modifica-"tion of its own, is thus admitted even by those philosophers "who still do not hesitate to deny the truth of the testimony: "for to say that all men do naturally believe in such a know-"ledge, is only, in other words, to say that they believe it on "the authority of consciousness. A fact of consciousness, and a "fact of the common sense of mankind, are only various expres-"sions of the same import. We may therefore lay it down as "an undisputed fact, that consciousness gives, as an ultimate

---

[1] Passages in which Sir William Hamilton expresses the above-mentioned opinion are numerous: as Vol. I. p. 223, "Dr Reid vindicated against the unanimous authority of philosophers, the universal opinion of mankind." Again, Reid and Stewart, Vol. I. p. 204, "hold with mankind at large, that we do possess an immediate knowledge of something different from the knowing self." See also Vol. I. p. 278, and in fact passim.

"fact, a primitive duality". This is another manner of proof, so to call it, of Sir William Hamilton's doctrine, from that which we have considered.

I am not fond of discussing whether a thing is or is not a fact of consciousness, because the principles upon which the dispute is to be settled are not very clear. If we appeal to what is felt, feeling is individual: we can only very imperfectly compare one man's with another's: but if we try to cure this defect by massing individuals together, we get rather, it seems to me, out of the region of philosophy. I must confess to caring not much what, on questions of this nature, men in general or masses of men think or are said to think. Not but that, if I knew that they thought and knew really what they thought, I should prize (speaking generally) the opinion of any one of them as much as my own, and their collective opinion much more: but I do *not* know these things, and I do not see how I am to know them: whereas I do know what I think myself, and know probably also (if I am a philosopher) that I have taken some pains to think, if I can, correctly. By philosophy, as the analysis of consciousness, I do not mean a report and record of the popular opinions of mankind.

The second reason why I notice Sir William Hamilton's saying that the common or universal opinion of mankind is on his side, is because I cannot the least understand the use of his saying so when he has got so shortly afterwards, in order for his view to hold, to use the extraordinary language about what it is that we perceive which I have in a former chapter alluded to[2], and of which I will now give a specimen.

"The report of consciousness", he says, "is that we perceive "at the external point of sensation, and that we perceive the "material reality[3]".

The word 'perceive', in the former part of the sentence, has in it exactly that confusion between physiology and philosophy which is what I want to prevent, spoiling as it does both. But I will not repeat my own often given view as to what takes place. Only how does 'consciousness' report as it is here said to do? "The too ordinary style of philosophising", says Sir William Hamilton in speaking of Dr Thomas Brown,

"is an easy way of appealing to or overlooking the facts of
"consciousness, as the philosopher finds them convenient or
"inconvenient for his purpose[1]". It is in the hope that the present generation of students of philosophy, who are likely to
learn so much from Sir William Hamilton, will not learn from
him their tone of speaking about other philosophers, that I
notice how thoroughly, if philosophers will not give each other
credit for a real love of truth, this same language may be used
of any, and of himself.

But the matter of importance is the second part of the
sentence. What is meant by 'perceiving the material reality'?

"In the first place", we are told, "it does not mean that we
"perceive the material reality absolutely and in itself, that is,
"out of relation to our organs and faculties: on the contrary,
"the total and real object of perception, is the external object
"under relation to our sense and faculty of cognition".

Have we not here even enough to make the appeal to the
common voice of mankind nugatory and unmeaning, for what
does that voice know about this notionalism of the absolute
and the relative, in which Sir William Hamilton qualifies his
statement into what Mr Ferrier, or I, or almost any body might
accept, supposing only we acknowledged *meaning* in it? The
common voice of mankind, so far as it says anything, says, We
perceive *the thing:* the thing is *what we perceive:* this common
voice would surely say to Sir William Hamilton here, You mean
then, we do *not* see *the thing* after all?

But the common voice, or feeling, of mankind must be still
more shocked with the answer to the next question.

"In the second place, what is meant by the external
"object perceived? Nothing can be conceived more ridiculous
"than the opinion of philosophers in regard to this. For ex-
"ample, it has been curiously held, (and Reid is no exception),
"that in looking at the sun, moon, or any other object of sight,
"we are, on the one doctrine, actually conscious of these distant
"objects; or, on the other, that these distant objects are those
"really represented in the mind. Nothing can be more absurd:
"we perceive, through no sense, aught external but what is in
"immediate relation and in immediate contact with its organ;

[1] Vol. I. p. 278.

" and that is true which Democritus of old asserted, that all our
" senses are only modifications of touch. Through the eye we
" perceive nothing but the rays of light in relation to, and in
" contact with, the retina".

If anything was wanted to justify my saying that there is
really no use in appealing to the common voice either of mankind or of philosophers, surely this extraordinary passage would
do so. Did any language ever, if we may take *that* as a specimen
of human opinion, talk about perceiving 'rays of light', and *not*
the sun or the tree which they proceed from? Common opinion
is asked, Do we perceive immediately, and what do we perceive? It answers, we do perceive immediately, and we perceive the tree, sun, &c. I might doubt as to the answer which
it would give to the former part of the question, but no one
could doubt as to the answer to the latter. Sir William
Hamilton then, who made just now the observation as to Dr
Thomas Brown which I quoted, answers common opinion, I
will accept you as representing human consciousness so far
as the former part of your answer goes, but cannot as to the
latter. And common opinion, it would appear, Sir William
Hamilton's self-chosen referee, considers that we perceive immediately something which, in his view, it is impossible that we
should be conscious of, namely distant objects like the tree or
the sun : going, it would appear to me, to prove, that though
we perceive the external world as *it* understands perceiving, we
are *not* conscious of it. I am myself indeed quite unable to
appreciate the greater philosophical difficulty of saying, ' we are
conscious of the sun', than of saying ' we are conscious of the
rays of light'. We are told that it was ridiculous in the philosophers who held representation to say that distant objects
like the sun were represented in the mind—would he have
had them say, as less ridiculous, that the rays of light were represented in the mind? But it is hopeless to make anything
of all this, and the philosophical reasoning which follows, and
to which I refer the reader, is as hopeless. We have seen
sufficiently then, I think, how Sir William Hamilton really
deals with the common voice of mankind.

But I have said for the present enough upon this subject.

CHAPTER VIII.

LOGIC—MR MILL.

I WILL vary the somewhat monotonous course of what I am now writing by a very little philosophical reminiscence.

The idealism, personalism, or whatever it may be called, which lies at the root of all that I have said, is not simply a doctrine or opinion, but seems to me to have been my earliest philosophical feeling, and to have continued, if not so vivid, yet not less strong, ever since. Experience in these things is all individual, but what from my own, I should guess, is, that that phenomenalism which seems to us to be everything, that world which is too much with us, that nature or universe into which, as time goes on, we seem to sink all our independent selfhood so as to be only parts of it, the highest animals in it, is something in a manner which we require to get *used* to : and that before this familiarity is complete, in earlier years, there is a disposition in us to be struck with what I may call our personal or conscious difference from it, or independence of it, or however else we may style the *individual* feeling: this is what is with me the root of philosophy: in respect of the problems, or difficulties, or as some please to call them mysteries of philosophy, I think that one reason why they have this character is on account of a kind of dullness which is superinduced over our disposition to higher thought by what the course of everybody's life is pretty certain to be. We get *then* the notion of philosophy as something only to be learnt with infinite labour, as indeed is the case when all this familiarity with life, and nature, and the phenomenal universe has supervened—but we have had it near to us, and still all this labour would be of little value except there comes now and then a glance of *insight*, which is the real *philosophy.*

I suppose there is more of what may be called personal or individual philosophy in the world than one readily hears of, but it is not a thing which seems much in people's mind that any real philosophy (or metaphysics, other than mere talk) is something that they must see for themselves, and that they must value any chance or early glimpses they may get about it, because the course of life and study will in many respects make it more difficult for them to get such.

Corresponding with the feeling, from early times, of the deep interest of personal consciousness, has been to me the feeling which I have alluded to already [1] of the dreariness, as I have called it, of the phenomenalist view, or knowledge as ot experience, taken to represent *everything* for us. I will not repeat what I have said about that.

In a similar manner, my condemnation in these 'rough notes' of what I have called 'notionalism' is not an opinion simply produced in me by the sight of what seems to me a wrong philosophy, but represents much effort in thinking what, as to these logical conceptions, *is* the truth. A belief in a real *substance*, or thing in itself, is what I have always had, and have most strongly: but it is this very belief which makes me revolt against the philosophy which would disjoin from the substance or reality of the thing every thing, it appears to me, which we do or can come to know about it: it is the assigning a character of unknowableness to the substance which is repugnant to me. So long as our knowledge is imperfect, which in fact all knowledge of every being (One Being only excepted) must be, we must *suppose* complete knowledge, to fasten our incomplete knowledge on : and the complete knowledge thus supposed includes of course a portion of ignorance, or unknown. But of the unknown there is no reason for us to suppose either that it is unknowable, or that it is (necessarily) more important to the thinghood of the thing about which the knowledge is than the qualities which we *do* know about it.

There is without doubt a sense in which we may say that knowledge itself is impossible—complete knowledge necessarily is, and in various points of view complete knowledge and knowledge are the same. In knowledge of thought, we suppose a

[1] Ante, p. 15.

subject or a substance, and knowledge is the filling this up with
its appropriate predicates or attributes. In knowledge of
acquaintance, our attributes and those of the thing communicate: but there is not proper knowledge except so far as *we*,
consciousness, thought, comes into play: there must be, for
knowledge, something in the thing with which *this* can come into
communication—is there? the thinghood of the thing, thus,
looking at the matter this way, is the thought locked up in it,
which by the key of our sensive power, fitting its sensible qualities, we try to open. But in either of the cases it may be
said, do we ever arrive at knowledge? Can we ever, in the
former case, convert our supposition into anything which we
can consider as *more* than supposition, and can we ever, in the
latter case, get at any thought in the thing in regard of which
we may consider that it is more than imagination on our part
about it? It appears to me, that what is to be said about this
is that which I hold strongly, that while there are two views,
there are not two parts, of knowledge, and consequently, that it
is not knowledge, or any one kind of knowledge, which we
cannot get at, but *complete* knowledge: the knowledge of the
thought locked up in a thing is not generically different from the
knowledge of its sensible qualities, which are all portions of its
thought or thinghood: in the same way substance is not different from the qualities, and we attain towards the knowledge of
it as we fill up the knowledge of the qualities. Knowledge is
thus a reality, though either of the two manners of knowledge
may be described in such a manner as apparently not to constitute it: the mere rubbing ourselves against fact (which, con-
cisely put, is the view which some have of *experience*) is not
knowledge, nor on the other hand, is the imaginatively supposing what after all may be chimera: *learning*, or the action
of the mind in *gaining* knowledge, is by these two processes in
conjunction, but *knowledge* does not consist of an union of the
two, which would be incongruous, but of a something between
the two, which may be conceived arrived at either way, and to
which we may approximate, and really approximate, each way.
As we *learn*, thought and fact may be said roughly to correct each other: but it is incongruous to describe knowledge
either as thought corrected by fact (as something different from

thought), or as fact converting itself, in the mind, into thought (as something different from fact). We may describe it as right thought, and then what such thought presents to us we call fact: or we may describe it as communication with fact, and then, supplementing something, which in this, the incomplete view, we must, we may suppose the communication accompanied on our part by feeling. In the former case we have the *knowledge* given us, with difficulty as to knowing its *truth*: in the latter case we have something given which so far as it is knowledge, must be *true*, but is it *knowledge*[1]?

I seem unable however to keep the thread of philosophical reminiscence, and will only mention one more particular, which is in fact the occasion of my having alluded to the subject here.

With respect to the psychology which I have rather strongly criticised, from my very first study of it I have felt, though indistinctly, the difficulty about it; what it was that it aimed at, or what it could result in. The sort of bewilderment or puzzle which Berkeley's views produce in many has always appeared to me to belong to the whole of this psychology. I

---

[1] One of the many possible ways in which the distinction between the two views of knowledge may be put, and of which I give, for illustration, as many as suggest themselves to me, is this: suppose a mirror reflecting the universe: and then make in succession the two suppositions, first, of the mirror simply feeling the reflection, or image, if we may use such language, *i.e.* of there being feeling in it, we cannot tell more, varying with the variations of the image: next, of an eye more or less identified with the mirror seeing the image. We have here roughly the two views of knowledge. In the first, the communication, that is, the reflection of the universe in the mirror, is a fact, there is no question as to mistake or error in it, *in its own way*: but it is not knowledge: for knowledge we must suppose an accompanying sensation, and as to the relation of such sensation to the image, or whether it is possible for it to have any relation to it, we cannot say anything at all. That is, with knowledge begins fallibility or uncertainty. In the second case, we have only the depreciated mediate or indirect knowledge: but it is knowledge from the first, it begins with thought; possibility of mistake, the test of *knowledge* as distinct from mere familiarity and habit, is in it from the first; there is activity from the first, or knowing what we are about. Not to dwell on this, I will just observe: these two views of knowledge cannot be put together. We are sentient mirrors in the one view, in the other we are contemplators of the universe as it is in our consciousness; but we are not contemplators of our sentience, because the two things are the same, put different ways. The supposed eye sees the image, not the supposedly coincident sensation. In the same way it would be unreasonable to say that part of the image is seen, and part felt.

never could understand how, if we took for granted, as we all
naturally do, that we were members of a spatial universe with
things round about us, it ever could be considered a question
whether things really existed, or how there could be any
meaning in giving an account (as by means of 'Common Sense')
of our supposition of their existence. The whole psychology
begins with human beings *knowing* that they are members of a
spatial world, and then, as an important defence against scepticism, it is established *upon this basis* that they *believe* (say on
principles of common sense) that they are so. What is their
actual state of mind on the subject seems in this way hard to
tell. I have always had a strong faith in philosophy and
thought, and have believed that the former existed for a better
purpose than to make itself a reductio ad absurdum by return-
ing upon its postulate and invalidating it. The uneasy state
of one's logical feelings thus produced is likely to concentrate
thought more strongly upon personality or consciousness as the
real starting-point, in distinction from which the phenomenal
point of view is an assumed one for certain purposes, so that
in the establishing that it does not hold for others there is nothing at all surprising.

It would be an interesting subject to consider how philosophers have got into what seems to me this singular position,
but I will not follow that now, but mention the point in this
psychology, a slight and small one, which is the immediate occasion of my introducing these experiences.

The relation of logic to the above psychology long ago
puzzled me. We are told in the books of psychology about
'perception', this is what the logicians call 'simple apprehension', without any reason given why the logicians should call
the same thing by one name and the psychologists by another.
I am inclined to think that the different ways of speaking, all
in my view meaning the same thing, coming some from logic
and some from psychology, cause in the minds of students a
great deal of puzzle, and in the minds of philosophers themselves a great deal of *notionalism*, by the converting different
accounts of the same process into different processes.

I am quite aware that the having, so to speak, different
philosophical sciences, and the yet mixing them, in some par-

ticulars, together, is a thing which has been from the beginning, and certainly was in Aristotle. But I am sure it is
desirable as much as possible to consider them together, and as
one subject, or we get into hopeless confusion. When logic and
psychology are pursued each by a different person, are they the
same line of thought in different language, or are they not,
and who is to know ?

In Aristotle, Logic, Physics, Metaphysics, and Psychology
all are connected with each other, or have common parts. But
Aristotle's psychology is much more pure psychology, as I
should call it, than the noö-psychology which we have been
speaking of.

The Aristotelian logic and psychology therefore confuse
each other very little. Logic is the theory of thought and of
correctness of thought and of advance of correct thought by
reasoning, almost for any kind of intelligence, almost for any
universe. There is assumed a subject of thought as a peg to
hang predicates on, and in these predicates is the knowledge :
the subjects, in virtue of the predicates attachable to them,
may be put together (as *terms*) in propositions, and the propositions again be put together in syllogisms leading to further
propositions. *Correctness* of thought is in proper predication,
in making propositions and putting them together : *advance*
of thought is in the fruitfulness of such predication, making of
propositions, and putting them together, in view of further predication.

Right thought, and its advance, being thus in right predicating, asserting, and syllogizing, what, to begin, is right predicating?

The 'subject' is to be supposed a something with only *one*
character about it, *viz.* a capacity for certain predicates and not
for others, and when we have attached all the right predicates
to it we thoroughly know it; when we have attached any wrong
ones (or for which it has not a capacity) we are mistaken about
it. How to attach what predicates to what subject, Aristotle
tells us nothing : that belongs to knowledge of the universe :
but he gives a rough list of heads of predication, (great or
summary predicates, predicaments, categories). The predicates
too may attach to the subject in different ways : he speaks of

these to some extent, and his successors catalogued them : they are a sort of higher predicaments or categories still, 'predicables'.

In all predications we assert, but when the subject has had any predicate attached to it, or is at all *clothed*, it becomes not only, in reference to other predicates, a subject, but in reference to the proposition, or assertion, a term, as does also that which in the proposition is predicated of it. For rightness of assertion, besides the relation of subjects to their possible predicates, there have to be considered certain other relations of the terms to each other.

Propositions put together in certain ways bear fruit in further propositions, or predications, by which therefore our knowledge of the subjects is increased : and thus knowledge grows.

Of the manner of this growth of knowledge I have at various times spoken. It is as I have said by imagination or speculation about things with constant self-correction arising mainly from our constant rubbing against things, as I a short time ago expressed it, which latter it is that in the main fixes predicates to subjects. The Aristotelian scheme may be regarded as an exceedingly abstract outline of a vast imagination about things, with certain ways and methods in which this imagination may correct itself and keep itself in order independently of this experience : still the imagination without the experience is entirely visionary; as the experience without the imagination or thought would be merely proximity or familiarity—not knowledge.

As I have said, whatever we rightly imagine we might conceivably have been in contact with : whatever we are in contact with we might conceivably have pre-imagined : there is nothing generically different in the *object* in the two cases : the difference is in the manner of our learning. We might therefore if we liked it, call Aristotle's list of categories a sketch of the great heads of reality or fact in all, or almost all, conceivable universes : the great category of 'quality' would I suppose be the repository of differences, and an universe in which (*their*) matter had what some would call different secondary qualities, or in which light, oxygen, magnetism, &c. were replaced, if we can conceive it, by other elements or natural agents, would differ from ours in *this* category.

The growth of knowledge being, as I mentioned just above, by the speculation and experience joined, it is obvious that the Aristotelian proceeding, running wholly on the former, or on the latter only in so very abstract a form, can be of little consequence as to this. I shall call a supposed method of Logic, of any kind, which so far incorporates into itself the notion of actual experience as to be able to take into account *the growth* of knowledge, whether in the individual or the race, a *Real* Logic, in contrast with such as the Aristotelian, which we may call if we like, when pure and by itself, Formal, and which may have various valuable applications, besides this, if we consider it one: as to verification, to grammar, or to digestion of argument.

The great mass of 'the Philosophy of the Human Mind' is in its details an attempt at a Real Logic of individual knowledge ; an attempt vitiated in various ways. For this Real Logic of the individual is of more complicated and difficult consideration than the Real Logic of the knowledge of the race, unless we may say that this, to counterbalance, has difficulties of a different kind. The greater difficulty is in this: that we are considering the growth of the knowledge of *one* mind in the midst of a quantity of others where the knowledge exists. This I believe, at bottom, is the origin of the mis-psychological error on which I comment so abundantly. 'A stone lies before me: I see it'. We put this down quite naturally in the account of the growth of individual knowledge, not apparently thinking that the *first* clause is *other* people's knowledge : the second is the step of *mine :* and, *now*, that the step is taken, I say the stone lies before *me*. Our collective Real Logic, which I shall shortly speak of, is not to the same extent puzzled with the *double* view of angels and superior beings of we know not how many amounts and kinds seeing the universe, and our seeing it with them, in the way in which the human race will (physically) see it, we may suppose, some hundred centuries hence, should it last so long, and *with this*, of our race coming step by step *to* see it in this real way. In respect of the race, we *can* understand and watch the *learning*, because we cannot and do not make the vast and absurd supposition of all the *to be known* in this way as already existing fact[1].

---

[1] I am not certain whether this is put in the best way, but I leave it. On the subject of advance in perception, and advance in knowledge of nature beyond

The fact of the one learning mind existing in the middle of a multitude of knowing ones is of importance in another way. While almost all books, I think, of the philosophy of the Human Mind make, as above, the already existing knowledge come in where it ought not, they do not make it come in where it ought. The course of individual knowledge is described not only without sufficient reference to the consideration, how much, as a matter of fact, we are taught by others, but also to the more important consideration, that whether we are actually taught by others or not, our intelligence is in its very constitution social, and our mind is the mind of a social being, a being such as our organization (tongue, &c.) shows us to be. We *think* of necessity socially: more socially perhaps in some solitude than in some society: we think with the minds of others as well as our own: thought is internal conversation and discussion. Language, which is social, goes to the bottom of our mind: not but that we might, and perhaps do, abundantly imagine without language, but that we should not, without it, come to anything like the results to which we do come, and that in respect of some of the earliest and simplest things.

The two sets of Lectures of Sir William Hamilton which have been published are one on Metaphysics, and the other on Logic, the two courses having some introductory Lectures in common. The Lectures on Metaphysics I have to a certain degree examined, because, though the subject is called Metaphysics, and the point of view, the purpose assigned being the analysis of consciousness, is more philosophical than that of several of Sir William Hamilton's Edinburgh predecessors, yet still the subject is considered 'the Philosophy of the Human Mind'; and the confusion of the wrong psychology is abundantly prevalent. In pursuing his subject of the Philosophy of the Human Mind, Sir William Hamilton discusses faculties &c. and gives several new names, but hardly seems to have said anything very important.

What I have criticized in those Lectures of Sir William Hamilton is his application of the term 'consciousness' to 'perception'. It may perhaps be remembered, that the point of view of the analysis of consciousness has been called by me what would be commonly called perception, and their relation to each other, I shall have a few things to say.

sometimes the *philosophical* (answering to Sir William Hamilton's metaphysical) and sometimes the *logical.* Sir William
Hamilton's error seems to me to have arisen from his having
before him the psychology of his predecessors, which prevented
him, as he was so abundantly able to do and one would have
thought would have been likely to do, taking the line of philosophical (not mis-psychological) metaphysics and logic in conjunction, going so naturally as they would together. As it is, I
imagine students ask themselves what his metaphysics and
logic have to do with each other: they read, I think, the former
more than the latter, with some wonder, of the kind which I
mentioned before, how the subject comes to be *two.* Locke's
Essay on Human Understanding is Logic and Psychology united:
most of the Philosophies of the Human Mind are intended to
supersede the necessity of the Formal Logic, and Dugald Stewart, whose memory Sir William Hamilton cherishes in a manner
which does him great honour, says of it that its 'inutility is
now pretty generally acknowledged, and it deserves our attention chiefly as a curious article in the history of science': while
a Logic of the kind which I have called Real Logic he describes
as the valuable logic, though still in its infancy.

The importance of all this is of the following kind : people
constantly talk about these different professedly philosophical
subjects as if they were like branches of physical science, say
geology and botany, in regard of which one man may know and
value both, another may know one and honour the other as a
co-science, another may know one and think, or pretend to think,
the other worthless, and all this be of no consequence in respect
of his knowledge of what he does know. But this is not the
case with these philosophical subjects. They are rival claimants
more or less for the same ground. The thinking wrongly about
their relation to each other may do damage in all sorts of ways.

Sir William Hamilton speaks, as we have seen, of matter
being the object of consciousness. It seems odd that he should
do this, when, in a different set of Lectures, those on Logic, we
have the real objects of consciousness, which he calls 'concepts',
treated truly and properly as such : we seem to have here, all
along, that difficulty which I spoke of, and the student of Sir
William Hamilton's Lectures on Metaphysics is astonished to

find that, when he has got through them, there are two volumes, as big as the others, treating knowledge and the processes of the human understanding in an entirely different manner and with different language—after all, he asks, have I only got half the subject, and now I know what 'perceiving' things is have I got to learn all about the 'forming concepts' of them, and is it a different thing or the same?

I have written this (and shall now not go further into the subject) for two reasons: first, to suggest that these things want putting together—we want to know, more than people are aware of, what different terms only express the same thing put different ways; and secondly, to account for my speaking of the *philosophical* and the *logical* view as in the main the same, though by the logical we may often mean what, as compared with the other, is an abstraction. If Sir William Hamilton had put his metaphysics and his logic together, I do not think we should have had the same confusion. The 'consciousness of matter' seems to me to be a jumbling together of the things impressing our senses and our forming concepts or ideas of them, which would not have been fallen into except that the whole theory of this forming concepts is made into a separate subject for a different set of Lectures.

I will say no more about the Formal Logic and the various books of interest and value upon it. What I protest strongly against is the *realizing* its terms (which is what I have called *notionalism*): but I do not at all call in question the great value of its language for its proper purpose. Its value depends in every way upon this non-realizing, upon its being kept formal and abstract. The attempt to apply it too much may very possibly I think by confusing it and realizing it in another sort of way, injure its value[1]. But that is not now my business.

What I am going to speak of is the Real Logic of the knowledge of the human race, which is at once an important branch of literature and an important philosophical subject, and the two books which I have taken as specimens of it are Mr Mill's and Dr Whewell's.

---

[1] An exact appreciation of the real bearing and importance of the extensions of this Logic by Sir William Hamilton, Professor de Morgan, the late Professor Boole, Dr Thomson, and others, would be of very much interest.

My concern, it will be remembered, is not so much with the advance of knowledge as with the beginning of it: not with *reasoning*, but with sensations; with conceiving and perceiving. But since this latter process or these processes take place in advanced knowledge, of course I am concerned with the ad_ vance; what I mean is that I shall say little about the manner or mental machinery of the advance, reasoning, syllogism, in_ duction, deduction.

Mr Mill's book is what I should call a Phenomenalist Logic with a starting point from the Aristotelian or Formal Logic.

It will be remembered that I described the phenomenalist view, as I called it, to be *an abstraction*, meaning this: that when we have got the knowledge, we may suppose the things we know to exist without any reference to our knowing them or to the manner in which we come to know them: but that in reality the manner in which we come to know them is by a great deal of imagination, speculation, and action of mind. However, when we know them, we say one of two things of them, both coming to the same: either, 'they exist': or 'we believe them'. There is a third thing which we *might* say: viz. 'We have learnt them'. In the first case the understood mental accompaniment is more or less of this nature: 'There they are: do you not see them?' In the second, 'I can give a reason for my belief, if you wish to hear it'. In the third, 'I have thought about the matter a good deal and made many observations, and this is the result I have come to'.

The view of knowledge which I understand Mr Mill to take is that which I should call the proper phenomenalist view, or the notion of 'adstance', 'presence at' anything (the French *assistance*), which I have already in some degree alluded to, and to which I hope to return[1].

---

[1] Mr Mill's phenomenalist logic is in effect a description of the facts of nature, the heads of this description being suggested by the relations and processes of logic, as these have been previously understood. Our knowledge is then, in his view, a following or tracing in one direction or another, a keeping close to, these facts.

Thus in respect of propositions, what Mr Mill considers is, that where the proposition is important for the advance of knowledge, what we are doing in it is not the assertion of anything as to the applicability of the terms or names (which is the same thing as the reference of things to classes), nor the making a judgment, in the sense that the result of the proposition is something in or having reference

The special character of this view is the avoidance as much as possible of any reference to activity of the mind—the saying but little, so to speak, of 'thought about things'. So far as the state of the mind which possesses knowledge, in face of the facts of nature, is to be described, it is to be described as a state of belief upon evidence. We are in phenomenal contact, so to speak, with every thing that we know: but this contact, in regard of a great deal of our knowledge, is not immediate, distinct, recognisable: it is mediate through the intervention of evidence on which we believe. We believe that the earth moves round the sun, and can, if we wish, exhibit a scheme of the grounds of our belief in this, for examination as to satisfactoriness: at the same time these grounds only represent a complicated and vast contact of the same nature as that in virtue of which we consider that a tree before us is green, or a bird in front of us is flying.

On this 'belief on evidence', as I am not at this moment going to dwell upon it, I will just remark so much : that the evidence upon which we should justify our belief is not at all likely to represent in any way the process by which the knowledge of it has actually been come to : that such evidence is a very vague term, and the manner of its possible exhibition,

to our own mind (a view, a change of view, a notion &c.) but the *assisting*, as it were, the standing by or looking on at, an (imagined or actual) natural fact, which the terms of the proposition, indicate. The proposition in this phenomenalist logic, is not the reference by us of a thing to a class, nor is a judgment, or opinion, on our part, about a thing, but is an expression of a natural fact or relation of things. What is important about the proposition is not the goodness and good employment of a classification of things which it may imply, nor the correctness of thought on our part which it may imply, but its trueness to the phenomenal fact.

The distinction between the *latter* two of these members is in fact the distinction between the logical (as I have called it) and the phenomenalist view. The object of the previous logic has been correctness of thought : that of Mr Mill's logic is true following and rendering phenomena.

In the distinction between the two latter and the former of these members, disallowing *this*, the reference in the first instance to classification, as the proper business of *any* logic, Mr Mill, as I understand him, has my hearty adhesion. His views as to the subordination of the classification of things to what I will call their nature, which latter, not the former, our propositions in the first instance refer to, are important and true for all logic alike. Reference of things to classes and the introducing in this way quantitative relation into logic may be a most valuable and important subsidiary thing to do, but logic looks at things as variously endued with similar qualities, and therefore as classifiable, not, except subsidiarily, as already classified.

in many cases, infinitely various : that, in fact between the
remote, hidden, or complicated phenomenon and human sense,
there are what we may call two threads of experience, contact
or communication, the one the *historical* thread by which the
knowledge has been arrived at, the other the thread of most
satisfactory justification of the belief, or nearest communication
between the sense and the phenomenon now.   So much as to
the relation of the evidence to experience and sensation.

Mr Mill's purpose, as I understand it, is to avoid as much
as possible what I have called. the logical point of view in
our simpler or more immediate knowledge of nature, and when
we come to the more complicated and mediate knowledge of it,
the historical attainment of which by the human race is what
we call the advance of science and is the object of Real Logic,
to treat this by what I may call the Logic of Evidence.   It
is the minor proposition in a syllogism, or that in an argument
which most corresponds to such minor proposition, which constitutes what we should call the *evidence* for the conclusion—as
distinct from the principle of the argument, or the considerations which give value to the evidence, or the theory upon
which we conclude from it, which vaguely represent what in a
regular syllogism is the major proposition.   Mr Mill's treatment
of the syllogism seems to me to go upon this view.

My business here however is very little with reasoning or
belief upon evidence, but with the general view of knowledge :
and I proceed to explain what I mean by saying that in respect of
our simple and more immediate knowledge, Mr Mill takes great
pains to avoid the logical point of view : which is in *this* way
remarkable, that he has taken great pains to preserve the old
logical language, and if I may so speak, utilize it.   In this I
sympathize with him much : but I think it has led him into
a certain amount of error, which I shall afterwards notice.

The old logicians had then these processes, ' simple apprehension' (perception, conception), 'judgment', and ' reasoning', and
one way or another this triplicity must always exist.   Thought
or language naturally divides itself into notions or words, judgments or propositions, and syllogisms or arguments.

It is for the two former members of this triplicity that
Mr Mill as I said carefully avoids the logical point of view.

For instance I mean that in regard of the *first* member of the triplicity he prefers not to speak of notions, ideas, concepts, or to use corresponding terms, but will take cognisance only of *things,* which things we express by *names.* His care in this respect is more striking on account of his equally carefully avoiding all *nominalism,* as it was called, that is, the ignoring more or less the reasons *why* things were collected as they were into classes, and had such and such names given to them, and the attending only *to* the classes and names. Mr Mill sees more in a thing than a mere member of a class and object of a name: he sees in it the properties in virtue of which it is such : but he will not allow of 'notion', 'idea', 'concept' of it.

This, so far as we have gone, is what I have called the *phenomenalist* point of departure in contradistinction to the logical: and for the better explaining what I say of Mr Mill, I will just say how *I* should have proceeded from this point of departure, which of itself is a very legitimate one.

I should have asked the physical, chemical, physiological, philosopher what it was to the best of *his* knowledge that the universe was made up of, and I suppose he would have told me elements, forces, tissues, organizations, I know not what more : he and I should both of us have understood that there must be space and time for all these to exist in : and though we should have in some degree diverged as to what comes next, yet we should have gone *some* way together; namely, as to laws, order, system, if I may venture to say, 'idea'.

Mr Mill's first proceeding however with his 'things' is to categorize them. This is a part of what I mentioned, his care to preserve the old logical methods and language, while altering their application and utilizing them.

I mentioned previously about the Aristotelian categories, that though they proceed from a logical point of view, yet they might be turned round to a sort of quasi-phenomenalist one, in which view they will represent the main constituents, so to speak, of almost any possible universe. Mr Mill finds, reasonably enough, that they are a very poor catalogue of the constituents of *this* universe, and proceeds to utilize the notion by substituting others for them.

I will make a few remarks on what he substitutes.

He makes four categories of things: minds: bodies: attributes of mind, viz. feelings: attributes of bodies, of which then he makes sub-categories.

This classification resolves itself, for use, into the two latter heads (as I have given them): for minds, and bodies (or substances), are only described as the unknown and unknowable substrata of the feelings and the bodily attributes or qualities: the categories therefore of things which are objects of knowledge are really to be considered only two, with the observation appended that these objects of knowledge are not independent, but involve in themselves (how can Mr Mill or anybody avoid saying in our notion of them?) a reference to something unknown as the substratum of them.

We are thus, at this apparently second step of our progress, only advanced as far as to say that the things (known to us are yet only as *nameables*) are attributes of a substratum, which, in reality, was Aristotle's *first* step, or was the notion, itself, of categories.

In *one* respect indeed we are further advanced, but, it seems to me, wrongly, or, at least, confusedly.

Mr Mill makes *two* sets of attributes of two substrata, mind and body.

The importance of this proceeding in Mr Mill is this. For the whole of what we may call his actual logic, *things* are with him only the attributes of body with their substratum (whatever is to be considered about this), and the above classification is of no application at all. It only receives application when it is considered, as Mr Mill does consider in the latter part of his book, that the same logic which he has exhibited and illustrated from an examination of the advance of phenomenal knowledge is applicable also to knowledge of the attributes of mind.

Now that it may be possible to find or exhibit a 'real' logic, (as I have used the word real) applicable both to the study of mind and the study of physical nature, I have no wish to deny. But I do not admit the propriety of the process of settling such a logic from observation of the advance of physical knowledge (my 'phenomenalism') and then at once saying, All this is applicable similarly to the study of feelings or mind.

The relation which facts of mind, so to call them, bear to facts of body is not this: nor on this supposition, can we deal properly with the great fact of mind, human liberty.

As the apparent purpose of this classification, in my view, involves errors, so the classification itself involves some curious danger of confusion. Mr Mill sees well, and has expressed in language which leaves nothing to be desired for clearness, the difference between feelings (or sensations) and physical fact or relations of any kind. He also says as distinctly as I or any one taking my view could say it, that, nevertheless, in the last analysis, all physical fact or relation is in fact our feeling of such fact or relation: this, our feeling or sensation, is what we come to in the last resort as to all. But yet again, in another place, he says, in effect[1], that it is conceivable that further physiological knowledge may resolve all our feeling, as we call it, into a sort of refined physical fact: into a delicate and special kind of physical relation. The complication here is great. There is a circularity which seems almost to result in nihilism: for if physical fact is at the bottom only a manner of describing our feeling, and yet again this our feeling is or may be a refined kind of physical fact, we seem to revolve endlessly without any logical standing for our feet. In fact, Mr Mill seems to try to take *at once* two positions which, in my view, can only be taken separately; we may choose which we will take, and there is one of the two which may be so taken as to embrace the other. But Mr Mill's view seems to me to puzzle phenomenalism as much as to annihilate the higher philosophy. The phenomenalist will, I conclude, say with Mr Mill, that as he looks upon physical science, it is within its purview, it is what he hopes will one day be accomplished, that mental facts, as he would call them, one such fact being what we call our consciousness of personality, should be recognized and understood as one kind of affections or circumstances of the organism, and nothing more, in the same ways as its size, colour, form, are another kind of circumstances of it. But I do not think such a person would be inclined to say with Mr Mill that the qualities of matter are after all only our feelings of something. The phenomenalist's test of reality is not our feeling

[1] Noticed afterwards, p. 197.

about anything, but things or elements as *he* understands them
—what I have before called ' natural agents', for instance. And
conversely the logician or philosopher who really looks upon
the ultimate test of reality, for us, as being our consciousness,
is, in truth, precluded by his initial view (and this, as I shall
have to say more fully, is what it seems to me philosophers too
much forget) from allowing the *possibility* that this consciousness can, by *any* process, be proved to be only a circumstance
or relation of matter.   It stands to him as his *basis* for everything else that he knows, and therefore, whatever may be
proved *from* this so as that he knows it, the utmost is that he
must hold it in *accompaniment* with that his original thought or
basis.   On this view it can never be the feeling itself, but only
something *about* the feeling, which on any supposition of phenomenalism, can be shown to be a circumstance of matter.

It seems to me then that the manner in which Mr Mill tries
to put mind and its feelings by the side of body and its attributes is not successful. It was open to him to take the phenomenalist view, to understand by ' things' body and its attributes, to take as ultimate realities chemical elements or primary
forces, to trace the logic of our knowing them and all about
them (supposing it possible), and to consider it conceivable that
future physiology might possibly bring into relation with them
the as yet incommensurable or unassimilated matter, not yet
things for this view, which we call ' consciousness', ' feelings'.
This view would have had its truth as what I have called an
abstraction.   Or it was open to him to take the other view,
which, made a co-abstraction with this, is the ' logical', and,
carried out, is the view of the higher truth and philosophy: to
this belongs the saying that *things* (bodies and their attributes)
are really to us what we think and know to be things. But
we have no right to bring in mind and feelings as matter of our
knowledge, except upon *this* view. Where they enter, they
must take precedence of phenomenalism, and be presupposed
to it, not be put by the side of it, subjected to a logic derived
from it, and considered as what may conceivably be reduced to
it. This last is what Mr Mill has done, I think wrongly, and in
spite of his concurrent and correct view of the real precedency of
consciousness.

The important point is the putting 'mind and its attributes' as a part of the 'things in the universe' by the side of 'body and its attributes'.   I have alluded to this already by anticipation in speaking of the partly similar, partly opposite, proceeding of Sir William Hamilton, in putting 'matter and its attributes' if we may so speak as a part of 'consciousness' by the side of 'mind and its attributes'.   It is what I shall continually refer to, as constituting the great groundwork of my differences with Mr Mill.

I acknowledge that there is a difficulty before Mr Mill here, and that there are reasons why, for his purpose, it is better that things should be categorized logically than sketched or roughly enumerated physically : because we are going to examine how men have come to the knowledge of their physical nature, and we ought not at the outset (like the bad psychology) to anticipate this knowledge : and also because our physical knowledge is continually improving, and our sketch now would not have done for readers of Mr Mill's book a thousand years hence.   But this goes with me to show that Mr Mill, since he cannot avoid the logical view, had better have taken it boldly, as what it is.   I think his *partial* taking it has misled him more than a more thorough taking it would.   Talking so much of 'things', I think he *realizes* some logical entities more than he would have done if he had allowed himself more to talk of 'notions'.

Mr Mill then (in this respect not unwise) takes 'things' from the dictionary, not from the universe, and understands by them 'nameables'.   It is not quite easy to follow this view, as an index to 'things', nor can it be accepted except as a very rough one.   'Things' are in this view 'that which names are meant to designate, and very much besides *like* that which is thus designated'—of all the infinity of 'things', it is only that part which has already come under human knowledge which is named : and there is so much human mis-knowledge, altogether one is puzzled—I think 'notions' and 'concepts' would after all have been easier : unless I have read Mr Mill carelessly, it hardly appears whether the 'things' he speaks of are assumed to 'exist' or only to be the objects of names, in which cases, like Centaurs, they may not exist, and never have existed—but I need not dwell upon this.   I need hardly say that I have myself sufficiently spoken of the importance of language in the advance of thought not to quarrel with Mr Mill for making such use of it as is possible.

Coming now to the second member of the triplicity, Mr Mill is as careful to avoid the use of the expression 'judgments' as he was before as to 'notions' and 'concepts': as 'things' exist in nature, and are expressed by names, so 'facts' or 'phenomena', relations of things, exist in nature, and are expressed by 'propositions'. And as effort was before made to categorize or classify the 'things', so the same is now done as to the facts or phenomena, and there are found to be five great facts or heads of fact[1].

On these I shall not comment, except very slightly, as *e.g.* on the mention of 'space' and 'time'.

They occur I think here for the first time, and I am not quite certain as to the position which they are intended to occupy—*i.e.* whether they are to be considered 'things', and to come under the category of attributes of matter, or of matter and of mind—or whether they are something præter-real which we are here introduced to, and with which 'things' have relations, such relations as we see here, forming the object of propositions. I scarcely know whether Mr Mill is quite aware of the great delicacy of speaking as he does about *co-existence* in time and again in space, and about 'order' in them. Two things or facts, both occupying or taking place in space, or one doing so and one not, or perhaps both not doing so, are co-existent I suppose in time if they occupy *the same* time. The same two things or facts, part of their nature being the occupation of space, if they occupy *the same* space, are just what are *not* co-existent, either in time or in space: they are non-co-existent in time, and though they have a special relation the one to the other, it is not one which any term of this kind can express. All objects filling space and co-existent in time may be called co-existent in space: but I suppose co-existence in

---

[1] Mr Mill gives five great heads of natural fact, just as he gives, with whatever success, four great heads or categories of *things*. The facts are facts about the things, or what the things enter into, in the same manner as propositions are about the terms, or what *they* enter into. These categories or kinds of fact are Coexistences, Sequences, Existence, Causation, Resemblance.

space means proximity, side-by-sideness—equally exclusive of occupation of the *same* space or of a remote one.

I mention these various things only to show that what Mr Mill is speaking about here is not at all a matter of easy consideration, or clear—otherwise I do not know that about space and time I am particularly likely to differ with him. Whether they had come in previously under 'things' or come in *here* first as something with which 'things' have a relation, is not a matter of consequence in my view. Things are in them, and yet if we like to extend the use of the term, they are things too : they are objects, so far as we can tell, of our right or grounded thought, and that is all that I mean by 'things'.

As space and time come thus in here, after we have categorized the universe, so there comes in at a later stage still, in the chapter entitled 'On the Ground of Induction', something which I should have thought would have come in sooner. But I will speak of this by itself in another chapter, though I fear it will not be in what I publish now.

In the same manner in which 'things' are 'nameables', so propositions are in Mr Mill's view, though he does not use the language, 'asseribles' or 'assertables'. That is, their object exists in nature in the same way as the object of names does. The universe is an infinite complication of the 'nameable' and the 'assertable' (or thing and fact) from the former of which we separate portions into distinct nameables or things, from the latter of which we separate portions into distinct assertables or propositions. A thorough philosophical language is the ideal of a good separation of the former kind. An ideally good separation of the latter kind would be a perfect scheme or rationale of knowledge.

As I said in regard of names, we are puzzled by the fact of human error, and by the vast mass of the *asserted* which is not properly asserted, that is, of propositions which do not correspond with any facts of nature. The truth of propositions is their so corresponding. And the case in regard of the propositions is different from that in regard of the names. It is in the asserting facts of nature, and only such, that is truth. And how do we know *how* to do this, and *when* we do do it?

This is proper Logic : and *here*, in respect of the third

member of the triplicity, Mr Mill does come to a certain extent
to a logical point of view, *i.e.* entertains the idea not only of
things being and our expressing them, but of our thinking and
reasoning about them.

I may perhaps however have spoken too generally about
this—but it is not of importance.   I am not writing to criticize
Mr Mill.   There is in him abundance of most valuable logic in
reference to definitions &c. (the earlier portion of the triplicity).
And, in reference to reasoning (the latter portion of it), there is
kept up fully, as with what went before, the notion that what
we want is *in nature*—that it is not supposition of ours about
nature.   Only that with reference to this third member of the
triplicity, the manner of our proceeding in reference to what
is thus in nature is given more elaborately : as is natural, this
being the most special and thoroughly necessary business of logic.

Without at all entering to or criticizing Mr Mill's Real
Logic as compared with others, which would be quite beyond
my present purpose, I shall just mention what in his view (so
far as I understand it) is in nature, and how we, in the progress
of knowledge, proceed in reference to it.

Mr Mill changes his ground (so I describe it, but *that* is of
no importance) from *things* to *fact*.

I mean by this, that *his* important continent of the universe
as something to be investigated, in other words, that which the
universe and its contents *exist in*, is *time*, not space : in other
words still, that which we are to investigate in the universe is
not (at least so much) what *is* or *exists* in the universe, but
what *goes on* in it.   Order in space is with him of *some* importance in the universe, but only apparently in reference to some
geometrical considerations, and so much as to occupy a few
pages: what is important in the universe is, its sequences, and
as I shall take the liberty of calling them, its 'contemporaneities' (or co-existences in time) or 'simultaneities' (I use the
word to prevent any misleading of the term 'co-existences').

But as the sequences are thus important in the universe, so
there is something most important in respect of *them :* there
are uniformities of them, or invariable sequences among them:
(these uniformities are, in a manner, quasi-identities or same-
nesses of sequence, *i.e.* of fact or occurrence, they are what we

should describe roughly as the *same* fact, their sameness being of the same sort as that which generic identity gives to things —they constitute *kinds* of fact—they are sequences different in time and place, and with different accompaniments, but alike in themselves.

These sequences have their conditions or antecedents (which answer with them to the qualities of things): but each sequence has what we may call a prime condition, or antecedent not only invariable, but really connected with it, and unconditional, which gives us the answer to the question, Why has it occurred? and which, as we conceive, accounts for the sequence being what it is: and this is its 'cause'.

In the case of contemporaneities or (definitely constituted) *things*, it might be considered there must also be some prime quality, corresponding to cause in the case of fact, giving the reason and principle of the thing, and making the thing what it is, in the same way as the *cause* does in the case of fact. This however Mr Mill does not allow: considering indeed, that we may indeed look for the cause or causes which have made the thing what it is, but that is all. I mention this, not as criticizing, but as showing what I mean by saying that with him what is important in the universe is the fact or sequences in it, not the things (contemporaneities or co-existences) which, he considers, *depend* upon the other. His proceeding has a sort of similarity of contrast with that of Bacon, with whom the causes of fact depended on the forms or prime properties of things, which he thought the important part of nature[1].

I mention it also for this reason. The regularity of the universe, that is, both the entire connexion of fact and the entire compages of *thing*, is composed, in Mr Mill's view, of a number of *regularities*, or different sequences and co-existences. Mr Mill speaks to this effect very quietly, without seeming to observe how much he is saying. I have already spoken of the circumstances, most complicated, under which there takes place this process, which I am quite willing should be described as we please, either as the universe separating itself in our presence

[1] Mr Mill criticizes Bacon's View, Vol. II. p. 128, 2nd Edit. See the accurate description given of this part of Bacon's method by Mr Ellis, in his General Introduction to Bacon's Philosophical Works, Ellis and Spedding's Edition.

into units of fact and being, or as our conceiving separate and individual facts or things.   In reality, the facts or sequences which
he speaks of—would rarely have any unitary character at all,
that is, would hardly be looked at as separate or particular facts,
without the notion of a cause or necessary antecedent, and it is
this which most strongly suggests the existence of such cause.
But the same is the case in regard of *things*.   Mr Mill's word
'coexistence' as I have before said, always puzzles me, and I
converted it into 'contemporaneity'.   But it is evident that
a thing is more than a contemporaneity of attributes (a crow
e. g. more than a *contemporaneity* of blackness, feathers, living
tissue, &c.) and yet the question is, *What* more?   Unless Mr
Mill flies to his unknown substratum, about which I shall shortly
have something to say, what is the nexus or connexion in virtue
of which we say '*co*-existence'?   Is it spatial? but what are we
to think of things indefinitely separated or indefinitely dispersed
in space, as the solar system, or a gas?   We seem to want, in
regard of the 'thing', to individualize it or separate it from the
rest of the universe, exactly that same nexus which the supposed cause supplies in the case of the sequence: or at least
the 'co-existence' requires some explanation—a better one
than the substratum.

This looking in the universe at *fact* rather than things, at
what goes on rather than at what is, is of course a part of that
general tendency to look at matter of knowledge as *history* or
occurrence, which belongs to positivism (I do not mean the word
at all in any invidious sense).

Such then being the matter of knowledge, *viz.* the facts or
sequences in the universe, and the circumstance of importance
in respect of each of these being its 'cause', what is our mental
position in respect of them?   Any *adstance* or presence with
them must be by an intermediation of some kind, and it might
have been considered what *sort* of intermediation there could
be.   Mr Mill however, as I have said, deals with the universe
as with facts, not with things: and the knowledge of these
facts he describes (most reasonably) as *belief:* by so doing he
takes what I have called the *logical* point of view, or considers
what is the state of our consciousness.   In other words, when
we use the term *belief* of anything, it is not the same view as

if we said, Such and such a thing is in nature, it is there whatever is the case with me, whether I believe it or disbelieve it,
whether I am alive or dead, whether or not there is or has
been anybody to know about it—in this case, if we *do* suppose
anybody by or present (adstant) to know, we must bear in mind
that the thing known is entirely independent of the knowledge.   When, on the other hand, we speak of believing, conceiving, &c., the thing known is a part of the knowledge: we
are at what I called the *logical* point of view: we must not
previously suppose the independent existence of the thing
known, because its existence depends upon the correctness of
our belief: we cannot speak with meaning of believing anything that is *in* the universe: we believe something about the
universe, and if our belief is correct, *then* we may say with
reason, if we like the language, the thing is in the universe,
but not before.   We believe then in the first instance, by a
belief counter-respondent to (*i. e.* the same thing as, looked at
the other way) simple adstance or presence with the thing
known, the existence of the facts or sequences: if we believe
anything as to the *causes* of them, it must be through an
intermediation, which is what we call 'evidence', and the
treatment of this evidence is the purpose of Mr Mill's Logic
proper.

Mr Mill's Logic then, like Bacon's, is simply a Theory of
the Evidence of the Facts of Nature, or Art of dealing with
it, in the double way of dealing with evidence which belongs
to all use of it, whether for legal purposes or for others, *viz.* to
find out by it that which we do not know, and to verify by it
(or prove to others) what we suppose we do know.   This is
one way in which the advance of knowledge may be looked
on: we go on from one to another fresh step of knowledge:
each must be fresh, and each must be knowledge: we have got
therefore first to have it suggested to our thought, and then
shown to be knowledge: the evidence acts to *both* purposes.

Mr Mill uses the word 'induction' in a wider and in a nar-
rower sense: first, for all inference, or in fact all mental
process, by which anything is added to knowledge, or knowledge grows: and next for the particular case of such inference
or process, in which the added knowledge is more general than

that which it had proceeded from. Hence the most important process of Induction in the first sense is Deduction, by which latter term is signified a triple process: first of Induction in the second sense: next of Ratiocination, which may be considered an extension or expansion, in the sense of a wide application, of the general truth thus approximately obtained: and finally, a continued Verifying or testing it as thus applied.

This language does not seem to me very happy for general use: by which I mean: every philosopher has a right to *his own* language: I think such language is generally best when it is most his own: and all this language is explained and used by Mr Mill with most perfect clearness. But the term ' Deduction', of which I do not very well know the history, was I suppose invented and used as an antithesis to Induction: and so, in books inferior to Mr Mill's, and in much philosophical language derived more or less from his views it constantly is: with him it scarcely represents such an antithesis: it is most expressly opposed to 'Experimental'. Altogether, I do not think the language is favourable to clearness of thought, and I question whether there is much significance in what Mr Mill says, as to the Anti-Baconian revolution (so to call it) now going on. But I will not dwell on this.

I am not at all going to criticize Mr Mill's System of Real Logic, if so we may call it. To do this with any utility would require much more space and care than belongs to my present purpose. I will only make one or two observations.

A Real Logic has in *one* respect two parts, thus: it contains always in some degree a sort of review of the manner in which knowledge has advanced, and also a scheme, system, and rationale of the manner of proceeding which is best for its future advance. Every Real Logic is to me of great interest on account of the *former* of these parts of it. But the different views taken of the circumstances under which knowledge has advanced, or, in other words, which have been the cause of its advance, make me put not much faith in the second part, or in any Real Logic as a kind of art of the advance of knowledge for the future. The logical language which the new Real Logic is introducing seems to me to be of a cumbrous character, as likely to be a load upon speculation and investigation, and as little likely to be helpful, as much of the old Formal Logic. I think there is still something to desire as to the way in which we ought, philosophically, to think of the vast advance in physical knowledge which man has made. And till we understand it in *this* way more than it seems to me we do, I think any conclusions from the manner of it as to our best way of proceeding now are very doubtful. According to Mr Mill, we are unlearning Baconianism—would it, or would it not, have been better for us never to have learnt it? or after all, is it *nothing* that we have learnt and are now unlearning, only a manner of speaking? Apparently, however, non-logical physical research has been too strong for our Baconian Real Logic—if this is so, I do not say that no purpose is served by our trying, in whatever degree, to direct this research by a fresh Real Logic, but only that the same thing may happen again.

In another quite different respect also a Real Logic has two parts: *viz.* it has a view of nature or of the universe, *and* it has a view of the manner in which our mind should proceed for the advance of the knowledge of it. These two are pretty certain of course to be connected together, and if the one is wrong, some things also necessarily in the other must be: but it may be *some* only, and it is quite possible that to a considerable extent the views may be separable.

In the case of Mr Mill his Logic of Evidence may be to a considerable extent separated from his phenomenalist view of nature: we may disallow, or think very insufficient, his view of the universe with its supposed sequences and their causes, and yet consider that the scheme he gives of the manner in which we may best find out the truth about something which we want to know, is most valuable, important, and useful. For all this 'Induction' is only what we are always about when we want to increase our knowledge of any kind, or to find out the truth about anything. This Mr Mill tells us, and truly. And this is important, in relation of my present discussion, in this way. What seems most important to Mr Mill's mind, and what many of his readers think most important in his researches, is the making a Real Logic for Social and Moral Science—the application of methods which have been so fruitful as to physical science, now to moral. I have not the least doubt but that

Mr Mill's book is full of most valuable hints and helps for such a Real Logic. But so far as this is so, I think it is quite independently of his view of nature and of the universe. So far as his book is a good Real Logic in *general*, applicable to Moral Science as well as physical, it might be taken in hand for instance by a lawyer, and there might be published, similar in method to it, and without a word about sequences and co-existences, a treatise *e.g.* on the manner in which we hunt out crime, and bring it home to any body—the word 'causa' is probably, like αἰτία, a quasi-legal word from 'caveo', signifying who or what is to blame for anything, to whom or what it ought to be attributed. I dare say Mr Mill's Deduction, with its three steps, would be the best way to set about this—a preliminary induction would fix upon some one for strong suspicion —suppose him to be the man, and argue then what other suppositions must follow from this—see if these suppositions are verified by actual fact. I put this in this manner only to show how thoroughly independent all of it is of Mr Mill's peculiar language or of his views of the universe: it is his Logic as a good logic of discovery of fact and belief of it on evidence which is of value for moral and social science, not his Logic as founded on any particular view of nature.

How far Mr Mill's view of the Inductive Deduction to which I have just now referred, is really different from Dr Whewell's view of fitting a conception to the observed facts, is not easy to say—I very much doubt whether it is greatly so. Mr Mill's discussion with Dr Whewell as to the 'conceptions' is in substance double: Do the conceptions belong to the mind, or are they, if right, in the facts? Is the process of two members only, a comparison of conceptions and facts, or is it more elaborate, induction, ratiocination and verification?

I have just alluded to this controversy, which I am not going to pursue, for the two following reasons.

My difference with Dr Whewell, as we shall shortly see, is in this: that I think the conceptions—which are described as taking their origin in the mind—are nothing but the other side, so to speak, of the facts which are described as independent of the mind, and to which the conceptions are to be applied. I regard therefore the first member of the above discussion between

Dr Whewell and Mr Mill as not involving *any* real matter of discussion. It is discussed in Mr Mill's Chapter on Abstractions : he makes great effort to prove that " the conceptions which we " employ for the colligation and methodization of facts, do not " develope themselves from within, but are impressed upon the " mind from without : they are never obtained otherwise than by " way of comparison and abstraction, and in the most important " and the most numerous cases are evolved by abstraction from " the very phenomena which it is their office to colligate[1] ". If the reader follows what I have written all along, he will see that one special value to me, of the view which I take, is, that it prevents this most undecidable controversy. Let us call knowledge whichever we please, an impression made by reality upon the mind, *or* a right view taken by the mind as to reality, but do not let us discuss *which* it is, for it is either and both : do not let us say it is one to the exclusion of the other, for then we shall infallibly become slaves of our terms, and think that we mean something really taking place, when we talk of 'conceptions being *impressed upon* the mind from without': in respect of each view, its counter-view is needed to prevent any such misapprehension: and last, do not let us say, which seems to me to be Dr Whewell's mistake, that knowledge is partly in the facts and partly from the mind: the highest conceptions are in the things as well as the most mate-rial and secondary quality: the most material quality, as a part of knowledge, is a notion of the mind, as well as the highest conception.

If *this* discussion is put aside, we come much more freely and hopefully to the other, namely, that as to the manner of the action of the mind in adding to its store of knowledge, and eli-citing truth. And, as I have hinted, it would probably be really the better for the Real Logic of Science, that it should not be too speedily involved with technical terms, but that the general principles of the logic of learning or finding out *anything* should be as distinctly as possible laid down first. Mr Mill appeals from his technical logic to the natural logic of us all : ' Let any watch the manner in which he himself unravels any complicated mass of evidence[2]': and then he goes on to de-

---

[1] Vol. II. pp. 223, 224.   [2] Vol. II. p. 20.

scribe how we speculate, and form our theories, &c. and see whether they will do, and so on. In reality, I doubt much whether any purpose is served by speaking, in a manner which I have described as 'cumbrous', about the 'Hypothetical Method', for instance—the disadvantage is, that we get hard and sharp technical distinctions, of little use, as it seems to me. This 'Hypothetical Method', says Mr Mill, 'out of the three processes, induction, ratiocination, verification, suppresses the former': now the former, surely, at least exists in the shape of 'suggestion', and considering that in the proper 'Deduction' the preliminary induction is avowedly incomplete, the limits between such suggestion and the incomplete induction are very vague: and then the distinction between the preliminary induction and the final verification is by no means very absolute: as the terms are technically used by Mr Mill, no doubt it is so: but as I have said, the technicalism ought to stand upon a general basis of good *mathetic* logic, or the logic of learning, finding out, arriving at truth, and then we have to *apply* this.

The reason why I do not say any more about Mr Mill's account of the various Inductive and Experimental processes, is because what is of interest in his book for my present purpose is his view of nature and his view of the general action of the mind. I shall investigate to a certain degree how far he is or is not free from what I have called 'notionalism', and from what I have called wrong psychology: I shall allude to what he says about the logic of the moral sciences: and after an interval, shall make a few additional remarks upon his *most* general views of the universe, of truth, and of the manner of our arriving at it, and the extent to which we do so arrive.

CHAPTER IX.

MILL'S LOGIC CONTINUED.

IF any person would have been likely to avoid notionalism (or relativism) and the wrong psychology, one would have thought that Mr Mill would, on account of his strong view of 'things' as the objects of knowledge, and of his clear observation of the difference between 'sensation' as 'consciousness' and 'sensation' as (so to call it) 'bodily affection'. I do not think he does avoid either of them, and the present chapter is a discussion as to his doing so: the conclusion which I draw from this is, that phenomenalism, with a philosophic mind like his, will not stand alone, and if it cannot have (what seems to me) right philosophy to support it, must have wrong.

1. In speaking of an unknown and unknowable substratum of things, Mr Mill seems to me amenable to all that I said in speaking of Mr Ferrier, about the error of those philosophers who speak about 'things in themselves', or use any language of that kind, from a *logical* point of view, converting their mere logical supposition into a supposed reality. I will leave this however for a moment, and before saying more about it, will say a little about something else.

2. I think Mr Mill is inconsistent with himself in the following manner. All facts of body are ultimately facts of mind, *i. e.* the truth about them is capable of being reduced to truth of thought in the thinking mind. This is what I understand him to say, what I heartily agree with him in, and what seems to me the same as my saying, that the phenomenalist view is a partial one or an abstraction, and that the philosophical view, or that from the point of view of consciousness, is the comprehensive and complete one. But in this philosophical view, that which we are conscious of in the first step of immediateness is

on the one side our own feelings, on the other side something which gives occasion to them, which latter developes itself, as our intelligence goes on, into the facts of body or phenomenalism. Thus, on the philosophical view, these facts of body stand at a further remove from our consciousness, the test of certainty, than our feelings do: which Mr Mill himself seems to consider, in saying that the facts of body may be ultimately referred to feelings of mind. But then these feelings of mind ought not to be put on the same level of thought as the facts of body, as phenomena together with them, to be treated conjunctly with them, and to be considered as forming, along with them, a class of nameables in the universe. Still less ought a system of logic, formed upon the basis of the observation how we advance in the knowledge of the phenomena of body, to be applied to them, and to be considered as the instrument by which we shall advance in knowledge of them. And Mr Mill's attempting to do this seems to me inconsistent with his saying previously, that the facts of body are ultimately referrible to feelings of mind—*i.e.* that these latter stand at a higher stage, in the *complete* view, than the former. The immediate result of this logic, which I have called phenomenalist, is the denial of the existence of will, and of causation as action : *i.e.* as soon as the feelings of mind are professedly set by the side of the facts of body as co-phenomena, they are really subordinated to them, no longer treated as facts of mind or consciousness, but dealt with according to principles which the phenomenalist logic has given. It is quite possible that our supposed consciousness of will or activity may be a delusion : but it is possible in exactly the same manner, and at the same stage of thought, in which it is possible for our supposition of the existence of an universe independent of us, or a spatial, external world, to be a delusion. Our feeling of our activity or of our being sources of change exists by the side of, and at the level of, the entire and general feeling that there is a universe independent of us. We follow out this latter feeling into phenomenalism, and lay down (or describe) the facts of the universe : but it is not a proper course to put by the side of these facts, and to consider as phenomena analogous in any way to them, our various consciousness, or our feelings, which belong to a higher and different region. Our

feeling of there being a universe at all, upon which all phenomenalism depends, is but one of these feelings. Our feelings,
viewed from the philosophical point of view or point of view of
consciousness, are not phenomena of the universe or capable of
standing by the side of such, but the universe, if we like to use
the language, is a fact or phenomenon of *them.*

I do not quarrel with the looking at our feeling, so far as it
can be so looked at, from the phenomenal point of view. Each one
of us is a corporeal organization in the universe, filling space as
a tree fills space, and sensitive more or less as a dog is sensitive.
Of this sensitiveness which we share certainly with the dog,
perhaps with the tree, for there may be an infinite number of
degrees and kinds of it, we may, from the phenomenal point of
view, have some notion: it *is* a fact of the universe: we may
call it if we like consciousness: we may apply our individual
feeling of consciousness towards the gaining this notion, so far as
we can: we may imagine what the dog's feeling must be, and
judge from what he does, how far it is like our own: I have no
quarrel with all this. All I say is, that with each one of us (if
we say 'each one'), with me, with you, the one great reality which
absorbs all others is that I, you, think and feel, and we only
talk of a universe because we think and feel that there is one;
that our thought in this way surrounds or embraces the universe and cannot therefore be embraced by it in such a manner
as to be liable to have said of it, This, or that, matter of consciousness, is inconsistent with such and such laws of the universe which we have discovered, and therefore cannot be true.
We may, to a certain extent, be able to treat of our thought or
feeling as embraced in the universe, as a fact of it: but we have
no right to conclude that because we may do this we may conclude things about it, from its being a fact of the universe,
which the thought itself, as consciousness, disowns.

There seems to me, in all this attempt to apply phenomenalist logic to the consideration of thought and feeling, to
be the same confusion of two views which I have all along
been noting. We are, for physical and physiological study
(which is what I call phenomenal) one species of animal upon
the earth, the highest that we know, with communicative
tongues and constructive hands, so that we can make all sorts

of things and combine together, with common and mutual understanding, to make them, and talk about them, and talk in our own minds about them—we may study the facts of our own nature, including our thought and feeling to the extent I have mentioned above, in our place in the universe, as we may study any facts of any nature, phenomenally. But we are, and we cannot help really feeling ourselves, for purposes of philosophical and moral study, not *this*, but something different—what I should call, 'higher'. We feel with, and we feel ourselves as having, a free consciousness, a disposition to look at things generally, a curiosity, or love of knowing, a disposition to do things for a purpose and to try to do them well, all which with kindred feelings besides, makes us occupy, in our own view, the position, not of animals, however high, *in* the universe with a sphere and environment, and with our own existence subordinated to that, but of observers of the relation between ourselves and this universe, with *its* existence subordinated to ours, believing in it not because we are inferior to it but because we think it, judging about it as well as studying it, and when we are settling upon our action, thinking, from this free point of view, what is worth doing, what wants doing, what it is well *should* be done; not simply considering that our experience in the universe as the animal *man*, is to guide our action in the same way as a dog's experience or instinct as the animal *dog* guides his, which is what *he* cannot help.

I have put this a little strongly just to mark how it is at the point of *human* nature and human action that we must take care that we keep the views distinct. I have been noticing, throughout what I have been saying now, the confusion, as it seems to me, of the two views, in reference to *philosophy* or the study of knowledge: Mr Mill, in respect of the application of his logic to knowledge, does not much fall into it, but he does when he thinks to apply his logic to social science and to morals. Because for these, in my view, we must start, not from phenomena, but from consciousness, in the same way as we start for the higher philosophy of knowledge. I have just tried to describe what I mean by this. The putting our feelings as co-phenomena with the facts of the universe is the bringing them from a higher level to which they do belong to a lower to which they do not. It is analogous in a different application of thought, to the want of clearness of view in setting before ourselves the question whether we are thinking of ourselves as corporeal and local, or whether we are considering how we gain the knowledge, or conceive the notion, of corporealness and locality.

From what I have said as to the extent to which our feelings may be treated phenomenally it will be understood that I do not wish to deny the possibility of much valuable result from this line of thought—but it must be kept within its proper limits for this, and must be subordinate, as a logic of philosophy and morals, to the logic of the higher point of view which I have mentioned. Whereas Mr Mill considers, and I believe has influenced many to consider, that by what he has said he has opened the way to a new and better method, promising much advance, in respect of social science for instance and morals. This I think is mistaken.

I should perhaps have said, that for the phenomenalist study of human nature and morals, we have now, at this stage of the world's life, something beyond physics and physiology, in the facts of the history of human society. All this I most fully allow, and the very valuable results which may result from the study of these facts or phenomena. But even these, though phenomena if we like to call them so of a higher order, do not alter what I have said, that our starting point must not be from them. All that man *has* done, whatever aid it may give, can never teach us what man *should* do or what it is best for him to do, any more than the facts of the universe can.

Before however proceeding further on the logic of the moral sciences, which is what comes last in Mr Mill's book, I had better finish what I have to say about the 'unknowable substratum' of things, and mention one or two points in which there seems to me confusion.

3. I am not at all now criticizing Mr Mill, which could not be properly done except at much greater length than I wish here to go to, and without going into details which would interfere with the general view which I want to give. I take

his book, a book well known and of universally acknowledged merit, as a type of a kind of thought, and so far as he is concerned, it is quite sufficient answer for him to say that I have misunderstood him. This is not unlikely, but in that case the criticism of the view which I suppose in him remains the same.

This may be not an improper place to call attention to a possible misunderstanding of the term 'phenomenal', as I use it. I use it as an adjective formed from 'phenomenon', in our present acceptation of the word phenomenon, as synonymous with physical fact, or fact of nature, or fact in the universe, or however we describe it. The word 'phenomenon', in this use, is a relic of the old philosophy which taught that all in nature, as sensible, was *appearance*, and that the process of learning or gaining knowledge or forming true notions was a coming, through the intervention of this appearance, and by proper thinking about it (dialectic) at the *idea* or true reality of things, and forming our notions in conformity with this. The word 'phenomenon', as I use it, means to those who are what I call wrong phenomenalists, or positivists, simply *fact*, they recognizing no other reality: to me it means what it does to them, so far as used for *their* purposes, but also *besides*, for philosophical purposes, what it meant, in the main, to the old philosophers. That is, I look upon our complete and right conception of things as something in relation to which our view of the universe as fact or nature is something incomplete—I do not call it deceptive appearance, but I call it partial and an abstraction.

The words 'phenomenal', 'phænomenal', 'phenomenology', and other such, as they are used by Sir William Hamilton and a great many philosophers at present, carry with them a different reference. *I* recognize in '*noumena*', their opposite, only mental creations, temporary notions, if we like so to call them, formed as aids to, or in the way towards, the notions which we want to form, not at all the things themselves or our *final* notions of them. What the physicist considers facts are 'phenomena' (significantly) in the eye of the philosopher, because he takes cognizance of something further back than the physicist goes, *viz.* that he only calls them 'facts' because they *seem* to him so, which *last* is the real fact, the fact of facts: the universe is all a dressing up of one side of this fact: he wants to escape from the word 'seem', not, as the simple phenomenalist does, by ignoring this latter great fact, but by *facing* it, and trying whether he can arrive at, or approach towards, anything, in regard of which the word 'seem' would lose its meaning, and be felt as identical with 'is'—at anything which *is* to him with the same completeness and conviction as, in his own view, he himself *is*. In *this* view the *idea*, the proper reality, is the true *object* of knowledge: it is what all our efforts are directed towards: to say that it is *not* matter of knowledge, that it is something which from its nature cannot be known, is negativing the view altogether: it is just what *can* be known, and the only thing which can be *known* in the full propriety of the term, so far as we can attain to know it.

All this is entirely different from the notion of an unknowable *noumenism* with which phænomenism (as I here on purpose write it) is contrasted, phænomena being supposed only the dress of the *noumena,* and the latter, though in their nature unknowable, being the things in themselves, the substratum, the true realities. Our consciousness, the ultimate test, suggests to us, we may say, ourselves, as a continuing substratum of our varying feelings; but it does not suggest to us this as *unknown,* for it is just what we most *do* know: and it is quite a false parallel to suppose that in any way our consciousness suggests to us a (supposedly) similar unknowable substratum for the occasions of our sensations, or phenomena. What our consciousness suggests to us on this side is not at all *this,* but is a universe or existing order of things of which we form a part at the same time that, in the first instance, we in our thought comprehend it. What suggests the supposed substratum is merely *notionalism,* or wrong conclusion from the manner or process of our knowledge, which is the describing things by predicating qualities of them, so that in *the process* of knowledge, we have to suppose the thing (for it is only temporary supposition), independent of each, and therefore of all, its qualities.

I hope what I have said may make it clear how *my* use of the term 'phenomenal' differs from Sir William Hamilton's in that passage of his quoted in Mr Mill's later editions[1], where

[1] Vol. I. p. 65, 4th edit.

he says, "All that we know is therefore phænomenal—phæno-
"menal of the unknown." All that we know is but a small part
of the knowable, and since we all hold whatever we know *as a
whole*, since our knowledge is a view of things or of the universe, since there is given us in our mind so to speak a frame
for our knowledge, which the particular things which we know
more or less fill up—all that we know may be regarded as that
appearance which the universe or reality takes *to us*—as
phænomenal of the unknown whole—the whole unknown and
unknowable as a matter of fact, but not unknowable in its
nature or philosophically.

It seems to me a strange perversion of the notion of knowledge to suppose that we can know that anything is in its
nature *un*knowable, except so far as the notion 'knowledge' is
inapplicable to it, in which case nobody would talk of knowing
it, or would call it unknowable. We do not talk of colours as
inaudible, and if we do of sounds being invisible, it is because
of the wide and loose way in which sight is used as the type of
all sense. It is the giving a mere logical puzzle as a supposed
wholesome humbling of the intellect which is what I call 'notionalism' or 'relativism'.

To return from these observations on phenomenalism to
Mr Mill. In that passage[1] which I have just referred to, I
doubted, in the former edition, *where* he ceased to speak the
language of Kant, and where he began his own: in the latter
it appears more clearly. He preserves in his note the passage
of Cousin which expresses, as pointedly as could possibly be
expressed, the relativism with which I have expressed my dis-
agreement, now evidently as expressing his own view, and he
adds the passage from Sir William Hamilton which I have just
quoted.

"It may", says Mr Mill, "be safely laid down that of the
"outward world . . . . . we know and can know absolutely nothing,
"except the sensations which we experience from it[2]".

[1] Page 78, 2nd edit.; page 64, 4th edit.

[2] I am in a difficulty as to what to quote here, but perhaps, I had better print
in this note the whole passage of Mr Mill (since I shall return to it again), as it
stands in the fourth edition, omitting only the long passage from M. Cousin,
which the reader may imagine. I will first give the text.

"But although the extreme doctrine of the Idealist metaphysicians, that

I mentioned some time since that a good test of a philosopher's manner of thought was his use of the term 'object of

" objects are nothing but our sensations and the laws which connect them, has not
" been generally adopted by subsequent thinkers; the point of most real importance
" is one on which those metaphysicians are now very generally considered to have
" made out their case : viz. that *all we know* of objects is the sensations which they
" give us, and the order of the occurrence of those sensations.   Kant himself, on
" this point, is as explicit as Berkeley or Locke.   However firmly convinced that
" there exists an universe of 'Things in themselves,' totally distinct from the
" universe of phenomena, or of things as they appear to our senses ; and even
" when bringing into use a technical expression (*Noumenon*) to denote what the
" thing is in itself, as contrasted with the *representation* of it in our minds ; he
" allows that this representation (the matter of which, he says, consists of our
" sensations, though the form is given by the laws of the mind itself) is all we know
" of the object : and that the real nature of the Thing is, and by the constitution
" of our faculties ever must remain, at least in the present state of existence, an
" impenetrable mystery to us.   'Of things absolutely or in themselves,' says Sir
" William Hamilton, ' be they external, be they internal, we know nothing, or
" ' know them only as incognisable ; and become aware of their incomprehensible
" ' existence, only as this is indirectly and accidentally revealed to us, through
" ' certain qualities related to our faculties of knowledge, and which qualities,
" ' again, we cannot think as unconditioned, irrelative, existent in and of them-
" ' selves.   All that we know is therefore phænomenal,—phenomenal of the un-
" ' known.'   The same doctrine is laid down in the clearest and strongest terms
" by M. Cousin, whose observations on the subject are the more worthy of atten-
" tion, as, in consequence of the ultra-German and ontological character of his
" philosophy in other respects, they may be regarded as the admissions of an
" opponent.

    " There is not the slightest reason for believing that what we call the sensible
" qualities of the object are a type of anything inherent in itself, or bear any affinity
" to its own nature.   A cause does not, as such, resemble its effects; an east
" wind is not like the feeling of cold, nor heat like the steam of boiling water.   Why
" then should matter resemble our sensations ?   Why should the inmost nature of
" fire or water resemble the impressions made by those objects upon our senses ?
" Or on what principle are we authorised to deduce from the effects, anything con-
" cerning the cause, except that it is a cause adequate to produce those effects ?
" It may therefore safely be laid down as a truth both obvious in itself, and ad-
" mitted by all whom it is at present necessary to take into consideration, that,
" of the outward world, we know and can know absolutely nothing, except the
" sensations which we experience from it.   Those, however, who still look upon
" Ontology as a possible science, and think, not only that bodies have an essential
" constitution of their own, lying deeper than our perceptions, but that this essence
" or nature is accessible to human investigation, cannot expect to find their refuta-
" tion here.   The question depends on the nature and laws of Intuitive Know-
" ledge, and is not within the province of logic."

    I will now give the note.

    " Sir William Hamilton even goes so far as to assert that this opinion not only
" now is, but always has been, held by nearly all philosophers.   'It has been com-

knowledge': I will now mention another, which is, his use of the term 'outward' or 'external'. For instance, Mr Mill speaks in one place of something being 'external both to the body and the mind' as if the term was in the same sense applicable to both. This is just the way of speaking which I do not understand, and which I have called a confusion between two views. The mind, as distinguished from the body, is the knowing (thing) or the subject of the attribute knowledge, in regard of which the question is, not whether anything is or is not spatially external to it, but whether it is or is not, in any way, independent of it. Not however to dwell on this: as to the passage quoted, I cannot see the force of it, because I cannot understand what *the outward world* means or can mean more than the (supposed) occasion of the sensations which, in Mr Mill's language, 'we experience from it'. What I understand by the term 'outward' is a reference of it to these sensations: so far as we know any more, if we do so know, than these sensations tell us, the term 'outward' so far ceases to be applicable to it: that is all that seems to me to happen: as I should express it, we are taking no longer the phenomenalist view. And what I differ from Mr Mill in as to the last sentence is this, that while condemning apparently Ontology, or the notion that bodies have a

---

" 'monly confessed, that, as substances, we know not what is Matter, and are
" 'ignorant of what is Mind. With the exception, in fact, of a few late Absolutist
" 'theorisers in Germany, this is, perhaps, the truth of all others most harmoni-
" 'ously reechoed by every philosopher of every school.' And he supports his
" assertion by quotations from seVenteen thinkers of eminence, beginning with
" Protagoras and Aristotle, and ending with Kant. Gladly, howeVer, as I should
" learn that a philosophical truth destructiVe of so great a mass of baseless and
" misleading speculation had been uniVersally recognized by philosophers of all
" past time, and that Ontology, instead of being, as I had hitherto belieVed, the
" oldest form of philosophy, was a recent inVention of Schelling and Hegel ; I am
" obliged to confess, that none of the passages extracted by Sir William Hamilton,
" except one from the elder Scaliger and another from Newton, conVey to my
" mind the conclusion that the writers had eVer come within sight of the great
" truth which he supposes them to haVe intended to express. Almost all the pas-
" sages seem to me perfectly compatible with the rejection of it ; and in most
" I cannot, by any legitimate interpretation, find anything more than a recog-
" nition of the far more obVious principle, that our knowledge of external things
" is necessarily conditioned by the laws of our knowing faculty : a Very different
" thing from the assertion that the laws of that faculty are such as to deny us
" all knowledge of outward things, except that of their mere existence."

super-perceptional constitution which we may hope to find out, he seems to countenance the belief that they have one, which, from its very nature it is useless for us even to try to find out. This is the 'notional' Ontology, if I may so call it, which seems to me worse than an attemptedly Real Ontology. It is what I have alluded to above as the Kantist manner of thought—I give no opinion as to proper Kantism. I say nothing at all as to whether there is any meaning in speaking of 'an essential constitution of things': I say only this, that if the notion is to be entertained even so far as to say that such a thing is *possible*, this constitution must have some relation to the facts about things which we know by our sensations, along which relation there is a road for our intellect towards the knowledge of this constitution—how good a road is a question I do not enter upon: the question is as to a chasm or discontinuity in virtue of the nature of things.

I do not allude to this in Mr Mill for the purpose of criticizing his sentences—it requires much fuller consideration than I am giving here to know how far a particular sentence expresses a philosopher's full view—but because it is all a part of that which is my difference with him—his not indeed ignoring the philosophical view, which would be the course of many phenomenalists, but his attempt to bring it in along with the phenomenalist, in a way which confuses both. He thus seems to consider that the semi-Ontology of Kantists and Sir William Hamilton (which seems to me a mocking of our intelligence) *will* come in by the side of his phenomenalism, while a further going philosophy will not. I have taken as the real or important line of thought with him that which seems to me really inconsistent with this, and in which 'notionalism' is just what he opposes. What we see and name are 'things', and propositions express 'facts' or 'phenomena'. Ideas of things, and judgments about things, may in this view, and I agree with him in it, be left out of consideration.

I cannot resist dwelling still however for a moment on this page of Mr Mill, in which every sentence, both of his and Sir W. Hamilton's fills me with a sort of wonder—how so much knowledge, and so much ignorance or nescience, of these 'things in themselves', can go together, I cannot understand.

"Of things absolutely and in themselves", says Sir William
Hamilton, "be they external, be they internal, we know nothing,
"or know them only as incognizable: and become aware of their
"incomprehensible existence, only as this is indirectly and acci-
"dentally revealed to us, through certain qualities related to our
"faculties of knowledge, and which qualities, again, we cannot
"think as unconditional, irrelative, existent in and of themselves.
"All that we know is therefore phænomenal—phænomenal of
"the unknown[1]".

I go with the description so far as this—we know the object
through certain qualities fitted to our faculties of knowledge—
these, in language I have used, fit each other. I generalize:
whoever, whatever mind, even an all-knowing one, knows the
object, knows it by qualities fitted to *its* faculties of knowledge.
Qualities and faculties of knowledge go together. Suppose one
single universal faculty of knowledge, in place of various special
and particular ones, what the mind having this must know is—
one universal quality of the object and no more. *Who* then
knows the object *itself* if even omniscience does not and cannot
go beyond quality? Here we have doubtless got at an unknowableness of the 'thing in itself', but it is an unknowableness
I think of *my* sort, viz. because there is nothing to know. Or
was I wrong in generalizing as I did above, and should I have
said, Some minds, including ours, know objects through qualities, and some know them independent of knowledge of their
qualities, by themselves? They know them then I suppose
without faculties of knowledge. And what then is meant by
qualities? By qualities or properties of an object I mean nothing but what (by one mind and another, if you like, according to its faculties) can be known about it: *here* we seem
to have an object unqualitied, unpropertied, unconditioned—
But I do not pursue the subject. There can be little doubt
but that in all this there is the confusion I have spoken of,
and that the philosophers who have thought in this manner
did not know whether they themselves meant that we could not
know *the thing itself* because we could only know qualities,
or because with *our* intelligence, we could only know *some*
qualities.

[1] Page 65, 4th edit.

The real being of things is doubtless uncomprehended by us: how do we know that, and how do we know why, it is *incomprehensible?* How do we know that the revelation of the things to us by the particular qualities by which we know them is 'indirect' and 'accidental'? Can anybody imagine there is any meaning in these terms as thus applied? Or can there be a worse, and a more vain Ontology?

This is the worst form of realism: the realizing of logical notions, and then pacifying our intellectual conscience by saying that we only know the things, the result of this our realizing process, as 'incognisable'. How do we know them as *that*, I ask? There is truth within its province in *phenomenalist* realism, so to call it, by which I mean the supposition that the *chemical* elements or constituents of the universe, forces perhaps, are the ultimate realities: and if this does not satisfy us, as it does not me, because the universe consists not only of such things as *these*, but of these going together to make other things, bodies as we call them, organizations, systems, constitutions, more or less after the analogy of the manner in which we make them go together to compose things which we want for our use, ploughs, houses, &c., in regard of which, besides the elements, there is, at once in our mind and in them, plan, meaning, purpose—then we may consider this plan, meaning, purpose, *itself* a reality, of a different and higher nature than the elementary reality, and as constituting the real *thinghood* of the things, the reason why we notice them and call them *things:* here we have the *ideal* reality of things, in contradistinction to the phenomenal: we know the things by a process which may equally well be described in either way, either as *putting* meaning into the things, or *seeing* meaning in them, for the simple reason that in reality the thinghood is a something *between* the two sides, the subjective and the objective—it is the meeting of the two. The thinghood of a thing is the proper *thoughtness* of it—what it is rightly thought to be: the right thinking about it is indeed on the other side the thinking of it as it is, but the two do not exactly counterdefine each other, because *mind comes first*—the cardinal point of philosophy in my view: the thing as thought, pre-contemplated by its Creator, contemplated by beings with created faculties of knowledge with such following of his thought as they can attain to, is the idea, the ideal thing, the ideal reality, the truest reality.

This of course, when carried to *this* extent is abstruse and may seem visionary: no one *need* carry it further than he likes: what I have endeavoured to show is that to whatever extent we go along it, so long as we are in this road, we have a true reality: I accept the notion of phenomenal reality most fully, when not misapplied. What I protest against is the wretched ghost of this higher philosophy which is furnished by the realizing our logical notions. It is Sir William Hamilton, not I, who says that the real existence of things is only 'indirectly and accidentally revealed to us' by the phenomenal knowledge which we have of them. It is an accident of the things we know that they are known *by us*, but that they are known by means of faculties of knowledge such as ours is no accident of them—they are so known in consequence of their having qualities which those faculties fit, which qualities are as much a part of their constitution or thinghood as anything else of them is. *Indirect*, we may indeed call the revelation of them if we like, in *this* way: whatever higher realities, so to call them, we may be able to know about them *might* have come to our knowledge without the necessity of so much lower reality—of so much communication and contact, to be used by intelligence, of our corporeal or sensive frame with the particular natural agents, elements, constituents, of the universe. But I do not think there is really reason in this. I do not think man is the worse for the fact, that for such knowledge as he has of the universe, there has been obliged to be such a vast amount of particular observation or communication between his senses and phenomena. Were our knowledge direct, it would be, I suppose one great, single, monotonous act: we know the higher properties of things with the same sort of *indirectness* of knowledge with which we know that the earth turns round the sun, and I do not know that directness of knowledge or immediateness of feeling would be any advantage.

I suppose that Sir William Hamilton, in his attempt to unite logic, Reidian psychology, and Kantian criticism, really did confuse together the logical view of knowledge as a forming proper notions of what (no matter to logic *what*) in virtue of the notions thus formed, we call *things*, and the view of knowledge as a communication or presence with something supposed existent. The idea of the essential unknowableness belongs to the former: the solemnity with which it is talked about, as if this *unknowable* were something real and awful, belongs to the latter.

I write with genuine self-distrust here, in spite of the firmness of my conviction, on account of my wonder not only at Sir William Hamilton's saying what he does, but at Mr Mill's receiving what he says as *he* does. In spite of Mr Mill's admiration of what Sir William Hamilton says here, whether he and Sir William Hamilton really understand each other, is what I cannot make out: Sir William Hamilton says the doctrine which he gives has been held always and by almost all philosophers, and cites, textually and in order, seventeen philosophers to prove this: Mr Mill, judging from Sir William Hamilton's own citations, thinks all but two of the seventeen hold a doctrine different and apparently wrong, the doctrine which I and (it would seem) most people hold. If we consider that what Sir William Hamilton really holds is that which is taught by the fifteen, and understand his text by this comment, then he is, I suppose, on my side against Mr Mill. Nor can I make out from Mr Mill's own description whether his doctrine is really the same as Sir William Hamilton's: the latter says, we are aware of the existence of things, aware that it is incomprehensible, and aware, accidentally, of various qualities about the things: Mr Mill says, as I understand, 'The laws of our knowing faculty are such as to deny us all knowledge of things, except that of their mere existence'. And the unexpected fraternization of such an Ontologist, in Mr Mill's view, as Mr Cousin, whom Mr Mill quotes with approval, might almost make him suspect.

I dwell on this in Mr Mill rather for my own satisfaction, in this way: in order to convince myself that I really do him justice in treating his *phenomenalist* view and logic as really his *true* view, and that it is only his dread of Schelling and Hegel which makes him fly to such a very doubtful auxiliary in *these* points as Sir William Hamilton. He says, shortly afterwards[1],

---

[1] pp. 69, 70, 4th edit.; 83, 84, 2nd edit.

that *qualities* and *attributes* are not real entities, but the result
of the convenience of discourse (what I call *logical*)[1] : and he
describes, no one could do it clearer, the various *sensations* which
are the real *fact* when we use the logical language, such and
such *qualities*. The confusion arises from this : that while,
as clearly as can be, he points to us the two worlds, or two
points of view, to which the expressions 'quality' and 'sensation' belong, he makes the mysterious unknowable which we
have been speaking of a citizen of *both* worlds—a something
underlying *both* sensations and qualities. Sensations may very
likely have something beyond them—*i. e.* they may not be proper
knowledge themselves, but a means towards knowledge : if so,
that which they are the road to is just what we *can* know, and
ought to *try* to know. Qualities again, as a logical expression,
may involve the notion of a subject or substance : but this latter,
then, by the notion of knowledge, is something which we know
when we know the qualities, and only know by knowing them:
knowing it is predicating all its predicates of it : to try to know
it otherwise is like trying to hear a colour. Speculation about
the basis of sensations (if we like to use the language) or
qualities as they are *phenomena*, may be fruitless, but is not
foolish : speculation about the knowledge of the *subject* of
qualities or attributes as distinct from knowledge of the qualities, and the treating it as a grave and real fact that the former
is unknowable, is foolish.

4. The manner in which, in his categories, Mr Mill speaks,
rather reiteratedly, of facts and phenomena being resolvable
into states of consciousness, *after* he had put facts of body and
facts of mind by the side of each other as going together to
make up the universe of things, is another part of the same
bringing in of philosophy when it should not come. The necessity of this reiteration in reference to particular facts, and
as it seems to me, puzzling of things, would have been spared
by the saying in the beginning, as I should do, that the existence of body itself, the universe, anything, is a fact of mind

---

[1] From the fact that the *qualities* are *not* real entities, Mr Mill apparently
draws the conclusion that the substratum (the thing itself, or in its own nature,
supposed unknowable) must be real: from the same fact *I* draw the conclusion,
that it is only a supposition rendered necessary by the supposition of *them*, and
has the same reality, or non-reality, with them.

or mental supposition in the first instance, and of course therefore every developement of it is: then, with this preliminary
supposition made about body and all the facts of it, we might
proceed to categorize and treat them without continually and
puzzlingly repeating this supposition as to particulars. In
reality, Mr Mill's continually saying that facts of body are resolvable into facts of mind is, to my view, a refutation of the
view with which he starts that facts of body and facts of mind
go by the side of each other, as co-phenomena in the universe.

This view of Mr Mill's is of course the view of the ordinary, or, if I may call it, Lockian, psychology, and Mr Mill
cannot help, as, it seems to me, the whole of that does, confusing the philosophical and phenomenalist views together. I
cannot understand such a sentence as the following : " I infer
" that the object is present, because it gives me a certain assem-
" blage or series of sensations[1]". If this means, as I suppose it
must, ' because I feel that *it* gives me the sensations', then I
am aware of its presence before the inference. If it means,
' because, as a fact, it gives me the sensations', then the fact
is not properly described as inference : the phenomenal fact is
the communication (as I call it) between the natural agents
concerned with what we call the object, and our organs, and this
is accompanied with the feeling or fact of consciousness, which
makes us use the language, 'Such and such an object is present'.
No person describes more clearly than Mr Mill the distinction,
as he calls it, between the sensation itself, and the state of
the bodily organs which (as he says) precedes, (as I should say)
accompanies in time, the sensation. The difficulty begins
when he goes on to say, 'and which constitutes the physical
agency by which it is produced', the same language as in the
sentence I quoted, 'the object *gives* sensations'. 'Physical
agency' seems to imply a sort of intermediation of means of
some sort: and what intermediation or means can be conceived
between a physical state of the organ, some mode suppose of
motion, and what we call feeling or consciousness ? Nor does
Mr Mill seem able to keep hold of his own distinction when
he uses such language as " When a stone lies before me, I am
" conscious of certain sensations which I receive from it : but

---

[1] Vol. I. p. 83, 2nd Edit.

" when I say that these sensations come to me from an external
" object which I perceive, the meaning of these words is, that
" receiving the sensations, I intuitively believe that an external
" cause of those sensations exists[1]". In this sentence does 'receive
the sensations' express a part of the consciousness, or express
simply a fact, a second fact besides the fact that 'the stone lies
before me'? If it expresses a part of the consciousness, then I
cannot understand the distinction made between the consciousness of the sensations and also of the reception of them from
the object, in the first part of the sentence, and the intuitive
belief that the object exists, in the last. This is the same as I
said in regard of the last sentence quoted. If the consciousness is simply of the sensation, or feeling, which according to
Mr Mill's distinction it should be, then the stone giving me the
sensations, or my receiving them from it, is simply a matter
of fact, like the stone lying where it does lie, and then there
seems to me the confusion between the two views, which is no
particular fault of Mr Mill, for I conclude it to belong to all
the psychology which he here represents. Instead of describing
a thing in either of two ways in which we might describe it,
we seem to describe it in a manner confused of the two. 'When
a stone lies before me, i. e. corporeal me, filling space in the
universe, it gives me (or I receive from it) certain sensations':
this is my manner of describing the fact that light comes from
it in such a way that my optic nerve and brain are in a particular state, simultaneously with which state I, knowing subject, feel or think, There is a stone. Or we might say, I,
knowing subject, am conscious of something or have a feeling
—a double feeling, viz. of a feeling and a supposed occasion
for it; and this, taken along with my past and my other contemporaneous consciousness, is what I express by saying, I,
corporeal I, see a stone before me in a phenomenal universe,
filling space as I myself do. All that I say is, that we must
take the one view or the other, and that it is mere confusion of
thought to try to blend both, except so far as the phenomenal
one may be absorbed in the conscious. If 'the stone lies
before us', then we are making our supposition already of the
phenomenal world and ourselves as part of it, and anything

---

[1] Vol. I. p. 70. 2nd Edit.

about ourselves which will not come into relation with this
phenomenal world is so much *besides* this view and showing it
incomplete : of this nature is our consciousness as feeling,
which it is right, with Mr Mill, to distinguish from its bodily
accompaniments, but as to which it is otiose and useless to talk
of its being produced by physical agency, for no notion which
we can form of physical agency can make us at all understand
how it can produce what we call 'consciousness' or feeling. If
on the other hand 'we are conscious of certain sensations', then
we begin with the *conscious* side : *I*, then, is the knowing subject : we interpret the sensations into the thought of ourselves
as corporeal or phenomenal, and of the stone, we will say, lying
before us and being seen by us : but on this supposition and
previously to the supposition of the interpretation it is idle to
talk of 'the stone lying before us'. The stone lying before the
knowing subject is like such a phrase as 'external to the mind'
which I commented on before.

  Whatever is wrong in all this Mr Mill shares with a very
large number of others, most of whom have gone *less* far than
he has in drawing attention to the distinction between consciousness and bodily state or phenomenalism.

  To come now to the logic of moral science.

  I do not want to go into any detail on the subject of social
or moral science, on the logic of which Mr Mill has several
chapters, though in reality it is with a view to that that what I
am now writing is written ; namely, in order to test, by comparison with the views of others, the general intellectual or
philosophical spirit in which I should look on moral questions.
But what I have said will be made clearer by a word or two
on these chapters.

  They are full of value. I agree with Mr Mill, that, according
to the title of his third chapter, 'there is, or may be, a science
of human nature' in the manner in which he describes such a
science in that chapter: such a science does exist, more or less,
as a practical science: we do study human actions, and more or
less, accordingly, predict them: this prediction, or even attempt
at prediction, shows that we consider they go upon laws. Such
a science as this may be in some degree, but only in some
degree, brought into relation with phenomenalism, and studied

by phenomenalist logic. Actions are determined by motives, circumstances, and character : this character again is itself largely determined by circumstances: to a certain extent we may consider this to be analogous to the occurrence of natural phenomena according to their laws, and to this extent we may put these facts of mind as co-phenomena in the universe with facts of nature: this extent is not I should think determinable: and under the circumstances of this indetermination, there is an extensive approximate or inexact science of human action, by which we may learn a great deal about it, and to a considerable extent, as I have said, predict it.

But the point where I differ with Mr Mill, and that which makes me say that we must not, as he does, except to a small degree, put facts (so to call them) of mind on a level, as co-phenomena, with facts of nature, is this. We seem, in my view, to have in the above but a small part of what is wanted for moral and social science. Mr Mill speaks[1] of ' the laws of Mind, and the laws of Society', and says, 'it is still a controversy whether they are capable of becoming subjects of science, in the strict sense of the term' : and thinks that ' the principles' (*i.e.* of phenomenalist logic) ' laid down in the preceding books will be useful' to settle such controversy.

No doubt they would, and they would settle it, if we were to allow their application, but that is what, except to the extent described above, I should not be disposed to allow. Take ' the laws of Society', mentioned above : what do we mean by the term ? In my view (I am not now speaking of any religious view we may entertain besides), what we call ' society ' is a creation of man, which then he (that is certain portions of the human race) has been endeavouring during all his collective life upon earth to improve, according to his notions of improvement. The result we call ' civilization'. We have got to form *our* notions of improvement, in order to do our part, in our time, for this work, and it seems to me that the first and great point of a social science is to aid us in forming *these* notions. We may examine the laws, so to call them, upon which society has developed itself (so again to call this): or in other words, we may study what man *has* thought about society, and by what

---

[1] Page 482, 2nd edit.

means man has succeeded in creating the society which he has created: I should be the last person to deny the importance of all this: and we may study these laws, so far as we can study them in that manner, as we study the laws of nature: anthropology like geology.

But before we can *act*, which is the important thing as to society, as Aristotle told us long ago, we must know *what we want*. In social and moral matters, art comes first, science afterwards, and therefore the phenomenal view will not be sufficient for us, in which, as Mr Mill rightly describes in his concluding chapter, science comes first, and art afterwards as an application of it. Suppose we know perfectly how society *has* developed itself, or how, and with what views, man has created and developed it: still, before acting, we want to make up our minds what society *ought to be*. That is, we come here into the region of ideals. We are at the point of view, not of phenomenalism and observation, which has become subordinate, but of consciousness and activity. The laws which *have* developed society *may* in virtue of their having done so, guide us now, for one of two reasons: either because that they *have* been is taken by us for an argument or proof that they *ought* to have been, and were what was meant to be and should be now, in which case full account should be given of the nature of this argument: *or* these laws may guide us because we are not really active and have not really power of choice, though we seem to have—we may say that they will guide us *because* they will guide us. Upon this manner of speaking, which is the *complete* application of phenomenalism to human action, I will say nothing now. No person can really, in moral and social matters, consistently adhere to it. There cannot but be an oscillation of expression between, 'This is what you will do anyhow', and 'This is what you ought to do'. I think the reader will see this in M. Comte: it is never exactly clear whether we are to be positivists (I mean in his earlier philosophical application of the term, not with reference to any later extravagances) because we *ought* to be, or because it is certain we *shall* be, and is what we have come to.

Having said so much about the laws of society, let us now take the laws of mind. A good deal of what Mr Mill says in his chapter with that title I agree with, and will only notice one point of difference, because it is important to illustrate my own view.

In the paragraph[1] which begins 'Whether any other portion of our mental states (besides sensation) are similarly dependent on physical conditions', he appears to me to confuse the views from the point of consciousness, and from that of phenomenalism, in the way which I have frequently alluded to.

What I am unable to see is, that supposing physiology were carried to such an extent that every association (so to call it) between thoughts were proved to be accompanied (as I should call it) by an association between two states of the brain and nerves: that even then 'mental science', in Mr Mill's language, 'would be a mere branch, though the highest and most recondite branch, of the science of physiology'.

I mentioned in the introduction to what I am now writing, that, in my belief, the more genuine and thorough, in a proper way, is our phenomenalism on the one side, the more genuine will be our philosophy on the other. Mental science, as the analysis of consciousness, seems to me to be unaffectable by anything that physiology can possibly discover. Whatever may be proved, from the side of phenomenalism, about what, simultaneously with thought, takes place in the brain, seems to me to have nothing more to do with mental science as the analysis of consciousness than anything which can be proved about what similarly takes place in the eye or hand. I may be wrong, but it appears to me that in all that Mr Mill says here, he is neither true to the distinction which, as we saw a short time since, he rightly draws between feeling and bodily states, nor to his own view, phenomenally I suppose correct, of causation as antecedence. He uses such expressions as 'thoughts being generated through the intervention of material mechanism', and similarly 'produced' and other terms in the same application, as we have seen before, as if they involved the thing generated being in some way of the same nature as the generating—speaks (*e. g.*) of 'derivative uniformities'. If, as he tells us himself, the feeling is something in its nature different from any bodily state, how can anything that is discovered about the bodily state convert

the science of the feeling, such as it is, into a science of the
bodily state, or physiology?

I have alluded to this, because it appears to me that nothing
is more important at the present time than that physiologists
should not attempt by their science to prove what it is not in
its nature to prove, and on the other hand, that much most
unreasonable jealousy of physiology should cease.

But what is of most consequence for my present purpose is
what Mr Mill says in his chapter entitled 'Ethology': on which,
in relation to the laws of mind, I have the same to say as what
I have just said about the laws of society.

Mr Mill says[1], "If we employ the name Psychology for the
" science of the elementary laws of mind, Ethology will serve for
" the subordinate science which determines the kind of character
" produced, in conformity to those general laws, by any set of
" circumstances, physical and moral. According to this definition,
" Ethology is the science which corresponds to the art of Educa-
"tion". It seems to me that either for the science which corresponds to the art of education, or else for that art in such a
manner that the 'science' becomes something in comparison
subordinate, you have got to know something which Mr Mill
takes no notice of here, as he took no notice of the same kind of
thing in reference to society—namely, the kind of character you
want to produce. It is very well to know what circumstances
will produce this and that character, but it is subordinately important, i.e. as something to be applied: what is first to be
discussed is the comparative merits of the characters. That is,
here again we have come to 'ideals': art goes before science.
The consideration of the laws by which character is formed is
something comprised in a wider view from a different point, viz.
the consideration what we ought to do and be, or had better do
and be, and had better try to make others.

Ethology, Mr Mill tells us, is still to be created: and in
describing how it should be studied[2] he apparently considers
that it takes for granted what are the 'qualities in human
beings which are most interesting to us, as facts to be produced, to be avoided, or merely to be understood': and that
what it studies is, 'the origin and sources of these qualities,

---

[1] Page 528, 2nd edit.   [2] Page 534, 2nd edit. ad fin.

in order to consider what circumstances would promote or
prevent them'.   As I said in reference to Mr Mill's science
of society, I yield to none in my estimation of this ethology:
but there seems to me to want a science, so to call it, besides
and above this ethology, to discuss and tell us what *are* the
qualities which are thus interesting.   In fact there needs a
whole science, in my view, to explain the meaning of the word
'interesting,' as it is thus applied.

In his later editions, Mr Mill has added something at the
end to what he had said before on this subject, and has given,
or adopted the name 'Teleology' to represent a science, in effect,
such as I have just described.

This science, in the domain of practice or of life, must be
considered I suppose to correspond to what, for the domain of
thought, Mr Mill frequently (as I have mentioned) alludes to at
the beginning of his book as 'the higher metaphysics', and to
which he refers various problems as to the nature and grounds,
for instance, of belief, which, he says, it does not belong to logic
to touch.

All that I have said amounts to this.   Mr Mill, as belongs
to him to do, limits his own subject, and excludes 'Teleology'
from the Logic of the Moral Sciences as he excludes 'the higher
metaphysics' from the logic of physical science.

This being so, logic, in both cases, stands as a subordinate
science to a higher one: but subordinate, in the two cases, in
very different degrees.   Phenomenalist logic, as I have called
it, will stand for the physical world, in many ways, well by itself,
and one of the reasons why I am writing what I am writing is to
make this more fully appear.   I have endeavoured to show that
Mr Mill introduces into his phenomenalist logic more metaphysics than he need, and puzzles the simplicity of his view of
it with notions from Sir William Hamilton of relativism and an
unknowable substratum.   If the simply phenomenalist view
satisfies any one's intelligence, I have no care to urge him
beyond it.   Religion, as a matter of positive revelation, has
grounds or roots in *that* as well as in philosophical thought,
however I may think that without this latter, it is exceedingly
imperfect.   All that I want is that the phenomenalist should
not conclude *beyond* his phenomenalism from data that belong

to that alone. As, for instance, that he should not be under the delusion that in anatomizing the brain and accurately watching states of nerve he is getting really any nearer to the expressing and explaining in terms of what we often call *matter*—*i. e.* in sufficiently describing by any language of *motion* or chemical change—that which Mr Mill, as we have seen, distinguishes so justly from any bodily state, the feeling, the subjective feeling, which corresponds to the bodily states, so far as it does correspond to them, *really* in quite another world of notions, and which corresponds to phenomenal fact, not as actual or possible co-phenomenon (except to the very small extent which I have described), but as cast and mould, mould and cast, correspond the one to the other. Let the phenomenalist or physiologist either leave this subjective feeling alone, or else take his stand fairly *within* it and look at things from *that* point, in which case, in my view, he will find, not that phenomenalism absorbs it, but that it absorbs phenomenalism. That is, that if we are to say one or the other, there is more reason in saying, that the phenomenal world of chemical elements and mechanical forces, as we suppose it, is an imagination on our part perhaps ungrounded, than that God, freewill, the notion of something which we ought to do and of a purpose to which all action should be directed, are so.

The phenomenalist logic then may, in many ways, stand alone without metaphysics if we are satisfied with physical phenomena and speculation about them, though, as I hope to say shortly more fully, I do not think it is by the use of it, at least as commonly understood, that physical science has made the advance which it has, and I think that the supposed scientific sterility of the pre-Baconian period arose quite as much from want of imaginative enterprize and speculation as from want of observation and experiment—from inability to digest or make anything of known matter of fact as from an attempt to exercise the intellectual digestion without matter of fact for it to act on. That however does not belong to us now, and is rather a matter of the phenomenalist logic itself.

But the logic of the moral sciences, or what Mr Mill considers such, will not at all in the same degree stand alone without Teleology, and the attempt to make it do so is almost certain to be an abuse of it as *logic*—that is, there will be a supposition more or less express and distinct, but always without reason given for it, that *it*, the logic, is to supply us with the *end* as well as the means. This is precisely what I understand as the proceeding of M. Comte, and it seems to me the proceeding, to some degree, of all those who, like Mr Mill, put moral phenomena in the universe simply by the side of physical. Suppose 'sociology', a science of the *logic*, and treated as such by Mr Mill, tells us that it is a fact or law of human history that at a certain stage of civilization man passes through a metaphysical stage in which he talks of the ideal of the good and right, and then passes out of this into another, the positivist, in which he looks at all this as figment—on what principle are *we*, individual men, to infer from this that *we* are therefore to look upon it so? The *logic* of the moral sciences is to guide us in sciences of the fact—what men *do* do—what are the laws by which they *do* act—what they *ought* to do, what we *ought* to think, belongs to the supposed *teleology*. By what right, and on what principle of logic, so to call it, does the *sociology* settle the *teleology*?

This greater importance of the teleology in reference to the moral sciences, above that of the metaphysics in reference to the physical sciences, is what I meant when I said that in the former, art came before science. In another way we may put it thus: the moral world is man's creation: the phenomenal world is not. All the *uses* to which we put our physical knowledge, all our inventions and applications, are a small thing compared with the vast amount of that physical knowledge, and a main reason why they are so large as they are is that we have pursued the physical knowledge to a considerable degree for its own sake, and independent of them—science first, art afterwards. But sociology and ethology (Mr Mill's)—independent of the consideration how far societies and individuals *have been right* in what we find, by these sciences, they do do and have done—are matters of quite a different sort of importance—they will not at all stand in this way as simple sciences of fact, even if we can conceive them so. The truth is, that the conception of them is *not* clear—History and Teleology are mixed in the conception of each science—sciences of this kind are *not* truly analogous to phenomenal and physical science: so far as they are really carried out according to the conception (I speak of course mainly of sociology and of the other only as a supposed parallel of it) they will be a bad mixture of history and speculation, the former rendered inaccurate by the latter, the latter not recognizing its proper position, and trammelled by the former, instead of hand-in-hand with it.

Since adding to his later editions what I have been noticing, Mr Mill has published his 'Utilitarianism.' On this I say just so much, in illustration of the *present* matter, that it seems to me to show how logic, that is, a principle of decision among conflicting claims to truth, is wanted for the *Teleology*, more than for the subordinate science. Without saying here the least whether Mr Mill is right or not in considering 'human happiness' to be the great end or ideal, I look only, and that for a moment, at the principles upon which he considers himself to be justified in saying so. Roughly, these seem to me to be, that with human happiness thus taken morality can be made an inductive science, and that happiness is what men do desire. Suppose both these things to be so, I ask myself, do they establish what Mr Mill wants, that human happiness is that to which men *ought* to direct all their effort, or their highest effort? that it is the *proper* end, the end to be chosen in preference to other conceivable ends? Have we in this a real *Teleology*, or merely the same thing which I have just noticed in M. Comte? Are fact and ideal rightly put together? I do not the least here want to press upon Mr Mill, being quite willing to go on, Can *anybody* make a Teleology, or put fact and ideal properly together? Does not this carry us back to the hopeless discussions of Ethics long, long ago? Perhaps it may: all my point is, that *here* are the real difficulties of Ethics, and that Mr Mill's sociology and ethology will only solve subordinate ones.

CHAPTER X.

DR WHEWELL'S PHILOSOPHY OF SCIENCE.

I COME now to Dr Whewell's series of works, originally constituting in conjunction 'The Philosophy of the Inductive Sciences', which he has since amplified and made into three
works, the 'History of Scientific Ideas', the 'Philosophy of Discovery', and the 'Novum Organon Renovatum'.

As I understand the arrangement, the first of the three
above-mentioned works or portions may be considered as the
philosophy of the History of Science, which history Dr Whewell
had first investigated, and exhibited in detail, as a basis (certainly much the fittest basis) for all speculation about the
advance of the science, or Real Logic.

The last two of the three works may be considered as upon
Scientific Method, the former being a History of such Method,
i.e. of the views which have been entertained about it, and of the
manner in which men actually have proceeded in advancing,
or trying to advance, knowledge : the last being the Philosophy
of *this* History (so to call it) which of course is the exhibition of
the proper method, the Real Logic itself, for which all the rest
is foundation and preparation: the actual 'Novum Organon
Renovatum'.

We have then two histories, or a double Rationale, of Human Thought: the one of Human Thought about the universe,
which is the history of the progress in Science itself: the other
of Human Thought about Real Logic (as I have called it), that
is, about the way in which knowledge ought to be pursued and
advanced.

We each one of us learn, and the human race learns, and
between the two processes there must be some, and may be a
very great, analogy. Real Logic, as I have described it, belongs

to both. So far as there *is* analogy, the history of learning by the race must be that of learning by the individual, 'writ large'; and must aid the understanding of the latter in the same kind of way in which Plato expected (rightly or wrongly) that politics would help the understanding of morals. And the growth of knowledge in the individual, on the other hand, is something conveniently at hand for us continually to notice, and within a compass possible for us to notice: it may, on *its* side, greatly help our understanding of the other. In fact, however, in the manner which I have noticed, this learning by the individual is not a thing of which the rationale has been traced out very accurately; as happens with things near at hand to us, we do not know much about it.

Dr Whewell's starting point is then in many respects the same as that of those Philosophers of the Human Mind, who describe, according as they conceived it, the growth of *individual* thought and experience. As by that practice of the limbs and senses which results in greater sharpness and skill in the use of them, coupled with activity of mind and of reason, we learn individually to see and think of things about us in the manner in which we all of us do, so the race—by that continual use of sense in fresh and fresh observation, which is experience, and the continued *improvement* of sense, so to call it, by the invention of instruments, all *this* also coupled with continual activity of mind, in reasoning, speculating, and discussing— has learnt (as represented by its instructed and scientific intellects) to see and think of things in the way in which it now does, and which we describe as its present stage of knowledge or scientific attainment.

Dr Whewell's book, though not starting like Mr Mill's from the science of Logic, yet starts with what I describe as a more logical point of view. That is, his book is a view, substantially, of change in human thought: not a view, as I have described Mr Mill's to be, of the objective world such as we may be supposed, standing by, to see or know it. The history of the growth of human thought about the universe forms a subject of consideration in some respects analogous to the past history of the universe itself, and to some minds it may be quite as interesting. It is a history not likely to have sug-

gested itself as a special subject of consideration before our
time : and in our time, what has made it do so has been without doubt one science in especial, astronomy. The ideas of
human scientific progress would probably not have been what
they are, or even like what they are, if it had not been for that
science, assumed, with more or less reason, as a type of the
others.

This change of human thought about the universe is a
matter of fact, quite as much as the universe itself is, and it is
a matter of fact which is a more convenient starting point for a
Real Logic than a description (or anything of the nature of
a description) of the universe itself and the facts of it, because
the manner in which we must describe the universe is a varying manner according to this change of thought about it, and it
ought to come *last* in our logic, rather than first.   In spite of
Mr Mill's desire to escape from notions to things, his Real
Logic, it seems to me, is more *notional* than Dr Whewell's.
There seems to me to be in Dr Whewell's book more of what
I might call an *open air* effect, more of contact with living
thoughts of men and with nature and actual fact.   A description of the universe, or what amounts to such, *set before* a
view of the logic of our knowing it, can hardly avoid either
being notional, or else anticipating what should come afterwards,
and, so far as the logic may really act practically, hindering the
growth of knowledge.   Mr Mill's old logic of substances and
attributes, and his newer logic of co-existences and uniformities,
are safe from the latter of these dangers, but still they seem to
me (it may be prejudice) less in harmony with actual phenomenal nature before us, and with the way in which men have
fruitfully and profitably speculated about it, than Dr Whewell's
language and way of speaking.   This is what I should mean
by describing the latter as more real, less notional, than the
former.

The view, such as Dr Whewell has given it, of the growth of
knowledge in the human race, is invaluable, not only in respect
of our understanding this knowledge in the race, and the best
way of our pushing it further, but in respect of the comparison
between the growth of knowledge in the race and in the individual.   I have said on a former occasion, that the growth of

knowledge is a perpetual self-correction as well as a perpetual aggregation or self-enlargement. Seeing little is seeing wrong. If we are to talk of real *stages* in an advance of knowledge, one character by which the reality of any such stage may be known is that it is a mistake in regard of what follows it in the same manner in which it is a truth in regard of what has preceded it: if it is not afterwards itself corrected by being included in a broader view, in the same manner as it has itself corrected by inclusion what has gone before *it*, it is out of the line of advance of knowledge: a deduction or analogical conclusion, but not fruitful: its fruitfulness is in its correctibility.

Our first act of knowledge then is not only a seed or cell in which is contained, seminally or as in a focus of aggregation, all that comes after, not only like a word of a language, what could not exist or be in the mind without the supposition of the existence of the whole which it belongs to, but it is a real, though utterly insufficient, indistinct, even mistaken, look at the entire universe. I am not at all *here*, it is to be observed, speaking the words of Dr Whewell, though I am saying something which it seems to me his view suggests : and I am doubtful whether the bearing of what I have said would be on his side in the question of ' inconceivability ' as a test of falsehood, and of the difference between our knowledge of space, &c. and our other knowledge. I observe these things *now*, in the view of the interest of human knowledge as a *course:* and this interest is doubled, when we compare the course in the individual and the course in the race. It is interesting to think in what respects the learning of the individual to see a distant object, and the learning by the race to see, for so it virtually is, what is the real motion of the heavenly bodies, are and are not in analogy. The one and the other is a continued correction of first (and even of second, third, &c.) impressions by putting them together in conjunction with a continual activity of mind in respect of them : there is in the former all that Dr Whewell calls ' colligation of facts ' and ' induction of conceptions' in a rudimentary state : in these earlier stages with changes of consciousness so rapid that we cannot follow them : whereas each one of the corresponding changes of thought or view in later science may be the work of generations, involving observation heaped upon

observation, and the trying fruitlessly conceptions after conceptions. So far there is first a tolerably complete, and then a
very imperfect, analogy : in what follows there is no analogy at
all : namely, that the first lands us in a normal or habitual
state of thought and view from which all the latter, to whatever extent carried, does not, and does not seem likely to, dis-
lodge us. This is a circumstance which, apparently, depends
upon the relation between the time which we take to learn
anything and the duration of our individual existence. We
learn to say that we *see* the distance between a tree a mile off
and another many times that distance, but I suppose we should
hardly say that we *saw* the sun to be further off from us than
the moon is, though we know this fact as perfectly, and have
learnt it *really* in very much the same manner. In the same
way we never feel, and I suppose never shall feel, that we turn
round the sun or round the centre of the earth, though various
things which we say we do feel or know by sensation come to
our knowledge in really as distinct and intellectual a manner as
these facts do. I mention this analogy and want of analogy
between the course of knowledge in the individual and in the
race, because the comparison between the one and the other
seems to me in its *truth* one of the most important, and in its
error one of the most deceiving and injurious, of comparisons
possible.

I have mentioned that I say very little about the *merit* of
books, one reason for which is, that my view of merit of this
kind is rather my own, and what in the common talk of criticism might not be accepted as praise. In any branch of knowledge which is advancing, a view or a book without something
of incompleteness, and undigestedness, and consequently mistake,
would seem to me as little to be desired as full developed manhood in a growing boy ; and in estimating the value of a book
I look quite as much at the openings which it makes in front
of it for fresh knowledge, which are not unfrequently in the
way of mistake, as at the points which it definitely secures.
And besides this, I have a grounded disbelief in that view of
the nature of the advance of knowledge which is implied by the
Baconian expression 'intellectus sibi permissus', used in a de-
preciating sense. I do not want to have the intellect unshackled

from sloth, and prejudice, and misapplied authority, to be re-
shackled by a perhaps mistaken logic. This makes me look with
less interest upon Real Logic as a means, method, or instrument
of discovery than many would. But it makes me look with *more*
interest upon it as a rationale of what man has actually, from time
to time, thought. I have not the smallest belief in Bacon's having
reformed the methods of discovery (believing rather that if he
had had any success in this way, in the manner he wished, it
would have been most calamitous for science): nor, to the extent
of my knowledge, which is not great,· should I judge with
Dr Whewell that a reform is wanted in this respect now[1]. But
I think that the history of the advance of human thought
about the universe is only inferior in interest and profitable-
ness, if it is that, to the history of the universe itself, and that
the vigorous manner in which Bacon conceived this advance,
as possible when not actual, sets him in the highest *intellectual*,
as much as the earnest manner in which he urged it on sets
him in the highest *moral* rank. What Bacon had to look back
upon was not in many respects satisfactory, and he misconceived
it by making it worse than it was. Dr Whewell looks back
upon a far brighter retrospect, and has the advantage of Bacon
in the absence of such misconception. This advantage and the
tone of mind belonging to it, runs through the book. Dr
Whewell shows us how the human mind *has* acted in the
advance after truth, how its very mistakes have been of advantage to it, and how great men have trodden down the way
which may after them be the more easily followed. Bacon had,

---

[1] "It will be found, I think," says Dr Whewell, "that some of the doctrines now
"most widely prevalent respecting the foundations of truth are of such a kind that a
"Reform is needed. The present age seems, by many indications, to be called upon
"to seek a sounder Philosophy of Knowledge than is now current among us." (*Hist.
of Scientific Ideas*, Vol. I. p. 7.) I suppose this refers to positivist or ultra-phe-
nomenalist doctrines, and if so, I heartily sympathize with Dr Whewell's efforts
against them. But to know *what* philosophy of knowledge, or whether any, is
current among us, seems to me to be a very hard task, and the desire to find it out
is one of the things which has prompted my present employment. What Dr Whewell
assigns as the task of the present age seems to me to be the duty of every age.
To improve the philosophy of our age in the direction which seems to us the right
one is the duty of all who can do it—but to understand it to such a degree as to be
able to judge that it ought to be reformed, seems to me very difficult. How great
is the complication, for instance, of all the controversies with which I am dealing.

whether necessarily or not, the far less enviable task of a con-
demner, critic, corrector.

In my view then of Dr Whewell's book, I consider it a good
Real Logic, because it does exhibit the action of the human mind
in large as the same, in its great features, with its action in small,
and because it recognizes not only as interesting, but as important in the past history of the human race, that varied
experience, that feeling after truth, that approach towards it at
once by way of mental activity and variety of experience of
fact, which is the same way as that in which we gain our simpler
and earlier knowledge.   With full justice done, in this way, to
the value of past imagination and even error, there is no fear
of too shackling or restraining an *art* of logic for the future.

Logic of all kinds, Real Logic included, is likely to be in
some difficulty as to its way of dealing with first principles of
belief or knowledge—that is, whether it shall include within itself
notice of them, or not.   Mr Mill professes *not* to do so—dealing
only with logic of inference: some difficulties, we have seen,
arise from this.   Dr Whewell goes to the bottom—*does* deal
with them[1].

We may view knowledge, as I have said, from the logical or
from the phenomenalist point of view.   The pure phenomenalist
point of view is what, in speaking of Mr Mill, I have called the
supposition of presence with things, or 'adstance', on our part—
in this case notice of our faculties of knowing, or our manner of
thinking, does not enter into the consideration: there is supposed the universe with its facts: it so happens that it is we,
with and by our faculties of knowledge, who know them: but

---

[1] Mr Mill, I think, is rather too free in his references to a supposed 'metaphysics', to which the consideration of certain fundamental difficulties belongs.
That is to say, he does to a certain extent deal with such difficulties, to such
an extent, it seems to me, as to preclude himself from saying with reason that
they belong to a different subject from that which he treats of.   In my view, as I
have mentioned, philosophy is all one subject, and the reference of a difficulty from
one to another supposed branch of it is one of the most tempting subterfuges for
bad philosophers, and with good ones, like Mr Mill and Sir William Hamilton, is
likely to lead to mistake and insufficient consideration.   Of course there is a difficulty in this: no one book can contain everything.   But the reference of things to
a different subject is a shelving them, different from a simple declining, for whatever reason, to enter upon them.   I think Dr Whewell's view faces difficulties more
fully and thoroughly, in this respect, than Mr Mill's.

so far as the view of the universe (or the proper physics) is concerned, it might be a different being with and by different faculties who did so. The facts, not the knowledge of them, make here the important consideration.

The logical point of view is that of correctness of thought. So far as we say 'correctly' of thought about *things*, we must be aware that by 'things' here we only mean a formless non-ego; the thought is not about the really existing things until, or except so far as, it is correct: *i.e.* there must be supposed something distinct from ourselves which we think about, but from this point of view it is no more than an assumed object, or rather subject, in one sense of the word subject, of our thought: we have no business with any supposition as to what it may be, or may not be, in itself: knowledge of it is the thinking rightly about it, or investing it with the attributes which the laws of our thought induce us or compel us to invest it with. Any supposed real essence of *itself* is in this view left out of account exactly in the same manner as any specialty of the faculties of knowledge is left out of account by the phenomenalist.

It will be remembered that, using the word 'sensation' to express the whole of our consciousness, from the most agitating feeling of nervous or concrete pleasure or pain to the merest abstraction of thought, I supposed a scale of this, in which relations such as those of space would concern about the middle. The logical view takes notice *first* of the top or thought end of this scale, and proceeds downwards, considering what it meets with as of less and less intellectual importance, till the lower part will be neglected altogether, or treated as that unreason or nonsense which it is the business of the higher part to convert into knowledgē. And each higher part, as I said, is *form* to what is below it.

The phenomenalist view, so far as it deals with the scale at all, begins with the lower end, as, for it, the most real. It then proceeds upwards, attributing more and more of an empty, non-material, visionary character to what it in succession meets with: till that which the logicalist begins with, that which constitutes what I have called the *thinghood* of things, is with the phenomenalist unnoticed or treated as a delusion. The thing is, with him, a *co-existence* (say), in regard of which any supposition of reason for the co-existence, anything beyond its being a fact, is unmeaning.

In my view, it is a difference in manner of thinking rather than a difference in absolute truth, whether we speak of the whole scale or of any part of it as belonging to ourselves or as belonging to things, as part of the subject, or as the object, of knowledge. Our faculties of knowing and the things which we know are plainly in adaptation, however arising, the one to the other, and I do not see what principles we have to go on in saying what, in the act of knowledge, belongs to the one and what to the other. Except so far as this; I have represented sensation as a *scale:* so far as we speak of subject and object about it, we might represent it by two converging and meeting lines. Subject and object, at the lower or *feeling* end of the scale, are widely separated, there being between them (I mean the subject and object of *intelligence*) matter or body, phenomenalism, which is the vehicle of their communication: our body on the one side, extraneous matter on the other. Higher in the scale they converge, till in thought they meet. Let us say, *e.g.* as Dr Whewell would be inclined to say, that in an organized animal there is plainly indicated purpose or a final cause. Now *here* it seems to me an identical way of speaking, and only different in *words*, whether we say that the purpose is a fact of the organization, or a thought which we with reason have about it. If we disputed whether it was one or the other we should be disputing only about words. Being a *thought* in any case, it is just the same thing whether we consider it embodied in the organization or existing, with reason to exist, in our minds. Lower down in the scale, if we discuss whether whatever it is that we are speaking about is in the subject or in the object, in ourselves or in things, it is more than a question of words, though less than a question of absolute truth ; it is a difference of view. We mean different things, though we might mean either not incorrectly. This I conceive to be the case, for instance, as to space.

If there is to be any meaning of importance in our saying that space is subjective and not objective, an idea or form of thought as distinguished from a fact of objective reality, we must mean that we could conceivably, though not in *our* particular and necessarily spatial conception, think of things in a way other than spatial, or with some form of thought replacing that of space. Unless with some conception or quasi-conception of this kind, the saying that space is subjective, is otiose and resultless. If we separate space as subjective from certain other notions about, or qualities of, the universe which we consider objective, we must mean, if we mean anything, that we could, conceivably, apply our spatial thoughts to another sort of objective universe, and that, similarly, another set of beings, differently constituted from us, might look at our objective universe with other than spatial thoughts. I do not think we are prepared to mean all this. Our knowledge all goes together. The universe is what we, in the correct course of our thought, make for ourselves, if we *so* like to consider it, and again, our knowledge is not knowledge, unless it is knowledge of what actually *is*, independent of us, in the universe.

I have said that the thinking differently of the different portions of the scale of sensation is of cardinal importance : but the dividing them between subject and object I do not think is so : and for the same reason for which I dare not say of any such division that is not true[1], I do say that it is unimportant, namely, because we have nothing to go upon in judging of its correctness. The analogy of the subjective and objective relation with the relation between thought and the sensive organs of our body is not applicable, and will not suggest any division of this kind so far as it is, or rather would not if it were. Our knowledge, subjectively, is different kinds of sensation or consciousness, giving us no idea, or rather precluding idea, of any analogy of parts of it with material organs of sense. And in the case of the sensive organs, what we have, as I have many times said, independent of the correspondent stream of consciousness, which, *to us,* is out of relation—is only contemporaneous

---

[1] I have preserved on purpose the gradual change, or rather perhaps increasing fixedness, of view, presented by these pages, which were not written entirely in the order in which they appear. It will be observed that I speak a little more strongly on this in what will shortly follow. But I think the cause of truth, which is all that I care for, is best served by leaving what I say as I here leave it. The reader may perhaps think I am right here, and have gone, in what follows, too far. If so, perhaps his own thoughts will conduct him afterwards where mine have me.

—with what goes on materially or phenomenally, is the same thing on the one side as on the other. If it could be imagined that at this moment all light ceased to exist and the laws of optics were forgotten, but eyes remained, and, in some mysterious manner, a possibility of anatomizing them : and not only of anatomizing them, but of knowing all their possible movements and affections : I conclude that, were the intellect acute enough, a considerable portion of the laws of optics, the theory of a now absent light, might, from a knowledge of them, be recovered. The constitution of our body involves and implies the existence of light as much as light involves the existence of eyes for the knowledge of it. Just as our body fits the phenomenal universe, so under the important qualification which I mentioned just now (as to the different circumstances of knowledge in the different parts of the scale), does our mind or consciousness the wider or whole objective universe[1]. Knowledge is the link or communication between them : all of it is objective, or all subjective, as we describe it.

The difference between parts of the scale of consciousness is not of this nature, nor is it well described by saying that a part of our knowledge is gained by sensation, a part not. If we mean by sensation something distinct from, and opposed to, thought and idea, *no part* of our knowledge is due to it : if we mean by it something which must be superadded to thought or idea, or must mingle with it and go with it, in respect of each particular of our knowledge which is more than inference or deduction from what we have known before, then *all* such knowledge is due to it.

These matters are difficult to write about, and I have some hesitation in saying to what extent Dr Whewell is right, and to what extent wrong, in his 'Fundamental Antithesis' of knowledge. Knowledge is a relation between two members, commonly called by philosophers the 'subject' and 'object' of it, which relation we may call an antithesis if we like, though we must be careful in doing so. And there are various other terms in use as to knowledge, which will admit of being compared together, and

---

[1] Our thought outflanks (if we may so speak) or comprehends, all phenomenal possibility, which, on the other hand, does not outflank or comprehend it.

exhibited in a form more or less what we may call antithetical. The question as to this is, whether we gain any advantage from so exhibiting them, and considering them various forms of the same antithesis. There is one character which seems to belong to *most* of Dr Whewell's exhibited forms of this antithesis, and which is connected with what I have said of him, *viz.* that his view really proceeds from the logical point of starting : this is, that it is generally on the *objective* side (so just now to call it) that the member of the antithesis is indistinct. That this is the case with the term ' object' itself is not his fault, and belongs to the consideration that the relation of ' subject' to ' object' is a logical relation (by which I mean one in which ' object' is viewed from ' subject', or, in other words, in which ' subject' represents the viewer of the relation) : ' object' therefore is a word of very various signification according to the view which we take of knowledge, and the relation, ' subject' to ' object' is not one antithesis, but many, while one signification of ' object' may well stand quite as much in antithesis with another. In the antitheses, ' thoughts and things', ' ideas and sensations', ' theories and facts', which in certain respects do doubtless represent a single antithesis, it is to be observed that it is the former member which is distinct, the latter which, as standing in opposition to it, is indistinct. The former member of the antithesis in each case is the clearly viewed creating and active power, the latter in each case represents something mentally created, out of whatever material, by the former, and then when thus created, it stands in antithesis to the former, its creator, as material for this to create or produce something more with. This is what I mean by saying that the *latter* member in each antithesis is indistinct as compared with the former. Each latter member involves the former, and not vice versâ.

I do not at all complain of this, because I think that in the main it represents the truth, but what I doubt about is the desirableness of exhibiting it as a distribution of the various things or circumstances which enter into knowledge into two portions, the one supposedly, we will say, subjective, the other objective. I see the supposedly subjective portion, but I do not see the objective. On the objective side I see something as truly subjective as what is on the other side : not indeed so

purely so, but still so much so as that it ought not to be put in
this way in antithesis to the other. It seems to me that the
test of our being able to exhibit the *ideas* or supposedly subjective side of knowledge by themselves and independently is
our being able to do the same by that which stands in contrast
with them. And this we cannot do. A thing, as it is probable
the etymology of the word indicates, and as Dr Whewell himself
most clearly describes, is made what it is, and understood for
what it is, by *thought*—there is no antithesis between thought
and it, but only between thought on the one side and on the
other whatever the thing would be, if it would be anything,
without essence, thinghood or reality. In the same way with a
'sensation', a term used by Dr Whewell, as generally in the last
century, in a very dangerous manner. A sensation as it must
here be understood, so far as it carries with it attention to it
or distinct consciousness of it, has got thought mixed with it
already, as much as 'a thing' has. The only thing which can
be opposed to thought or idea in this respect is the crude blind
undistinguished feeling, so far as we can suppose such, with
the attention to it abstracted[1]. On the subject of the antithesis between 'theory' and 'fact', which is the fruitful and
it seems to me really valuable one of Dr Whewell's antitheses,
he has himself spoken fully, and described how the now-recog-
nized fact is really just and verified theory.

I do not think that we can really separate our knowledge
into its material on the one side and on the other its form or
that which makes it knowledge, or in other words, and invert-
ing the order, into ideas on the one side and something which
is not ideas on the other: except so far as I have said, that
we may consider each higher part in the scale of (my) sensation
(or increasing abstractness) to stand in the relation of 'form' to
the part below. The attempt to divide our knowledge thus, so
far as it has meaning, and it may have a great deal, is really
only a proceeding in the logical method, and studying the manner in which the continual addition of thought to thought produces the growth of knowledge. What thought in the first in-

---

[1] I have so put it, but even this cannot properly be so opposed, but only the
corporeal approximation, contact, communication, which I have several times referred to.

stance is added to or superinduced upon, is something which it
seems to me we cannot in any logical manner (that is, by any
term having anything to do with knowledge) describe, and just
in the same manner as we cannot describe this, I do not think
we can describe the particulars of thought itself as separated from
this, *i. e.* ideas. And I think we are in error if we do attempt
to describe them thus distinct and separate, and consider them
as thus described, the criterion of truth. So far as Dr Whewell
does this, I differ with him, and consider that with his right
view, that advance in knowledge is the growth of correct
thought, he mingles a wrong one, that this correct thought
can be exhibited separately from, and set antithetically against,
the universe of fact : that under the name of 'ideas' it can be
looked upon as something native to our mind in a manner in
which something else, also a part of knowledge, is *not* native ;
and as, in virtue of this nativeness, the proper truth.

What ideas are superinduced upon is, in the first instance,
vague, undistinguished feeling, undeveloped consciousness[1]: and
everything which is superinduced upon this is idea, if *anything*
is. In saying then that we ought not to consider with Locke
that we have an idea of everything we know, but that we have,
for instance, an idea of space, language in no respect wrong to
use, what I should understand would be, that the knowledge
which we have of space is in this respect different from the
knowledge which we have, *e.g.* of heat, that it is much more
abstract and less accompanied with feeling, more of the nature
of thought and *less* requiring comparison or experience, which
is what I have meant by considering it as high on my scale:
but that the one, unless it had thought or attention superinduced on the experienced pleasure or pain, would not be knowledge, and that the other would be at best but a bare possibility
that an idea might arise, if we think *that* anything, till the idea
did arise on the occasion of some movement, for example, or
pressure : and this being so, it is a mere arbitrary difference of
language to say that our knowledge of heat arises in consequence, not on occasion, of the application of a hot iron to the
hand, but that our knowledge of space arises on occasion, not in
consequence, of the conscious movement of our hand from one

[1] See the note in last page.

point to another. Both are sensations, so far as we call our knowledge by the name of sensation: both are facts, so far as we say that it is of facts that we have knowledge.

The best meaning perhaps which can be given to the saying that knowledge higher on my scale is more of the nature of thought than that which is lower, is, that any single experience, so to call it, of the former is endlessly fertile in the region of thought, and a similar experience of the latter very little so.

One single perception of space, and, were our thought in *strength* powerful enough, we need no more experience, and the whole of geometry might be evolved. How far the difference in fertility of an experience *here* and *e.g.* in respect of heat depends upon the constitution of our minds and upon the constitution of *things* respectively, is what, it seems to me, we cannot determine, because the relation of our mind in general and things in general, of subjective and objective, what *absolutely* belongs to the one and what to the other—since they are given to us only in conjunction and no ποῦ στῶ, nothing *besides*, is given to us—is what, as I have many times said, we do not know. It is here that arise the ideas of necessity and contingency[1]. Truth connected in *thought* with other truth we call 'necessary': truth connected with other truth as being matter of similar *feeling*, or experience involving little of thought, we call ' contingent'. We say, it is impossible for us to conceive the former otherwise : the latter we readily may. But the tiro in geometry is as readily able to conceive the angles of a triangle being equal to three right angles as to two, and the pre-Newtonian astronomer was as readily able (I suppose) to conceive the law of the central force, if there were such, being the inverse cube, as the inverse square: the tiro arrives at his after knowledge by way of thought or understood demonstration, the astronomer has arrived at *his* by the way of thought coupled with manifold observation, *i.e.* by induction : the former now cannot possibly conceive that the thing he knows could ever by

---

[1] 'Contingent truths', says Dr Whewell, 'are truths which *it happens* (contingit) are true', (as that a lunar month contains 30 days). This is making the conveying term *too* significant, for Dr Whewell would hardly like the length of the lunar month to be called 'an accident' of the universe, which in this view it might. *Hist. of Scient. Ideas*, Vol. I. p. 25.

any possibility have been otherwise, the latter is most likely in
a *mixed* state of mind, and to the extent to which the truth he
knows depends upon past observation he can see various ways
in which it might have been otherwise, to the extent of which
it depends upon past reasoning and thought he cannot. Necessity, the inconceivability of the contrary, depend upon, and are
an expression for, seen reason. Whether the reason, the necessity, is in our understanding or in the things, is what, so far as
anything which we are now speaking about goes, we cannot tell.

Inconceivability of the contrary is only so far a test of truth,
as, with thought, we can see, more or less distinctly, the *reason*
of the inconceivability.

The mark of the clearness and the firm hold with which
we possess our knowledge is our being able, and our *not* being
able, at the same time, though in different respects, to conceive
the thing (or the truth as to the thing) being different to what
it is. Such truth as we hold in the way of fact is held the
better and the more really for our imagining various ways in
which the fact might be otherwise, for it is its being what it is,
in contradistinction to its being any of these, that is what we
do hold, and the lively hold of the fact itself is really the perception of the distinction. But when in addition to the thing being as
it is, we are able to understand *why* it is as it is, all supposition
that it might have been other than it is is of course excluded.

As the human moral activity, to speak in homely language,
does not know its own mind, but aims at rest with a restlessness
which will not allow of acquiescence in it: so the human intellectual activity does not seem to know what it wants in its
eagerness at once both for reason of things and for ultimate
fact to rest in. Its desire after reason of things will not let it
rest in anything as ultimate fact, at the same time that its
earnest desire for a basis to its reasonings makes it most eager
to suppose such fact.

Mr Mill and Dr Whewell discuss much the value, as a test
of truth, of this 'inconceivability of the contrary'. Mr Mill, whose
notion of knowledge is as I have said the supposition of fact,
and then the supposition of a knowledge of it, holds it, as on
that view he should, as a false or unimportant one. Dr
Whewell, whose view of the advance of knowledge is the sup-

position of the human mind judging about things more and more correctly, thinks, as is natural, the opposite way.

I do not like the applying of the test of inconceivability of the contrary as it is often, perhaps indeed usually, applied, to supposed first principles. Argument in this case is too often only reiteration on the one side, with counter-assertion on the other. These first principles are supposed to be held as *fact*: and as I have said, we really hardly hold a thing as fact at all, clearly and forcibly, unless we make an effort to suppose the thing other than it is: in knowledge of fact, a main part of knowing what a thing is is the knowing what it is not. And can we set any limit to human conceptiveness or imaginativeness? Can we say of anything that no mind of whatever power in this respect can possibly conceive the contrary of it? We may say it cannot *reasonably* conceive the contrary, but then it is not conceivability, but *reasonable* conceivability, in fact reason, which determines the truth.

I am rather straying, but still what I say has some reference to Dr Whewell's book. He is, it seems to me, most eminently right in describing the course of human knowledge to be what I will call a theorizing on facts, and the mental generating, in this way, of new fact to be theorized on. The view does not necessitate the expression of it being in what I have called the logical direction: we might describe it, if we liked, as the proceeding from the looking at or knowing a fact or facts to the looking at or knowing a fact more general: but the advantage of the logical or Dr Whewell's view is the bringing into relief the activity of the mind in the looking at this second more general fact. The facts do not present themselves to the mind in succession, but the new fact comes into knowledge as the result of a very various activity on the mind's part, which Dr Whewell well describes. I think that the description of the process as the superinducing an idea or conception upon the facts and so making them into a unity to be marked by a term is an admirable one; but it is only for the nonce, for this process, that the idea is to be considered as belonging to the mind, the facts to objective nature: the facts belong to the mind, for they are nothing but verified theories: the idea, so far as it is correct, belongs to objective nature, for as soon as we have

verified it and found it answer the facts we shall consider it a
new fact of objective nature, to be itself theorized upon. But
I do not see that there is any reason to join this view with the
other, not necessary to it, that there are certain ideas which we
can enumerate and distinctly exhibit belonging to the mind, as
facts, things, or however we describe them, belong to objective
nature. The two views, instead of holding well together, hold
ill together. Just as right theory is the side turned towards us
of what, turned the other way, is natural fact, so ideas, even the
highest and most abstract, are the side turned towards us of
what equally, turned the other way, exists in the universe as
fact, if we choose rather *so* to look at them and describe them :
were it not so, they would not be true ideas.

A more important antithesis than that between some things
or circumstances as subjective and others as objective, is the
contrast between knowledge as of fact and knowledge by way of
reason. What Dr Whewell says is valuable as it is on account
of its full recognition of this. Each fact involves in itself an
abundance of thought—has an abundance of form : but so far as
it is known *as fact* only, it is isolated: on account of this absence of connexion it might be conceived as being variously
otherwise: we only know as matter of fact (as we call it) that
it is what it is. We want to cease to be able to conceive it as
what might be otherwise, and to this end to bring it into connexion with other facts, to view it as part of a wider fact: we
make a theory, a provisional or supposed fact, which will include it and other facts, and see how far the truth of this is
consistent with the entire truth of the facts. When we can
make the suppositions which want actuality fit with the actuality which wants more of form, order, connexion to be given to
it, we have got really valuable knowledge.

I have said that the attempt to exhibit ideas which are
purely subjective seems to me the same sort of thing as would
be, on the other side, the attempt to exhibit facts, so we will
call them, which were purely objective and unmixed with
thought (if we might call this 'objective'). I will notice now
one way in which the doing the one and the other of these
things would have something of a similar result. The purely
subjective and objective would be with great difficulty brought

into relation with the advance of knowledge. What is the nature of the advance, for instance, in respect of the idea? As the advance goes on, is the mind in a *better* state as to its manner of holding the idea, or in a worse, or in neither, it being, so far as the *idea* is concerned, in the same state, but the advance in knowledge consisting in the advancing perception of the relation of the idea to that which is not idea?

I shall not enter into this, only making an observation or two about it. The state of the mind, as Dr Whewell recognizes, in its advance, is quite *different* as its advance has reference to different ideas among those which Dr Whewell describes. Space, for example, exists clearly in the mind in the first instance, is developed into *geometry*, which is variously, almost endlessly, applicable to phenomena and in aid of observation: but observation adds nothing to it, either in the way of amount or clearness. The case is exactly opposite in reference to the idea of 'polarity': this the mind has no hold of at the first or the slightest suggestion of it: only with far advanced observation it shows itself. In the case of the idea of resemblance, what happens is that it takes, with advance of knowledge, the character of a different idea: the growing *definiteness* attaching to it is an alteration of its nature, this definiteness being, in reality, an increasing perception of law, order, reason, meaning, underlying the resemblance, and substituting itself in the mind for it, making the sciences which Dr Whewell has called 'classificatory' continually less and less so, and more and more what may be loosely called 'physiological'. As the idea of 'resemblance' is thus a temporary one, so the idea of 'a medium' seems to me a mistaken one, mistaken both in a logical and phenomenal point of view, and to disappear for this reason.

The great ideas of 'substance' and of 'cause' are the most difficult. With regard to the former, I should have thought that chemical speculations and researches as to the constitution of matter were not likely to be benefited by a comparison of the object of their search with the very difficult and doubtful notions, in which to disentangle logic from supposed phenomenal truth is scarcely possible, which the philosophical use of the word 'substance' involves'. If it is really an idea, it seems

---

[1] Upon this idea of 'substance', as well as upon that just mentioned, of 'a

to me that the advance of knowledge consists in the entire
transforming it, and gradually substituting a different one.

'Cause' Dr Whewell seems to look at in four manners.
'Efficient cause', which is what is connected with the sciences
of force: 'final cause', which is what is connected with the
sciences of organization: 'historical cause', which is what is
connected with the *ætiological* sciences, or those which concern
the history and origin of things: and what I may call 'physical
cause', the consideration of which is what differences certain
sciences or branches of science (astronomy, *e.g.*) as 'physical',
from certain others relating to the same subject and which
are called 'formal'.

I may observe that 'cause', as looked upon by Mr Mill and
phenomenalists, is a relation of time, and little else, in the
main like the third view above; cause being simply antecedent
with certain considerations indeed about it, in *some* respects
similar to those which belong to the fourth view above. And
I will observe in connexion with this, that the viewing of
things as much as possible in the relation of *time* is what,
substantially, the phenomenalist view amounts to, and it is
because this view of them is felt as a poor and insufficient
view that the phenomenalist view is unsatisfactory. The phenomenalist's knowledge of nature is the knowledge of the *history*
of nature. In that view, our presence or adstance, as I have
called it, is in face of what we are bid to call a series of
changes, without our being able to know what it is that
changes, or *why* the changes take place, in any other sense of
the *why*, than this, what previous change any present change is
the result of. The thought of 'cause', in the fourth view above,
is the asking the question, why the changes take place, in the
hope of an answer other than historical. The asking the question is in reality the theorizing about the change or fact, and
the bringing it, so far as the theorizing succeeds, under a
broader and more general fact: the quest of cause then, in this
fourth view of it, is—as instructed or trained by the advance of
knowledge—the desire of generality and simplicity, the tendency
towards them in our thought, the looking for them, and expec-

medium', I cannot enter into Dr Whewell's View at all. I will append in a future
chapter some remarks upon each of them.

tation of finding them, in nature. The tendency to proceed from formal science to physical is the same as that to proceed from knowledge by way of fact to knowledge of reason, and they are two ways of describing the general 'nisus' towards advance in knowledge.

The view of 'substance', and these various views of 'cause', seem to me attempts (but I do not think any attempt can be successful), to exhibit as distinct subjective ideas, that thought which belongs to the upper part of my scale of knowledge. I most thoroughly believe in or think one thing, which appears to me stateable with equal truth in either of two ways : namely, that there is in the universe, besides chemical constitution, besides solidity, shapes, and forces, something more abstract or as I should call it higher than these, I mean order, law, meaning, principle, purpose, however we may describe it : we are present or look on at this as much as at the other things : our *thought* is as real a sensive power for this purpose as our feeling is for sweetness or bitterness. It appears to me only to represent the same truth if we say from the other side, that we have sensations which we call the tasting and smelling things: that we have sensations again more refined about them, by some named ideas, and which we describe as the handling and measuring things: and again that we have thoughts about them (higher sensations or intuitions) certainly to be called ideas, as namely, that they have substance or real existence, that there is final cause or purpose about them, and many more.

But so far as these things are to be considered as in the universe, they would be by no means the first things that we should find out : and I do not think therefore that we ought to begin science with laying them down, or even attempting to do so. I think that if this came to affect our Real Logic as an art, *i. e.* to influence our action for the future, in attempts to discover, it would be injurious, as Bacon's method of a very different kind would have been injurious. And I think it injures our Real Logic as a science by confusing it.

Dr Whewell proposes his book to us as a Novum Organum for our time. It is, looked at simply as an Organum or guide to scientific thought, not only more suited to our time, but better than the Baconian Organum—I say nothing about the two

works in any other point of view. It seems to me to have far
more truth in it for all and for any time : no wonder perhaps—
there has been not only Bacon, but many others, to learn from.
But in reality it is a new 'Traité de la Méthode'—I mean the
thought of it descends (of its *actual* suggestion I know nothing)
quite as much from the manner of thought of Descartes as from
that of Bacon. This is a vast advantage. Bacon and Descartes
were two contemporary intellectual reformers with exactly opposite views, and the looking at them seems to me of the
greatest value in regard of all our view of such reform : the
general positive recommendations of each were I think in their
different lines equally wanted and have been since equally
valuable : the more particular recommendations, or more special
reform, have been nugatory. The scholastic stagnation of mind,
so far as it existed, wanted a Descartes to shake it up quite as
much as a Bacon. When Bacon urged attention, still attention,
and ever repeated attention, to nature, to fact, to observation, to
experiment, he was most right and useful: but so far as he said,
You must give less attention, in order for this, to books and to
reflection or self-concentrated thought (idle cobwebs of the brain)
he spoke without force or meaning. What was wanted in regard
of books and thought was exactly the same which was wanted in
regard of observation, not at all *less* attention to the one and the
other, but a wiser, better applied, more real attention, which would
really leave abundance of time for the *utmost* amount of observation of nature and fact, and would really *help,* instead of hindering it. In respect of this wiser and better reflection or thought,
Descartes was the apostle of it, as Bacon was of better and more
abundant observation. To complete the trio, there should have
existed at the same time some man doing in a special way what
was being done by many, and was a work quite as important as
either of the others, namely, urging the wiser and more thorough
study of *books,* better criticism : the intellectual revival of that
time was an awaking at once to more close study of nature—to
more accurate and methodical thought—and to better criticism,
and each one of them aided the other. The careful criticism
and study of what Aristotle really said probably aided the advance of science better than the putting him into the fire would
have done, in spite of Bacon's denunciations of him.

Dr Whewell then it seems to me joins with Bacon's view of the important thing about truth being its closeness to fact, Descartes' view of its being clearness and distinctness of thought, and is eminently right in doing so[1]. He has mixed with this what seems to me error, but I think it is *his* view on the whole which is the right and the fruitful one.

Any discussion of the particulars of his Method of Real Logic does not concern my present purpose, which has only reference to his general principles or view.

I shall proceed however in another chapter to enter a little more into detail on some of my points of difference given above, and to examine one or two passages which embody his views.

---

[1] I am not at all aware that Dr Whewell thinks as highly of Descartes as I do, and he does not I think say very much about him. He himself (*Phil. of Discovery*, p. 162), attaches the great reform of scientific method to Bacon, considers that Descartes set himself speculatively in opposition to it, but that still he and his disciples *did* attend very much to experiment and to the known facts, that consequently his physical philosophy (*then* the most important part of natural philosophy) was the best then current, and he came to be considered as the great hero of the overthrow of Aristotle. At the same time the *deductive* character of his philosophy, his rushing to general principles and deducing conclusions from them, his deducing effects from causes rather than causes from effects—this was a wrong side of his doctrine which gave nevertheless to it much of its charm, a 'gratissimus error' to human nature. When one reads this, one asks one's self, what really is the position of the two great controvertists in this matter of our day, Dr Whewell and Mr Mill, as to Bacon and Descartes? They both put forward the name of Bacon, they disagree nevertheless in their view of him, and neither of them really much follow him—do they take from Descartes' manner of thinking, the one his 'clear ideas', the other his 'deduction'? And do they each, more or less, consider that the other is in this 'setting himself in opposition to the reform which science needs'? I give no opinion about this, only observing how very difficult it is to enter into a controversy and see the real hearing of it.

CHAPTER XI.

THE FUNDAMENTAL ANTITHESIS OF PHILOSOPHY.

I SHALL proceed to put Dr Whewell's view and mine in conjunction in this way : by quoting various passages from him which indicate his view, and expressing my agreement with some of them, my difference from others.

At the basis then of all knowledge Dr Whewell considers there is that fundamental antithesis which I have already to a certain degree discussed. It is constant and essential, but without a fixed and permanent line dividing its members : it is variously modifiable, and variously expressible.

The simplest expression of the antithesis is the opposition of 'things' and 'thought'.

Upon these I begin as Dr Whewell ends : he says, after describing the antithesis, as a conclusion to his description, " Thoughts and things are so intimately combined in our know- " ledge, that we do not look upon them as distinct.   One single " act of the mind involves them both, and their contrast dis- " appears in their union.   But though knowledge requires the " union of these two elements, Philosophy requires the separa- " tion of them, in order that the nature and structure of know- " ledge may be seen[1]".   The first two sentences I hold : in the third, I do not accept the description of 'things' and 'thoughts' as 'two elements' of knowledge : and so far as Philosophy sepa- rates them, I hold that it presents us with two *aspects* of know- ledge from different sides, not with two *portions* of it.   It seems to me, that as soon as we begin, in the manner which Dr Whewell here describes, to make the separation he speaks of, his language will no more stand examination than that of Sir William Hamilton and of Mr Mill.

"Things", says Dr Whewell, " are something different from " ourselves and independent of us ; something which is without.

[1] *Hist. of Scientific Ideas*, Vol. I. p. 25.

"us: they are; we see them, touch them, and thus know that
"they exist: but we do not make them by seeing or touching
"them, as we make our thoughts by thinking them: we are
"passive, and *Things* act upon our organs of perception[1]".

Here we have, as before, 'without us' as quasi-synony-
mous with 'different from us' and 'independent of us'. But
what seems to me the case with Dr Whewell is, that the wrong
psychology which we find, carries in a way its antidote with
it: I will show how. 'We see the things, touch them, and thus
know that they exist'. This sentence *I* should put: we see,
touch (so we describe certain sensations), and in so doing know
that things exist, which last clause means, we become aware
of something to which we attribute an existence like our own.
In the wrong psychology the sentence would mean: three
steps, instead of my *one:* first, the things are by us to be
seen: next, we see and touch them: third, we infer from the
seeing and touching that they exist. The first step here is not
strongly marked in Dr Whewell: the transition from the second
to the third seems more strongly so: though still his '*thus*'
('we *thus* know that they exist') need not imply an inference[2].
The next clause of the passage quoted, it appears to me, should
be put with other passages of Dr Whewell, in which he seems to
me to say that we *do* make things the things that they are to
us by *thinking* them, that is, by superinducing 'ideas' upon
what he calls the sensations (the seeing and touching): when
some 'things', *viz.* the rays of light, act upon our organs of
perception, then, by *thinking* (as we make our thoughts), by
superinducing ideas (of space, &c.), we make other 'things', *viz.*
a tree or the sun, and *these* are the things which common
language describes us as 'seeing'.

The antithesis between 'thoughts' and 'things', and the
antithesis between 'theories' and 'facts', are in the main similar,
and are described in very much the same language. And I
speak of *them* in particular, because it seems to me that the

[1] *Ib.* p. 24.
[2] Of course if it does, the inference must be from a maxim, 'what we are to see
and touch exists': implying, previous to the commencement of knowledge, a notion
of existence independent of our own, and a sort of prescience of our seeing and
touching.

'antithesis', so to call it, has really, as Dr Whewell himself
puts it sometimes, much more the character of a contrast (or
counter-respondence) of view than of a separation of elements.
'That which is a Fact under one aspect, is a Theory under
another'. So says Dr Whewell in one place, and so say I,
and the same of 'thought' and 'thing', 'idea' and 'sensation'. 'Theories', again he says, 'become facts by becoming
certain and familiar'. That is, they become facts as we conceive facts: and just in the same manner if we look in the
reverse direction, 'facts' become in our mind true theories or
conceptions.

Speaking of theory, I will just comment for a moment on
a passage of Dr Whewell's, in which he gives a most interesting and fruitful illustration, and falls it seems to me into a
mistake as illustrative and important.

"The scene of nature is a picture without depth of sub-
"stance, no less than the scene of art; and in the one case as
"in the other, it is the mind which, by an act of its own, dis-
"covers that colour and shape denote distance and solidity.
"Most men are unconscious of this perpetual habit of reading
"the language of the external world, and translating as they
"read. The draughtsman, indeed, is compelled, for his purposes,
"to return back in thought from the solid bodies which he has
"inferred, to the shapes of surface which he really sees. He
"knows that there is a mask of theory over the whole face of
"nature, if it be *theory* to infer more than we *see*. But other
"men, unaware of this masquerade, hold it to be a fact that
"they see cubes and spheres, spacious apartments and winding
"avenues. And these things are facts to them, because they
"are unconscious of the mental operation by which they have
"penetrated nature's disguise[2]".

If any one will ponder this passage well, he will see, I
think, how the two things which I condemn, the relativism
and the wrong psychology, go together, and how they render
clear thought impossible.

What is it that we *want* to see, or, if we prefer the expression, which *ought* we to see?

It appears to me that Dr Whewell, in the above passage,

[1] *Hist. of Scientific Ideas*, p. 44.   [2] *Ib.* p. 46.

describes exactly the same proceeding on our part, in the earlier part of the passage as 'the seeing, not the face of nature, but a mask of theory over it', and in the end of the passage as 'the penetrating nature's disguise'. That is, in the same passage, the view of knowledge taken is changed to one exactly the reverse. The draughtsman does not see the cubes and spheres, but the surfaces, and it is *this* sight which is it appears the *real* face of nature: we *do* see the cubes and spheres, and this way of our seeing is described *first* as seeing nature in masquerade, and then as *un*masquerading her. Which is it?

I may be wrong in my understanding of the sentence, and so far as I am right, I say most unfeignedly that my view of the confusion is as of something which it is almost impossible to avoid, so long as the language about sensation and nature is used, which is almost the received language, and no peculiar language of Dr Whewell. I mean such language as 'the shapes of surface which the draughtsman *really sees*', and the language about 'inference', to which however I will return if I can again. And then, supposing the existence of this mask of theory (a most happy expression it seems to me, well understood), what does the mask cover? The face of nature? Nature, or fact, is to me, and I should have thought to Dr Whewell, the mask itself, if we are to call 'mask' what theory presents to us; and what is beneath the mask is not 'the face of nature', but the 'unknowable substratum' of the notionalists, the 'nonsense or contradictory' of Mr Ferrier. The notion of the mask over the face of nature is exactly that which I am sure Dr Whewell does not wish to fall into—it is what I have called 'relativism'. If 'the face of nature' is reality, then the mask over it, which is what theory gives us, is so much deception, and that is what relativism really comes to. Except that even the mask is less deceptive than the relativist's knowledge, for the mask does give us *some* features of what is within. If on the other hand, what theory gives us is real or fact, then, as I said, the mask *is* the face. And in either case, we have nothing to do with 'penetrating nature's disguise'; and this view of knowledge, anyhow out of place here, is not worth much anywhere. If nature does disguise herself, as the relativists believe, she is likely, as they also believe, to do so effectually.

My view then is precisely expressed by the antithesis as it exists between Theories and Facts. "As our knowledge", says Dr Whewell, " becomes more sure and more extensive, we are " constantly transferring to the class of facts, opinions which were " at first regarded as theories[1]". *Fact* is nature or the universe : and fact here, with Dr Whewell, is described as justified or verified opinion, just as I have described it as rightness of thought: the growth of our knowledge is the increase of fact for us by the conversion of opinion into it : I have described fact, or phenomenalism, as a deposit from imagination in this same way.

In my view, the antithesis between thoughts and things is just the same as this between theories and facts. How far they are the same with Dr Whewell, we have seen.

I will quote rather at length Dr Whewell's language on the antithesis as it exists between ' ideas ' and ' sensations '.

"Space, time, number, are not Sensations or Things. They " are something different from, and opposed to Sensations and " Things. We have termed them Ideas. It may be said they " are *Relations* of Things, or of Sensations. But granting this " form of expression, still a *Relation* is not a Thing or a Sensa- " tion; and therefore we must still have another and opposite " element, along with our Sensations. And yet, though we have " thus these two elements in every act of perception, we cannot " designate any portion of the act as absolutely and exclusively " belonging to one of the elements. Perception involves Sen- " sation, along with Ideas of time, space, and the like ; or, if any " one prefers the expression, we may say, Perception involves " Sensations along with the apprehension of Relations. Percep- " tion is Sensation, along with such ideas as make Sensation " into an apprehension of Things or Objects.

"And as Perception of Objects implies Ideas,—as Obser- " vation implies Reasoning;—so, on the other hand, Ideas cannot " exist where sensation has not been[2]".

If we begin, as in the case of the antithesis between things and thoughts, with the latter part of this language, I hold with it, giving my own meaning to ' sensation ' and ' percep- tion', and my own meaning to the calling the object of the

[1] *Ib.* p. 49.   [2] *Ib.* p. 46.

one and that of the other, 'two elements': but this meaning
is such as does not lead me to say that space is not 'a thing',
or that it is not, in another and more proper signification of the
term 'sensation', a 'sensation': nor can I understand the language, that space and time are 'opposed' to sensations or
things, and constitute an element 'opposite' to the other. I
will not say again what I have said as to 'the scale of sensation
or knowledge': I am equally ready (if only we take care *which*
we do) to use the term 'sensation' of all our knowledge, or of
knowledge such as our knowledge of secondary qualities : and
similarly 'perception' of all our just thought suggesting the
presence of phenomena, or of such thought as applied to the
primary qualities, united with sensation in the second signification above : and if any one likes to call knowledge such as that
of the secondary, and such again as that of the primary qualities
(knowledge *i.e.* at different heights on my scale), different elements, I do not quarrel with him. Only that in this view we
have really not two, but *many*, elements of knowledge : and to
me, Dr Whewell's 'Ideas' rise some of them as much above
others as any of them rise above his 'sensations'. This we
shall see better shortly.

What I quarrel with is the supposition of the *two* elements,
with the reason for it, *viz.* that the one is derived from the
mind, the other from things. I have described the extent to
which, in my view, this may be said justly : but as it is given
by Dr Whewell, it seems to me to involve all the wrong psychology which it is my chief business to oppose. 'Sensations' are
defined 'the impressions upon our senses': then these sensations are connected by us in perception according to relations of
space, time, number : these connexions of the sensations contemplated distinct from the things to which they are applied, constitute 'ideas'. The sensations are apprehended by the senses,
then relations of them by an act of the mind : the senses furnish
something, but these relations go beyond what they furnish :
the mind is passive, as well as active; there are objects without
as well as faculties within. The mind is always actively applying
ideas to the objects which it perceives, but at the same time is
passively perceiving them by means of sensations. This is Dr
Whewell's account.

I do not want here the least to be cavilling about language, and for that reason give a variety of sentences of Dr Whewell's, who is here giving nothing which is peculiarly his own, but only describing vividly and interestingly what a great many would agree with him in.   What I want the reader to judge for himself about, not by any one sentence, but by conceiving, as well as he can, the whole view, is this: Are there here *two* processes, or as I say, one? Is the mind's passivity, in so far as it is *receptivity*, or in other words, as there is knowledge, anything other than its activity looked at the other way?   Are objects objects to us any otherwise than as our faculties are exercised upon them?   What is the meaning of 'applying ideas to the objects'? Are the objects objects to us independently of this application? then we know without ideas: and what do the ideas add?   Or, on the other hand, are they not? then the application of the ideas is the knowing: and till they are applied there is no knowledge of any kind.   All I am concerned with is, that there are not two processes, but one described different ways.   And when Dr Whewell speaks of anything 'being apprehended by the senses', is he not doing the very thing which he condemned in the passage which I quoted before, and 'designating a portion of the act of perception as exclusively belonging to one of its elements', *viz.* (his) sensation?

I will not dwell upon this because what is wanted is thought, and not perhaps very easy thought on the part of the reader, and I speak of it in reference to Dr Whewell, because it seems to me, as I have said, that all that he says here is eminently instructive as to our view of knowledge, and that the wrong psychology is not essential, and has got, as I expressed it, its antidote with it.

It is chiefly by the aid of the sense of sight that this distinction between what comes from the mind and what from the thing is made out.   I will not speak of this now, because I should like to speak a little of this sense shortly by itself.

Let the reader only weigh such a sentence as this (it is 'seeing' that is being spoken of): "Who does not know how "much we, by an act of the mind, add to that which our senses "receive?[1]" What 'our senses' means here, I cannot understand.

[1] *Ib.* p. 45.

Is it the optic nerve ? *Then* the act of the mind adds *every-thing*, and we do not *apprehend* by the sense *anything*.   Is it ourselves as sensitive, so that 'what our senses receive' is the change of consciousness which we describe as 'seeing'? Then what needs any act of the mind besides this ? Is it not itself an act of the mind, if so we choose to describe it ?

I have perhaps said enough to make it understood in what manner I consider the antithesis right, and in what wrong. It is *right* in three ways : (1) as presenting the double view, in the way which I mentioned in speaking about theory and fact : (2) as applied through Dr Whewell's book, in bringing out pro-perly the manner in which the mind, in the process of learning or increasing knowledge, is active : and (3) in marking the dif-ferent *kinds* of things which are the objects of our knowledge, though Dr Whewell's view of these kinds is different in some degree from mine.

The antithesis is *wrong* in one way: that it divides a part of knowledge, as belonging to the mind, from a part as not belong-ing to it : whereas all knowledge is right thought, if we look at it *so*, as on the other hand all knowledge is fact exhibiting itself to us or at which we are present, if we look at it *so*.

The second way in which, as I noticed above, the antithesis is important, gives it probably its main value.

"An inductive truth", says Dr Whewell, "is proved like the "guess which answers a riddle, by its agreeing with the facts "described'". This account is incomplete, and is commented upon as such very severely by Mr Mill, because it is possible that various theories might agree with the facts described, and we want one answer, not several, to the riddle of the universe : but the describing the problem as the guessing a riddle puts it more aptly than any description of it as 'fact impressing itself upon us', because the real activity is on our side, and in all history of the process this is the important thing to bring fully out. Dr Whewell's view is I think more likely than many others to save us from that cardinal confusion in the study of the process of knowledge, the considering the things as known before we know them.

1 *Ib.* p. 29.

The mass of observed fact at any time, say upon any particular subject as to which knowledge is progressing, presents a double aspect: in reference to its past, and to the thought which *has* been expended upon it, it is *knowledge* and is orderly: but on the side opposite to this it is not knowledge but only the inform matter of possible future knowledge, and itself chaos or confusion. The idea or right conception is then applied to it: it becomes knowledge and order. The important thing to observe here is, that it is not to this *as to fact* that the idea is applied, *thereby* generating knowledge, but to this as *fact as yet unaccounted for*, and felt as unaccounted for: it is this, the unaccounted for, which is *the matter* of knowledge, and wants the idea or conception to make it knowledge: as fact, it *is* knowledge already, and *is* orderly, having been generated as Dr Whewell has himself described, from theory: this, the unaccounted for, is Mr Ferrier's non-sense, the not-yet sense. Now it is only in this way, it seems to me, that we can form a notion of this inform matter of knowledge, and therefore of what it is which the application of the idea effects. To form a notion of it, we must of course to some degree know it, *i.e.* it must in some way be no longer only matter of knowledge, but knowledge: but we may consider it in another way not yet knowledge, and this is just the state of Dr Whewell's 'fact with the idea as yet unapplied'. It is not therefore that the idea is of any different nature from the fact to which it is applied: it is not that the fact is something generically given *to* the mind, and the idea something generically proceeding *from* the mind: the fact, as known fact, does not want the idea, nor is capable of it: it is the fact in that aspect of it in which it is analogous to what I described the logical subject to be—in its aspect of the unaccounted for and undescribed, conceptible but unconceived, in which aspect it has no character but that of capability of the appropriate conception—in which it is waiting for its idea as the subject waits for its predicate—it is the fact in this aspect of it that wants the idea: and it is in *this* view that Dr Whewell's account of the growth of knowledge is true and valuable. We have epistemology, or the manner in which we make knowledge out of its præ-objectal matter or confusion, exemplified before us in an actual course or progress: and that without even so much of technicalism as I use here, with no cumbrous logical phraseology bringing us into danger of notionalism or mis-realization, but with, when *fact* is what we are concerned with, what I call a genuine and good phenomenalism, that is, a view of nature as our sensive powers actually communicate with it.

Such being the manner in which I look at Dr Whewell's proceeding, of course I set no particular value on his language, as distinguished from other possible language in conjunction with which the same proceeding might go on. This successive application of ideas to the matter of knowledge is a course of thought on our part about the universe, the great and primæval subject of knowledge, the vast unaccounted for and conceptible, but only *one* way, in substance, conceptible—capable only of the *right* account of it and the *appropriate* conception. Dr Whewell's ideas are a set of real categories or great predicates, of which the universe, as such a subject, is susceptible. And all this, as I view it, does not prevent our turning the thing the other way, and looking at these ideas as the great facts of the universe, if we like to begin with supposing the universe what we finally come to find out that it is: *then*, however, *we* are merely *adstant*, present at it, we must not make the incongruous supposition of ourselves thinking and learning about it. But since we *do* think and learn about it, and knowledge grows, and the Rationale of its growth is Real Logic, the best method for Real Logic is that of Dr Whewell, where the activity of our minds is fully taken account of, or *that* is the point of view.

Dr Whewell's ideas are in my view simply knowledge viewed as proceeding from the activity of the mind, in the same way as his *facts* are simply knowledge viewed as coming to the mind, or apparent to it. It seems to me that there is throughout an inconsistency in his language, arising from his mixing the notion (to me *right*) of the mind forming its conceptions and applying them to the facts (in the manner just described), with the notion (to me the *wrong* one) of the mind having *ideas* (the relation of which to the above 'conceptions' is confused) as *its* furniture, in the same way as the universe has *things* for *its* furniture. I accept, as against Mr Mill, M. Comte, and perhaps others, Dr Whewell's view in general of the manner of the growth of knowledge. But I think that the notion of the ideas being the furniture of the mind, so far from being necessary to what is good in the view, is incongruous with it. The whole purpose of distinguishing anything as belonging to the mind from something else as belonging to the universe, is in order that we may be able to contemplate reflectively the former in-dependent of that continuing change of view which progressive experience or growth of knowledge causes in us. But Dr Whewell's ideas have got nothing fixed or stable about them: even the value of space and time, as necessary and original ideas, is destroyed by the association with them of ideas in regard of which we are in no degree certain that we are really in right possession of them : the ideas cannot warrant any truth to us when so many of them want warranting themselves.

For the notion of the generic distinction of the idea from the fact, there needs to be substituted the notion which I gave above, that it is not the fact, quâ fact, which wants the idea as something to complete it, but the fact as unaccounted for. "We see two trees of different kinds : but we cannot know that "they are so, except by applying to them our idea of the resem-"blance and difference which makes kinds[1]". The superinduc-tion of the idea upon the fact as fact is just that same relativism and wrong psychology united which makes us suppose the ex-isting universe first, and then speculate how we know it. We then inevitably get the notion that our knowledge of it alters its existence to us, or is not of its true existence, which is what I call 'relativism'. And between the senses feeling and the mind perceiving we make the notion of knowledge utterly disjointed and confused. This is the wrong psychology. In the sentence above, I cannot possibly understand the meaning of 'seeing two trees of different kinds', and yet having still to know that they are of different kinds, by applying to them the idea of kind. When we first see the trees, how do they seem to us? of the same kind? then what leads us to apply to them the idea which makes us change our mind about them and think them of dif-ferent kinds? Or, on the other hand, do we see them of dif-ferent kinds? then we *do* know their difference already before the idea is applied. Or, again, do we see them of *no* kind? but then we do not see them as trees : they cannot be trees to us

---

[1] *Ib.* p. 32.

without the thought on our part of kind.   What I want to urge
is this : that the idea is not applied to the fact as fact, for, as
such, it is complete already, but to the fact *as idea* (if so for a
moment we may speak, following the analogy of some language
which I have formerly used), or in other words, to the jagged edge
of the fact, to the fact where it is incomplete, suggestive, causing
wonder, stirring imagination, leaving something to be accounted
for.   We see two trees of different kinds : what we want to
know is not that they are of different kinds, for that is what we
see, and it is very likely this difference which makes us notice
them : there wants no fresh idea applying for that : but no doubt
there is something we want to know, and a great deal, *viz.* what
I should call the *meaning* of their being of different kinds, the
reason of what we see : are they both the same thing, what
ought to be called by the same name, or are they not ?   What is
the meaning of their being so like each other, and yet so curiously
different ?   The answer to these questions is the development
of the idea of kind : whether this idea comes from the mind
or whether it is in the thing I do not care to enquire for various
reasons, which I have given.   What is of consequence is, that
there is no seeing *till* there is the idea : and after there is
seeing, the idea is not wanted *for that seeing*, though it is
wanted perhaps abundantly for what that seeing suggests.

What I agree with Dr Whewell in is the following : "Thus
"the Idea is disclosed but not fully revealed, imparted but not
"transfused, by the use we make of it in science.   When we
"have taken from the fountain so much as serves our purpose,
"there still remains behind a deep well of truth, which we have
"not exhausted, and which we may easily believe to be in-
"exhaustible'".   And such an account of space as that which he
gives, where he describes 'the perception of it as by a sixth
'sense[2]' and uses language in which I have entirely followed
him and others : 'we perceive space by motion': and much
besides of most interesting description, leaving me quite at a
loss why space is described, as we saw in another place, as
something *opposite* to sensations.

What I dissent from him in is expressed by such a passage

as the following, surely very different from the description above: "Whether we call the conception of space a Condition "of perception, a Form of perception, or an Idea, or by any "other term, it is something originally inherent in the mind "perceiving, and not in the objects perceived[1]".

The putting together the following two passages[2] from the same page may perhaps exactly express my difference with him. The first: "Ideas regulate the active operations of our "minds, without which our passive sensations do not become "knowledge". The second: "Knowledge involves an active as "well as a passive element; knowledge is not possible without "an act of the mind, regulated by certain laws".

Instead of this last passage, what I should say would be: Knowledge is all- active if we like to call it so, or all passive if we prefer *that* way of expressing ourselves : if we only *knew*, and did not *learn*, it would not matter which way we spoke : as it is the former is the better, because in learning we *must* describe the mind as active, and the description of knowledge as passive only applies to the mind after the knowledge has been gained.

Is Dr Whewell's latter passage here consistent with the former ?

If by 'sensations' in the former passage is meant what I have called 'bodily communication', then the former passage exactly expresses my view. But then the sensations, though they may be necessary for some knowledge, are no part or element of knowledge themselves. The knowledge is all super-induced upon them.

If by 'sensations' is meant consciousness in conjunction with the nervous affection, then it is wrong to say that without the idea superinduced there is not knowledge. This conscious-ness in the sensation is itself knowledge—in fact the idea *is* superinduced — in the sensation as felt is implied *notice*, *i.e.* mental activity—if sensation is more than unfelt bodily communication there is *thought* in it, and this thought is Dr Whewell's 'idea'. There are not two *elements* of know-ledge.

<hr>

[1] *Ib.* p. 94.   [2] *Ib.* p. 69.

Dr Whewell's argument that the idea of space is not from experience, but is inherent in the mind, is of the following character.

"I assert, then, that space is not a notion obtained by "experience. Experience gives us information concerning things "without us: but our apprehending them *as* without us, takes "for granted their existence in space. Experience acquaints us "what are the form, position, magnitude of particular objects: "but that they *have* form, position, magnitude, presupposes that "they are in space. We cannot derive from appearances, by "the way of observation, the habit of representing things to "ourselves as in space; for no single act of observation is "possible any otherwise than by beginning with such a re-"presentation, and conceiving objects as already existing in "space[1]".

What the first three sentences of this passage go to prove is, that the existence of objects in space is a presupposition to any particular experience, on our part, of them. Does this prove in any way that space may not be considered the first, and a general, experience? We cannot apprehend objects without apprehending space. How does this show that the space is more in the mind than the objects are? Dr Whewell's sentence — 'our apprehending things *as* without us, takes for granted their existence in space' — seems to me, naturally taken, to express *my* view rather than his. I say, our apprehending objects, and that in space, and the objects, to our belief, existing, and that in space, are two ways of expressing the same thing. Both objects and space either belong to the mind, or exist independently of the mind, according as we use our language. Space and objects both alike (phenomenalism, as I call the union, though not approving the term 'objects') constitute either the first great general experience, *or* represent a way in which we inevitably think, whichever language we like to use.

Dr Whewell's expression 'the habit of representing things to ourselves as in space', seems to me to suggest happily the truth as between the two parties. He says, You experientialists

[1] *Ib.* p. 239.

must then consider that the representing to ourselves things in space is a habit which we learn by experience, and that cannot be, surely : they say, No, the expression 'habit of representing things to ourselves in space' belongs to *you :* we feel the space as we feel them : it is with us an object, a part of objects, the first object : it is with *you* that spatial representation is a mental habit : with us the expression has no significance : space with us is a part of objects.

I have dwelt upon all this as I have, because I seem quite certain that in what Dr Whewell says about ideas there is a great deal that is true, and because it appears to me that this semi-Kantist or Kantoidic doctrine (of Kantism itself I say nothing) with its almost inevitable results of notionalism and relativism, does not properly belong to the right portion of Dr Whewell's views, however much it may seem inwoven with it. In looking at the 'Scientific Ideas' of which Dr Whewell writes the history, I want to be free to look at them as I please and according to the purpose which I have in view, *either* as, what certainly they are, so far as we can be certain we have fairly got hold of them, the great constituents, features, realities of the universe, *or* as, what is all that we can be certain they are till we have a reasonable confidence that we *have* fairly got hold of them, man's ideas *about* the universe, the results of the activity of his mind as in his history he comes into contact with one portion of the universe after another, and not only examines the things which offer themselves, but puts them into new circumstances for better examination. To me, the ideas are equally interesting in both aspects. To know, so far as we can, the world we live in, is one most glorious aim. To know the history of man's speculations about it, right and wrong, is to me scarcely less interesting.

But the saying, in this respect, that the ideas belong to the mind, and that the universe is something to which the ideas do not belong, seems to me to be a tearing in half what ought to go all together, and to spoil the whole view. When this is done, we can make nothing really of either the ideas or the universe. There is a necessary confusion about the ideas, whether they are something which the mind furnishes, ready to its hand from the beginning, or whether they are something

which we learn and gradually attain to. And so our notion of
the universe must be that confused mis-psychological one which
I have so often spoken of—the universe is before us and we can
describe it, and yet somehow or other we have *yet* got to apply
the ideas and to know it.

And besides, this wrong antithesis between the ideas on
the one side, and on the other the universe, not as confused
matter of knowledge, but as already fact and objects to us, prevents any proper examination of the relation of the ideas to
each other, and of their relative subordination and importance.
Notions most heterogeneous, as 'duty', 'cause', 'space', have to
be put into one category as belonging to the mind as against
what does not belong to it, and *this* antithesis is looked at as
so important that we are in danger of losing the proper notion
of the relations among the things thus put together.

On Dr Whewell's book I have perhaps said enough. Space in
my view is something higher, more mental, than oxygen or car-
bon, time than space, cause and kind than time, and in this way
there may be a continued succession, and a continued succession
of antitheses: the mind may go on supplying higher and higher
ideas; the universe, or fact, is not anything which receives the
idea, but is that which the idea constitutes before us. And
this is the same process as that which may be described as
man's finding the ideas in the universe: the history of the ideas
is alike the history of man's mental construction of the universe
which his mind lives in, and of his analysis, ever evolving higher
and worthier features, of the universe which he finds himself
bodily in.

CHAPTER XII.

THE INTERPRETATION OF NATURE.

On the famous metaphor of knowledge being the interpretation of nature, of which Dr Whewell speaks—and warms in the speaking of it to the consideration of it as something more than a metaphor[1]—I will say a few words: for this reason, that I think the metaphor *rightly* employed is a most instructive means of illustrating the wrong psychology, and wrongly used it is a very great support of relativism.

Let us suppose that I, ignorant of Sanscrit, purchase a Sanscrit book, without the slightest knowledge of its title or subject. It has been the property of other people before me, and they, or some of them, know that it is an account of the campaign of Alexander in India: but this knowledge of theirs is nothing to me.

The reason why the consideration of this is important in respect of the wrong psychology, is the following: (1) that it gives us a good illustration of what is the meaning of the matter, or inform (unformed) matter, of knowledge, out of which we, by activity of the mind (superinducing *form*, if we like so to speak), make knowledge in perception: (which matter of knowledge Dr Whewell erroneously supposes to be things known already to a certain extent by a kind of inferior knowledge or sensation): and (2) that it is likely to show us the wrongness of the mis-psychological supposition of the independence, first, of the things perceived, and of our then, as such, perceiving them.

A stone lies before me: I see it. This is very well to de-

[1] *Hist. Scient. Ideas*, Vol. I. p. 42.

scribe what we each of us do *now:* we know our Sanscrit: but if this manner of expression be used, as we shall find it continually used, in speaking of the manner of our coming to see things, or in giving a history of vision, it is just as if in relation to the book which I spoke of it should be said of me, He has got the history of Alexander's campaign before him: he reads it. He has really got before him a bewildering chaos of lines and characters, out of which, as he learns, he makes out, or in which, if we prefer the expression, he gradually comes to perceive, what he then calls, or finds out to be what others call, a history of the campaign of Alexander. This is the manner in which we perceive or know anything, whether rudimentary or advanced: whether the supposed stone lying before us, or the mighty fact equally lying before us, of the earth's revolution round the sun. And the illustration from language is useful, because it is only by means of an illustration that the truth on the subject can come home to us. We cannot *unsee* the prospect before us. Dr Whewell has well described, in a passage which I lately quoted, how the draughtsman (as *I* will express it) *unsees* to a certain extent, *i. e.* by effort divests himself of certain habitual ways of vision or inference from vision: but we have got to unsee and unknow much further back-than this, if we are in any way to attempt imaginatively to *reconstruct* our knowledge. The inform matter of knowledge of course cannot be conceived or imagined *as* inform, because the conception or imagination is so far giving it form, or making it actual knowledge: but we must remember that when we speak of the activity of the mind exerting itself in such a manner that there arises knowledge, it is upon *this* that we must suppose it exerting itself, or upon something in so far as it has *this* character, not upon something which *has* its form and character, so as to be known, already.

In the book, that which lies before me, independent of my understanding it, is a chaos of shapes and lines: that which lies before me, and I understand (supposing I understand it), is the history of Alexander's campaign. Our language, in our speaking of the universe and of our advancing knowledge of it, should follow this analogy. What lies before us men in the universe, independent of our or anybody's perceiving, who is there that shall say? is there any meaning in saying that *any-thing* does? What lies before us, *and we perceive*, is the universe, or what we call the universe, in all its particulars.

But let it be observed (and the illustration is equally good for the showing us this), what we want to know, what is the real thing to be known, is what *we do come* to know, or advance more and more towards knowing: this inform matter of know-ledge is not the thing in itself, or anything deserving the name of a substratum : knowing is superinducing form upon, *i. e.* thinking rightly about, this matter of knowledge, and it is merely in-congruous to lament or to feel humbled because it cannot be known otherwise than by being thought rightly about. The characters are our road to the knowledge of the contents of the book. The notion of the thing in itself and the unknowable substratum seems to me to be as if, in the case of the book, instead of learning Sanscrit, I should occupy myself in thinking what the characters are independent of their being Sanscrit or a language. No knowledge lies that road.

And on the other hand, as the inform matter of knowledge is no *thing in itself*, so neither is the real thing in itself, the true object of knowledge (in this case the history of Alexander's campaign), something that the characters *hide* from us, but something which they guide us to. The coming to understand *them* is the coming to understand what is in them or what they contain—different as the knowledge of *them* is from the know-ledge of this latter, the attaining to the one of these things is the attaining to the other.

This same fruitful metaphor may illustrate (for we must remember that it is all but illustration) something more about relativism. Using language similar to that of Sir William Hamilton on which I some time ago commented, we might say that there is a double relativeness in the knowledge which we have from the book of Alexander's campaign (the thing in itself or real existence): we know not it, but only a modification of it, *viz.* the knowledge or opinion which the writer of the book had of it: and we know *this* only through our knowledge of the Sanscrit language, as we know what we know only through our own special faculties.

Now of course there might exist an account of Alexander's

campaign in Greek written by a different person from the writer of my account of it, and another person might know *that*. He and I should then know Alexander's campaign differently, that is, should have, to a certain extent, different opinions about it. And what I want observed is, that there is no meaning in describing this state of things (and the parallel is exact with Sir William Hamilton's language) as our having two different relative knowledges of the history of the campaign, as our not knowing the history *itself* of the campaign, but only a modification of it—of course this is so, but it is simply because the knowledge is incomplete; and so far as we *do* know or as there is knowledge, what we do know *is* the history itself of the campaign, and nothing else. In the one case the one language and the one author's view, in the other case the other language and the other author's view, are successive stages on the road to *some* knowledge of the actual history, and we pass by them to this. The deceptiveness of the relativist view is in this, that it suggests that there is one sort of knowledge proper for people to whom *one* modification of existence is turned and who have *one* set of faculties, and another for another. But these, as the illustration illustrates to us, are only stages towards the attainment of the knowledge which is beyond them, which, so far as it is knowledge, is necessarily the same for all, and is unrelative.

CHAPTER XIII.

SUBSTANCE AND MEDIUM.

THE ideas which Dr Whewell gives seem to go each of them through a very different history. Some are seen with tolerable distinctness almost from the first: some are for a long time without there being any suspicion or glimpse of them: and some are at the first most vaguely apprehended or most strangely misapprehended.

The supposition that in *them* is the element of certainty or trustworthiness in our knowledge seems to have arisen from observation of the first of these three kinds, to which belong space and time, the foundations of geometry and arithmetic: and to apply this supposition to the other kinds, seems extraordinarily difficult.

As 'polarity' belongs to the second kind, so I suppose 'substance' does to the third.

Ideas of this third sort appear to pass through three stages, not at all like to, but still something in the manner of, M. Comte's three stages of thought. First a stage of most wild vagueness: second, perhaps, one of logical or philosophical consideration or rendering: third, the clear and developed stage.

Whether or not 'resemblance' goes through these three stages, I think Dr Whewell's 'substance' does.

So far as the first of these stages is of interest and importance, it can only be so in a very wide and general consideration of it, such as with reference, for instance, to the constitution of the universe or of matter, is contained in various portions of Dr Whewell's book. The history of early human speculation about anything is most interesting. But it can go very little way towards helping us to the right idea or portion of truth which such very vague speculations may contain.

And what Dr Whewell says about such early speculation
at the beginning of his chapter on the idea of 'substance' I
cannot enter into at all. It is exceedingly likely that in the
minds of some philosophers the 'gigni e nilo nil'—that nothing
can be produced of nothing—and views similar to it, may have
represented early speculations about the constitution of matter
which chemical investigation will now justify: but surely it is
not right to speak of any notion of this kind, in one and a consistent sense, as 'current as an axiom among the early philosophers of Greece', and to call it 'a steady keeping hold of the
Idea of substance'. There is not anything which can be called
either currency or tangible idea.

And so far as there is, it is surely something entirely different from the *logical* notion of the idea of substance to which
Dr Whewell then proceeds. The principle that 'nothing can
be produced from nothing' of the material philosophers, and
the maxim of the logical philosophers, that every property must
be a property of something, or must inhere in a subject or substance, seem to me to have nothing at all in common: and the
fact that they may be, and perhaps often have been, brought
into relation, appears to me to show that what we are dealing
with here is simply the history of human speculation, full of
interest, but full of error, and that it is not to this history that
we must look in our search for 'idea' as 'certainty' and what
we can rest in.

I have commented on Mr Mill's notion of substratum or
substance. That of Dr Whewell here should be, in the view
of both of them, worse, as it is decidedly more 'ontological',
and with both of them 'ontology' appears a term of reproach[1].

_____

[1] Mr Mill's horror of Ontology we have formerly seen—for Dr Whewell's I
refer to such passages as his character of Sir William Hamilton (*Hist. Scient. Ideas*,
Vol. II. p. 37). "This writer is a man of unquestionable acuteness and very exten-
"sive reading: but his acuteness shows itself in barren Ontological distinctions
"which appear to me to be of the same character as the speculations of the eminent
"schoolmen of the most sterile periods of the dark ages. That he should have no
"conception of progressive or inductive science is not wonderful, when we recollect
"that he holds, as an important part of his philosophy, that the study of mathematics
"perverts and obscures the mind." I quote this passage just to show how 'ontological' is used as a stone to fling at a dog, and in order to mention, that I think
Sir William Hamilton's error, really, is the making too much of logic and the occa-

"An apple," says Dr Whewell, "which is red, and round, and
"hard, is not merely redness, and roundness, and hardness :
"these circumstances may all alter while the apple remains the
"same apple. Behind or under the appearances which we see,
"we conceive something of which we think : or to use the
"metaphor which obtained currency among the ancient philo-
"sophers, the attributes and qualities which we observe are
"supported by and inherent in something : and this something
"is called a *substratum* or *substance*—that which stands beneath
"the apparent qualities and supports them[1]". And further on :
"The supposition of the existence of substance is so far from
"being uncertain, that it carries with it irresistible conviction,
"and substance is necessarily conceived as something which
"cannot be produced or destroyed[2]". If this is not 'ontology'
I do not know what is : not that its being ontology is any
reproach in my eyes, but its being, as I conceive it to be,
wrong.

The conviction which attaches to the supposition of the
existence of substances is in Dr Whewell's view of a double
nature : (1) "The Axiom of the Indestructibility of Substance
"(the principle mentioned a short time since, that nothing can
"be produced out of nothing) proves the existence of the Idea
"of Substance, just as the axioms of geometry and arithmetic
"prove the existence of the ideas of space and number[3]".
And (2), "We unavoidably assume that the qualities and pro-
"perties which we observe are properties of *things :*—that the
"adjective implies a substantive :—that there is, besides the
"external characters of things, something *of which* they are the
"characters[4]".

sional misapplication of it, in the same way as may be readily done, and as I
think Dr Whewell in a slight degrees does, with mathematics. I offer no apology
for Sir William Hamilton's illiberal depreciation of mathematics. But progressive
or inductive science is no more connected with mathematics than it is with logic.
Both are alike useful in their place, and both may be pursued into vain sterilities
or misapplied. The best thing for both of them is to be earnestly enlisted in aid of
progressive science. Dr Whewell has worked hard so to enlist mathematics—but
I think Sir William Hamilton endeavoured to do the same with logic—perhaps not
with equal success. Nor am I satisfied that the Scholastic speculations were altogether so sterile.

[1] *Hist. Scient. Ideas*, Vol. II. p. 30.
[2] *Ib.* p. 32.   [3] *Ib.* p. 31.   [4] *Ib.* p. 30.

It seems to me, that Dr Whewell's view of substance is 'ontology', while that of Mr Mill and I suppose of Sir William Hamilton is what I call 'notionalism': and I allude to this, to illustrate the difference between these : the ontology in my view is the better of the two. With Dr Whewell, the 'sub_stance' of the apple is something behind and under the appearances or apparent qualities which we see, and is also something as to which we necessarily conceive that it cannot be produced or destroyed. With Mr Mill, as I understand, the substance of the apple would be an unknown and unknowable substratum of its qualities.

The former of these notions seems to me exactly the same as that of the scholastic philosophers who conceived that a thing might be transsubstantiated, or have its substance changed, without any change in its apparent qualities : I call it, as distinct from the other, 'ontology', because this substance is conceived as the proper *matter*, as first matter as yet undrest, and if we do not know it, there seems no reason in the nature of things why we should not. I call the other 'notionalism', because it depends solely upon the realizing, in my view quite *mis*-realizing, of logical terms. Dr Whewell's view it will be seen depends *partly* on this, but incorporates with it the view of the substance being the real matter, that of which all things consist, which can neither be added to nor diminished : putting together, it seems to me, two things quite incongruous, but giving a kind of reality to the idea of substance, due to this latter incorporated view. For if we do like to call the ultimate element or elements of reality in the universe, so far as we can discover or imagine them, '*substance*', *this* notion is important and may be most fertile : material substance, as a physical notion, is well enough.

But from every possible point of view, the notion of *this* substance being the same with substance as the support of qualities is a confusion, as I presume was seen by the better of the schoolmen :—the substance of a body which supports its qualities is not its substantial *matter* at least by itself, but its substantial *form*. So far as we are not afraid of ontology, the substantial matter of a thing and its substantial form may together be conceived to constitute its reality : what is really meant by this is, as

I should express it and already have expressed it, that 'a thing' consists of various features, characters, or qualities if we like to use the word in our own way, which form a scale from abstractness to concreteness, and that the characters of a thing which are in the higher part of the scale which communicate more specially with the *intellect* may be called its form, while those in the lower part which communicate with the nerves of the body may be called its matter. But to put in the case of the apple the substantial matter, or material substance, as the support of qualities, is as I have said confusion on *every* view.

Setting aside *this* confusion, the difficulty or confusion as to the notion of substance or substratum of any kind has to do with our old enemy, the division of truth or reality between the thing and the mind. "Behind or under the appearances (of the "apple) that we see", says Dr Whewell, "we conceive some-"thing of which we think". This is the same thing we have seen so often before, two views put together which will not go together, while either by itself represents the fact. "Behind "the appearances (which are what we describe ourselves as "*seeing*), *there is* something of which *we think*". That is one view. *Or*, we *see* something, and this we describe as appearance or sensible quality: but we *conceive* something as behind this, and *this* we call—what we will; 'substance', 'form', 'idea'. That is the other view. But '*we conceive* something of which *we think*' is not significant. We may say, We conceive something, with a belief which we call belief in its existence: then there it is for us: *that*, so far as we are concerned, is its ultimate being. Or, from the other side; there is something, and it so happens that this something presents itself to our thought: its thus presenting itself is what we mean by saying that we think of it or conceive it: and this, so far as *it* is concerned, is the meaning of its being known.

The most *formal* part of the reality of a thing *may be* what we know *first* about it, or may be what we know *last*, or may be what we in fact cannot come at at all: *that* is matter of accident. To take a plough, as something familiar and at hand: the *thinghood* of that, that is, the reason of there being such a notion in men's heads and such a word in the dictionary, lies mainly in the *purpose of* it, *viz.* to turn up the ground in a particular (say sideways) manner. This 'idea', 'form', 'substance', of a plough is what we in England commonly come to know *first* about it: we are told, *there* is something used to turn up the ground, and it is called a plough: we have got the substance or idea to make our logical subject of, and we add according to circumstances the qualities or predicates—that is woodenness, redness, going upon wheels, or as the case may be. Supposing a plough abandoned in Australia, and found by savages who wonder at it much: they will clearly call it something, that is, it will be a subject with them for predicates, but probably they will never find out what it was meant for or what work it will do: they will then reason, I suppose, about it much as we do about the universe: they will say that the name which they give it represents something mysterious and unknowable, beyond the reach of human faculties: or they might with more truth, though more ontology, get *towards* the mystery by considering, perhaps not indeed that if instead of being wooden, and red, and on wheels, it was iron, and blue, and without wheels, it would be *the same* plough with one which they had seen of the former character (as the apple might be the same apple[1]), but that it might be *a* plough or that there was something about it the same, and in that case they would have the notion of the *genus* plough (or whatever they called it), which would be *some way* towards the meaning or purpose of it.

I will now speak about Dr Whewell's idea of a *medium*, the idea which belongs to the *secondary mechanical* sciences, as Optics and Acoustics.

What I have said about 'sensation' is, that it involves two facts; one, a corporeal communication with some part of the universe; the other, a feeling or unit of consciousness contemporaneous with this.

This *communication*, thus widely meant, is of course a vague term, and in my use it represents a relation of one part of our body to another, and of parts of our body with space, as well as a relation of certain nerves of our body or certain sensorially nervous surfaces with some independent material substance whose contact with them is accompanied with a feeling.

---

[1] Dr Whewell has judiciously chosen very fugitive and superficial qualities of the apple for his substance to underlie.

I have said that for good phenomenalism or physical science what is wanted is as much as possible to put ourselves and our manner of perceiving out of consideration. The physical world is what it is, and it is of the nature of an accident of it that it is known by us through the instrumentality by which we *do* know it.

But there are certain physical sciences, in respect of which this seems at first impossible. We seem obliged, in regard of the physical science of light, or optics, to have more or less of that confusion caused by considering the subject and object, or the two sides in the relation of knowledge, independent of each other, and yet modified the one by the other, which is what I have tried as much as possible, in the more *general* view of knowledge, to prevent.

The contact between certain sensorially nervous surfaces of our body and certain material substances, as between the retina and light, the ear and vibrating air, the nostrils or palate and that chemical efflux, or whatever it may be, from bodies, which we describe as their smell and taste, is described by Dr Whewell as 'perception through a medium'. It will be readily understood, from what I have said, that I do not consider this a good description. There is actual contact in each case between the material substances and the nerves, and in taste or smell the feeling or consciousness accompanying this is of a very simple nature. In the eye, on the other hand, besides the contact between the light and the retina, there is a most complicated process, and the accompanying sensation is most complicated, and is described by us as the perceiving of a perhaps distant object: but the describing this as the perceiving through a medium is a mixture of logic or philosophy on the one side, with physics or phenomenalism on the other, of the kind which I have endeavoured to condemn and to prevent.

The idea therefore of a medium does not seem to me in any respect a scientific one, nor do I see how it can be in any way even developed into truth.

I have said that Dr Whewell's parallel consideration of the growth of knowledge in the individual and its growth in the race seems to me interesting and fruitful. *Here* however, I should think it misleads. I speak with diffidence as to physical science,

but I should question whether the distinction between primary
and secondary qualities, which is a matter *of our sensation*, not of
nature considered independently of it, furnished a good principle
of classification or arrangement of the latter. The difference between primary and secondary qualities of matter, or as we might
with equal correctness say, primary or secondary sensation on our
part, is very mainly in this, that the secondary qualities, looked
at in their relation to the physical world, have as compared with
the primary, something of an accidental character. To use a word
which a short time since, I quoted from Dr Whewell: putting
all religious considerations for a moment aside: I look upon it as
a thing which only in the very minutest degree possible can be
said *to happen to be so*, that the universe has the qualities which
it has, or that, correspondingly, the reason or mind of reasonable
beings acts as *it* does. Coming then to particular qualities:
the first portion of the above sentence is still true: it is not a
thing that (with more than very slight significance of the word)
happens to be so that space exists : but with *more* significance,
though still not with much, it might be said to be a thing which
happens to be so that we *men* perceive it, for we just *might*
have been passive only, without power or notion of movement :
and in the same way we may perhaps say, there just might be
other primary qualities of the universe which we are not constituted in such a manner as to be aware of. In the same manner
it is not at all a thing *that happens to be so* only that there is
this or that secondary quality (as we call them) in the universe :
each one of them belongs to the universe as much as space does :
but it is a thing which in a very eminent degree *happens to be so*
that we men, or as we might rather say, we terrestrial animals,
we the terrestrial zoöcosm altogether, are with more or less
of directness aware or percipient of this or that secondary quality.
In order for this percipience, or sentience, we require, it would
appear, to have particular material nerves with very special
susceptibilities, and an organism, perhaps a most complicated
instrument, for bringing about the contact between the material
substance and the nerve. This our special sensive organization
may be called an *accident* of the universe with a much higher
degree of significance of the word than if we called the existence
of oxygen, or air, or light, or heat, an accident of it : and the

more so, since we are aware indirectly of various circumstances or qualities in the universe, such as magnetism, for which we might conceivably have had a special sensive organization, an eye or ear, so as to perceive them *directly* as secondary qualities.

Physical or phenomenalist knowledge, as I have said, should involve the notion of knowledge as *adstance*, that is, it should be independent of the manner, as regards the lower and more concrete circumstances of knowledge, in which it was known : as regards the higher or more abstract, it *could* not be so, and this belongs to its being, as I have all along called it, an *abstraction*, that is, a notion which cannot be carried thoroughly out. In other words, our physical science should be true so far as it had or would have any significance, not for beings with other *minds* than ours, nor for beings without *limbs* which they could move (this would be impossible), but for beings with a different *set of senses* from ours, so far as this is conceivable under the above conditions. Our physical science should be such, that if we lost as a race one of our present senses, and all the mental circumstances associated with it, yet the secondary quality which it took cognizance of should be still more or less indirectly indicated to us: and similarly that if we had a new special nerve and sensive power for some secondary quality now only indirectly known by us to exist, our present knowledge should be absorbed indeed but should still be confirmed and hold true so far as it went.

These principles are difficult perhaps to understand, and certainly to apply, but I think they hold good at least to this extent, that the scheme for arranging physical science should not be made to depend upon our manners of perception. I do not as it is quite understand Dr Whewell's arrangement as he does make it thus to depend : how for instance his secondary mechanical sciences, or sciences associated with secondary qualities, separate themselves definitely from the mechanics of fluids, &c. on the one side, and from the chemistry of heat, &c. on the other : and there seems no science at all, nor place for one, corresponding to his 'media' in the case of taste and smell[1].

[1] Of course I am not condemning the use of the term 'medium' for what is between our eye and the thing we say we see (and the same for other senses) if we like to use the term—but on sight, or rather on the use of language in respect of the sense of sight, I should like to say a little in the next part.

Optics and Acoustics, the latter specially (both of which I speak of very diffidently) do cause I presume some difficulty. But I suppose that the general physical science of light and the physiology of vision may be kept separate: when the former is known, all in the eye that is in front of the retina is simply a self-adjusting optical instrument: the laws of the self-adjustment, and the circumstances of the retina, belong to · the physiology of vision ; not to Optics as *photology*. As to Acoustics, such science in it as is separable from the Physiology of Hearing is I suppose of the very delicate vibrations of a fluid: the fact of these vibrations we discover by *other* means than hearing, in fact could not discover them by *that*, any more than we can *now* discover by *looking* or sight whether light is undulation or rectilinear motion: as to Acoustics therefore, what we have besides the Physiology of Hearing is a science which *I suppose* is a branch of the mechanics of fluids, and which is independent of the aerial vibration coming into contact with our ears, though suggested by its doing so.

I will finish by quoting a long passage from Dr Whewell.

It is as follows: "Though the fundamental principles of " several sciences depend upon the assumption of a Medium " of Perception, these principles do not at all depend upon " any special view of the Process of our perceptions. The " mechanism of that process is a curious subject of considera- " tion ; but it belongs to physiology, more properly than either " to metaphysics, or to those branches of physics of which we " are now speaking. The general nature of the process is the " same for all the senses. The object affects the appropriate " intermedium ; the medium, through the proper organ, the " eye, the ear, the nose, affects the nerves of the particular " sense ; and, by these, in some way, the sensation is conveyed " to the mind. But to treat the *impression* upon the nerves " as the *act* of sensation which we have to consider, would be " to mistake our object, which is not the constitution of the " human body, but of the human mind. It would be to mis- " take one link of the chain for the power which holds the end " of the chain. No anatomical analysis of the corporeal con- " ditions of vision, or hearing, or feeling warm, is necessary to " the sciences of Optics, or Acoustics, or Thermotics.

"Not only is this physiological research an extraneous part
" of our subject, but a partial pursuit of such a research may
" mislead the inquirer. We perceive objects *by means of* certain
" media, and *by means of* certain impressions on the nerves :
" but we cannot with propriety say that we perceive either the
" media or the impressions on the nerves. What person in the
" act of seeing is conscious of the little coloured spaces on the
" retina? or of the motions of the bones of the auditory ap-
" paratus whilst he is hearing? Surely, no one. This may
" appear obvious enough, and yet a writer of no common acute-
" ness, Dr Brown,' has put forth several very strange opinions,
" all resting upon the doctrine that the coloured spaces on the
" retina are the *objects* which we perceive ; and there are
" some supposed difficulties and paradoxes on the same sub-
" ject which have become quite celebrated (as upright vision
" with inverted images), arising from the same confusion of
" thought[1]".

I have quoted the passage for three reasons.

First, because, as to the three sciences (so to speak) of Metaphysics, Physiology, and Physics, it seems to me to represent
the truth, and almost makes me surprised at Dr Whewell's other
language which I have been criticizing.

Next, because, what more than anything I want the reader
to be accustomed to, is to learn from passages like the above
what is to be learnt from them, which is often much, without
being misled by their language. The tree (to take a particular
object), we are told in the passage, affects light, light through
the lenses of the eye affects the optic nerve, and by this nerve in
some way the sensation is conveyed to the mind. When language
like this is used, which itself is no harm, let the reader's mind
go with it. We may, if we like it, call the action of the various
laws ·of chemistry and light by which light proceeding from the
sun is partly (if it is so) intercepted from our eye by the tree,
partly absorbed, partly transmitted to our eye, 'the tree affects
light'. *There* is *one* use then of the word 'affect'. Again we
may call the highly complicated process which finishes with
what I may term a disturbance of the optic nerve when the light

---

[1] *Hist. Scient. Ideas,* Vol. I. p. 300.

reaches the retina, 'the medium affecting the nerves of the sense': this is *another* and different use of the word 'affect'. Again, we may call this affecting of the nerve by the medium 'a sensation', and we may say that the nerve 'in some way conveys this sensation to the mind'. Here we must dismiss all notion of 'conveying' meaning moving through space, transferring from one thing in space to another thing in space, or anything of that sort: in fact, as I have said, I do not see what the words can mean more than that there is a feeling or consciousness contemporaneous with the nervous disturbance. The 'impression' upon the nerve in the next sentence is the second 'affecting' above, and is quite appropriate.

Third, I quote the passage, because I want the reader to observe that the very same process which Dr Whewell in the first paragraph describes as the object affecting the medium, the medium affecting the nerve, the nerve conveying its affectation (or the sensation) to the mind, he describes in the second paragraph as 'our perceiving the object by means of the medium and by means of the impression on the nerve, while we do not perceive either the impression or the medium'. These two ways of putting the matter (if he properly attends, in the way which I have described above, to the language of the first) are exactly the two ways in which I would wish the reader to put it, only that, for his life, he must avoid mixing them. The act of his mind is 'perceiving': he perceives the object: between him and the object, in his perception, is much that he does not perceive, which is no part of his perception of the object, and which is only matter to him of indirect and subsequent, physiological and physical, knowledge. When physiology and physics take the matter in hand to give him this knowledge, *they* proceed in a different direction: they describe the object as affecting a medium, and describe the manner of its affecting it: they describe the medium as affecting a nerve, and describe the manner of *this* again: and then *without* description, for here they are brought to a halt, they simply say *in some way* the nerve conveys the sensation to the mind. I cannot conceive language more fitted than Dr Whewell's to show clearly the double view of the same process.

But the view which I think will be learnt from a good deal

of Dr Whewell's book, and from which I dissent, is that by
sensation something is given to us from the object : that to this,
by perception (or in whatever way it is described) we add something, to wit 'idea', from the mind : that there are thus *two*
processes instead of one : that knowledge is divided into a part
from the object and a part from the mind : the former sometimes appearing as knowledge, sometimes as not knowledge :
this is the putting of the two views together, which I have
urged the reader to avoid.

But on this I have said enough.

I will finish with remarking again upon Dr Whewell's scientific ideas that when the notion is introduced of their being
progressive and developable I do not see how, as ideas, they
can preserve any character of being original, universal, necessary,
convictions, or in any respect help, as ideas, the *certainty* of
knowledge. But though the notion of them does not seem to
me to be of value in *this* way, I think it is in many others,
some of which I have mentioned.

I now close this part of my work, hoping very shortly to
pursue the subject. In the interval, I trust to study the book
of Mr Mill's to which I have alluded in the Introduction, and if
I have done him any injustice, shall have an opportunity of
correcting it, and of avowing any error into which I may have
fallen. I am aware of some imperfections in what I have said
about him, more especially obscurities which it might be desirable to make clearer—now this will be done better. The
next Chapter (or one soon to follow), to which I have alluded
by anticipation in page 166, was intended to have reference
principally to him. In the other Chapters I shall follow out
the scheme indicated in the Introduction, and discuss the remaining works there mentioned : I may add some others to
them : and I hope to finish by putting the views here given
in a clearer manner than I have been able to do in the course
of the 'exploration', in consequence of the additional hold upon
them which I trust this may have given.

Printed in Great Britain
by Amazon

25043621R00172